Dialects of English
Studies in grammatical variation

Edited by
Peter Trudgill and J. K. Chambers

Longman
London and New York

Longman Group UK Limited,
Longman House, Burnt Mill, Harlow
Essex CM20 2JE, England
and Associated Companies throughout the world

Published in the United States of America
by Longman Inc., New York

First published 1991

British Library Cataloguing in Publication Data

Dialects of English: studies in grammatical variation. –
(Longman linguistics library).
1. English language. dialects. grammar
I. Trudgill, Peter   II. Chambers, J. K. 427

ISBN 0-582-02194-4

Library of Congress Cataloging-in-Publication Data

Dialects of English: studies in grammatical variation / edited by Peter
Trudgill and J. K. Chambers.
p.   cm. – (Longman linguistics library)
Includes bibliographical references.
ISBN 0-582-02194-4
1. English language – Dialects.   2. English language – Variation.
3. English language – Grammar – 1950–   I. Trudgill, Peter.
II. Chambers, J. K.   III. Series.
PE1711.E5   1990   89-14523
427–dc20   CIP

Set in 10/11 pt Times Roman

Produced by Longman Singapore Publishers (Pte) Ltd.
Printed in Singapore

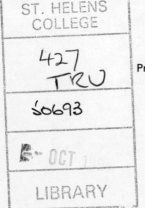

14.99

LONGMAN LINGUISTICS LIBRARY

DIALECTS OF ENGLISH

This book

LONGMAN LINGUISTICS LIBRARY

General editors
R. H. Robins, University of London
Martin Harris, University of Essex

A Short History of Linguistics
Third Edition
R. H. ROBINS

Structural Aspects of Langauge Change
JAMES M. ANDERSON

Text and Context
Explorations in Semantics and Pragmatics of Discourse
TEUN A. VAN DIJK

Introduction to Text Linguistics
ROBERT-ALAIN DE BEAUGRANDE AND WOLFGANG ULRICH DRESSLER

Spoken Discourse
A Model for Analysis
WILLIS EDMONDSON

Psycholinguistics
Language, Mind and World
DANNY D. STEINBERG

Dialectology
W. N. FRANCIS

Principles of Pragmatics
GEOFFREY N. LEECH

Generative Grammar
GEOFFREY HORROCKS

Norms of Language
Theoretical and Practical Aspects
RENATE BARTSCH

The English Verb
Second Edition
F. R. PALMER

Pidgin and Creole Languages
SUZANNE ROMAINE

A History of English Phonology
CHARLES JONES

General Linguistics
An Introductory Survey
Fourth Edition
R. H. ROBINS

Modality and the English Modals
Second Edition
F. R. PALMER

Generative and Non-Linear Phonology
JACQUES DURAND

Dialects of English
Studies in Grammatical Variation
EDITED BY PETER TRUDGILL AND J. K. CHAMBERS

Multilingualism in the British Isles
I: The Older Mother Tongues and Europe
II: Africa, the Middle East and Asia
EDITED BY SAFDER ALLADINA AND VIV EDWARDS

Semiotics and Linguistics
YISHAI TOBIN

Contents

Sources

K. Brown 'Double modals in Hawick Scots', unpublished paper.

J. Cheshire 'Variation in the use of *ain't* in an urban British dialect', *Language in Society* **10** (13): 365–81, 1981.

D. Christian 'The personal dative in Appalachian speech', unpublished paper.

E. Eisikovits 'Variation in the lexical verb in inner-Sydney English', *Australian Journal of Linguistics* **7** (1): 1–24, 1987.

W. Eitner 'Affirmative *any more* in present-day American English', *Papers of the Michigan Academy of Science, Arts and Letters* **35**, 1949. University of Michigan Press, 1951, *pp* 311–16.

C. Feagin 'Preverbal *done* in Alabama and elsewhere'. Excerpt from *Variation and Change in Alabama English*, *pp* 122–49. Washington, DC: Georgetown, University Press, 1979.

J. Gachelin 'Transitivity and intransitivity in the dialects of the south-west of England', *CIER Travaux* **52**: 91–9, Université de St.-Etienne. Translated from French by the author.

J. Harris 'Conservatism vs. substratal transfer in Irish English'. In N. Boretzky *et al.* (eds) *Beitrage zum 3. Essener Kolloquium über Sprachwandel und seine bestimmenden Faktoren.* Bochum: Studienverlag Dr N. Brockmeyer 1987, *pp* 143–62 (revised).

M. Harris 'Demonstrative adjectives and pronouns in a Devonshire dialect', *Transactions of the Philological Society*, pp 1–11, 1968.

A. Houston 'A grammatical continuum for *-ing*', unpublished paper.

O. Ihalainen 'Periphrastic *do* in affirmative sentences in the dialect of East Somerset, *Neuphilologische Mitteilungen* **77** (4): 608–22, 1976 (revised and abbreviated).

O. Ihalainen 'On grammatical diffusion in Somerset folk speech', unpublished conference paper.

W. Labov 'The boundaries of a grammar: inter-dialectal reactions to positive *anymore*'. Excerpt from 'Where do grammars stop?', in R. Shuy (ed.) *23rd Annual Round Table, pp* 65–76. Washington DC: Georgetown University Press, 1973.

H. Paddock 'The actuation problem for gender change in Wessex versus Newfoundland'. From J. Fisiak (ed.) *Historical Dialectology*, Berlin: Mouton, 1989, *pp* 377–95 (revised).

W. Wolfram 'Toward a description of a-prefixing in Appalachian English', *American Speech* **51**: 45–56, 1976.

Acknowledgements

We would like to thank Jean Hannah for her invaluable assistance in the preparation of this volume.

The Publishers are grateful to the following copyright holders for permission to reproduce articles:

Australian Linguistic Society for E Eisikovits, 'Variation in the lexical verb in inner-Sydney English' from the *Australian Journal of Linguistics* **7** (1) pp 1–24 (1987); Basil Blackwell Limited and the Philological Society for M Harris, 'Demonstrative adjectives and pronouns in a Devonshire dialect' from *Transactions of the Philological Society*, (1968), pp 1–11; Cambridge University Press for J Cheshire, 'Variation in the use of ain't in an urban British dialect' from *Language in Society*, **10** (3) pp 365–81, (1981); Georgetown University Press for Crawford Feagin, Preverbal *done* in Alabama and elsewhere' from *Variation and Change in Alabama English* (1979) pp 122–49, and W Labov, 'The boundaries of a grammar: inter-dialectal reactions to positive *anymore*' from 'Where do grammars stop?' in *Georgetown University Round Table on Language and Linguistics 1973* (ed.) R Shuy pp 65–76; Modern Language Society for Ossi Ihalainen, 'Periphrastic *do* in affirmative sentences in the dialect of East Somerset' from *Neuphilologische Mitteilungen: Bulletin de la Societe Neophilologique*, **LXXVII**, (1976), © Modern Language Society, Helsinki, 1976; Mouton de Gruyter and the author for H Paddock, 'The actuation problem for gender change in Wessex versus Newfoundland' in *Historical Dialectology* (ed.) J Fisiak, pp 377–95, (1988); The University of Alabama Press for Walt Wolfram, 'Toward a description of a-prefixing in Appalachian English' in *American Speech* (ed.) Professor R Butters, **51**, (1976), pp 45–56 © 1979 The University of Alabama Press; Universite Jean Monnet, Saint-Etienne and the author for J Gachelin 'Transivity and intransivity in the dialects of the south-west of

England' in Travaux No. **LII**, *La Transitivite, Domaine Anglais*, (1987), pp 91–9 © CIEREC; Universitatsverlag Dr. Norbert Brockmeyer for J Harris, 'Conservatism versus Substratal Transfer in Irish English' first published in Boretzky, Enninger & Stolz, *Beitrage zum 3. Essener Kolloquium uber Sprachwandel und seine bestimmenden Faktoren* vom 30.9–2.10.1987; The University of Michigan Press for Walter H Eitner 'Affirmative *any more* in present day American English' from *Papers of the Michigan Academy of Science, Arts and Letters* (ed.) Sparrow, **35**, (1949), pp 311–16.

Maps

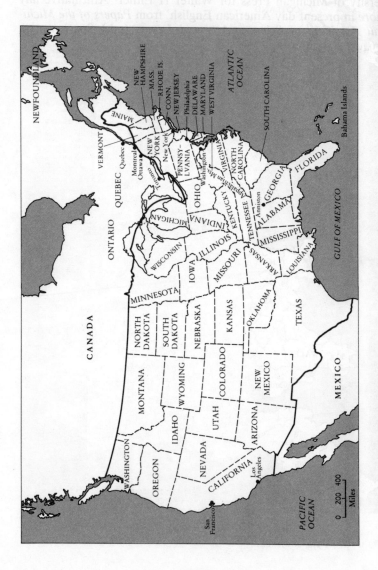

The United States and Canada

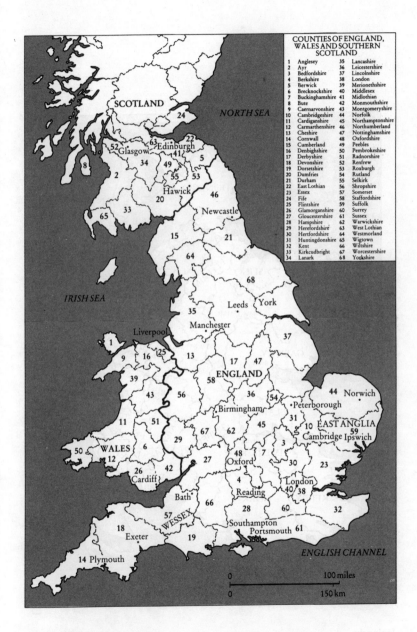

COUNTIES OF ENGLAND,
WALES AND SOUTHERN
SCOTLAND

1	Anglesey	35	Lancashire
2	Ayr	36	Leicestershire
3	Bedfordshire	37	Lincolnshire
4	Berkshire	38	London
5	Berwick	39	Merionethshire
6	Brecknockshire	40	Middlesex
7	Buckinghamshire	41	Midlothian
8	Bute	42	Monmouthshire
9	Caernarvonshire	43	Montgomeryshire
10	Cambridgeshire	44	Norfolk
11	Cardiganshire	45	Northamptonshire
12	Carmarthenshire	46	Northumberland
13	Cheshire	47	Nottinghamshire
14	Cornwall	48	Oxfordshire
15	Cumberland	49	Peebles
16	Denbighshire	50	Pembrokeshire
17	Derbyshire	51	Radnorshire
18	Devonshire	52	Renfrew
19	Dorsetshire	53	Roxburgh
20	Dumfries	54	Rutland
21	Durham	55	Selkirk
22	East Lothian	56	Shropshire
23	Essex	57	Somerset
24	Fife	58	Staffordshire
25	Flintshire	59	Suffolk
26	Glamorganshire	60	Surrey
27	Gloucestershire	61	Sussex
28	Hampshire	62	Warwickshire
29	Herefordshire	63	West Lothian
30	Hertfordshire	64	Westmorland
31	Huntingdonshire	65	Wigtown
32	Kent	66	Wiltshire
33	Kirkcudbright	67	Worcestershire
34	Lanark	68	Yorkshire

Britain (pre-1974 counties)

Ireland

Chapter 1

Introduction: English dialect grammar

Peter Trudgill and J. K. Chambers

In recent years there has been a move, as far as interest in dialects of English is concerned, from a concern with purely phonological, lexical and historical issues towards a deeper interest in the grammar of different English varieties. This is especially true of syntax, which has traditionally received much less attention from dialectologists than morphology. This upsurge of interest has been particularly noticeable, in the 1980s, in the British Isles. North American linguists have for two decades or so been studying the syntax of non-standard varieties, particularly those spoken by Black Americans, but in Britain the increase in involvement with grammatical issues has been much more recent. Indeed, as the contents of this book show, much of the best work on English dialect grammar in Britain has been carried out by scholars who are not British: five of the chapters in this volume that include data from England have been written by linguists from overseas (Gachelin, Houston, Ihalainen, Paddock).

The publication of this collection of papers reflects this increase in interest, and of course would not have been possible without the recent increase in scholarly activity in this field: four of the fifteen papers here are from the 1970s and nine of them from the 1980s. Our aim with this book is therefore to make available to a wider audience a selection of what we believe to be the most important, exciting and interesting papers in the area of English dialect grammar. The data presented here are in themselves fascinating in their diversity, and of interest to anyone who has a concern for varieties of English.

It is also our hope, however, that our demonstration of the availability in English dialects of grammatical devices, categories and distinctions which many an English-speaking linguist would associate only with, to them, more exotic languages will have one other rather specific effect. We would like grammarians of English to realize that by concentrating, as most of them do, on their own native standard or other mainstream (see below) varieties of English, they are missing out on some intriguing problems and important data, and that they are thereby doing both theoretical linguistics and descriptive English linguistics a disservice.

The papers published in this volume have been selected because they combine descriptively interesting and, from the point of view of English as a whole, often unusual data with discussions of important theoretical linguistic, historical linguistic and sociolinguistic problems.

A majority of the papers deal with data from what we can call, following Wells (1982) and others, traditional dialects. We take it that English speakers who normally employ forms such as:

> We're not coming.
> We aren't coming.
> We ain't comin.

are speakers of mainstream English dialects. Speakers who, on the other hand, say:

> Us byun't a-comin.

are speakers of traditional dialect. The same point can be made from phonology. Pronunciations of words such as *bone* as [boun], [bɔun], [bæun], [boːn] are typical of mainstream varieties. Traditional dialect pronunciations of the same word would include [bɪən], [beːn], [bwʊn].

The vast majority of native English speakers around the world differ linguistically from one another relatively little, with more differentiation in their phonetics and phonology than at other linguistic levels. Most English people, for example, betray their geographical origins much more through their accents than through their vocabulary or grammar. This vast majority speaks mainstream varieties of English, standard and non-standard, which resemble one another quite closely, and which are all reasonably readily mutually intelligible. Differences between these mainstream varieties may be regionally and socially very diagnostic, but they are generally linguistically rather trivial, and where not trivial, quite regular and predictable. Grammatically, in particular, these varieties are very close to Standard English. We associate mainstream dialects with upper- and middle-class speakers throughout the English-speaking world; with areas out of which Standard English as a social dialect grew historically, *ie* the south-east of England; with most urban areas; with areas which have shifted to English only relatively recently, such as the Scottish Highlands and western Wales; and with recently settled mixed colonial dialect-speaking areas, such as most of North America and Australia.

Traditional dialects, on the other hand, are spoken by a (probably shrinking) minority of the English-speaking population. These dialects differ very considerably from Standard English, from other mainstream varieties and from each other. They also differ in unsystematic and unpredictable ways, and in their grammar as well as in phonology and lexis. Some of them may not be readily intelligible to speakers of other dialects. And they are to be found only in long-settled and, especially, remote and peripheral rural areas, although some urban dialects in northern Britain should also be included under the heading of traditional dialect.

Traditional dialects are of particular interest to us here precisely because they do diverge most markedly at the grammatical level from the already relatively well-known standard and other mainstream varieties of English. It is true that we do include in this book a number of chapters based on data from non-standard mainstream varieties, such as those by Cheshire on Reading, England, and Eisikovits on Sydney, Australia. But a majority of the chapters in this volume deal with the less well-known traditional dialects, which is why the geographical emphasis of the book is on geographically peripheral areas of Britain, such as Scotland and the south-west of England, and on the long-settled and remoter areas of North America, such as Newfoundland and the Appalachian Mountains.

We have not included material in this book on the grammar of those other varieties of English which differ markedly from the mainstream varieties, namely English-based creoles and varieties with creole ancestry. Many of these have already received much greater coverage from linguists than the traditional dialects, and could in any case easily fill several volumes by themselves.

It is of linguistic interest to note that a majority of the papers that we have found to qualify for inclusion in the book on the grounds of quality and theoretical and descriptive importance have to do with English dialect verbal systems. Our first section, however, is devoted to pronouns.

Part one

Pronouns

Chapter 2

Pronouns and pronominal systems in English dialects

Peter Trudgill and J. K. Chambers

English dialects demonstrate a considerable amount of variation in their pronominal systems, in form, function and usage. The pronominal system which is common to all varieties of Standard English around the world can be presented as follows:

I	me	my	mine	myself
you	you	your	yours	yourself
he	him	his	his	himself
she	her	her	hers	herself
it	it	its	its	itself
we	us	our	ours	ourselves
you	you	your	yours	yourselves
they	them	their	theirs	themselves

Differences from this system in the mainstream non-standard and traditional dialects include the following:

1. Possessive *me*:
   I've lost me bike.
   This is very common in many parts of Britain, and occurs even in colloquial Standard English speech.
2. Singular *us*:
   Give us a kiss.
   This too is common in colloquial Standard English speech in certain locutions, such as the above. In certain regions, however, notably the north-east of England, *us* has a much wider function as singular object pronoun:
   He hit us in the face.
3. Possessive *us*:
   This is common in many dialects in areas of the north of England:
   We like us town.
4. Second person singular *thou, thee*:
   I'll let thee have some.

Many traditional dialects in the north and west of England retain forms descended from *thou* and *thee* as second person singular pronouns addressed to friends and intimates. In some cases distinct second person singular verb forms are retained also. In these dialects, *you* functions as the second person singular formal and plural pronoun (see Chapter 9).

5   Singular *you*:

In many dialects of English around the world, the historical loss of the second person singular/plural distinction that went with the loss of *thou/thee* has been repaired by the introduction of new second person plural pronouns, such as *youse,* which is found in North America, Australia, Scotland, England and especially Ireland. The American South, as is well known, has *y'all,* and, less widely and less well known, *you 'uns.* The traditional dialects of East Anglia, England, have *you . . . together,* in this function:

Come you on together.

In these dialects, *you* is singular only.

6   Third person *that*:

That's raining.

I don't like it – that's no good.

In East Anglian dialects of English, *it* occurs only as an object pronoun, with third-person neuter singular subjects being indicated by *that*:

7. Possessives in *-n*:

In the traditional dialects of central England, as well as in some parts of North America, the so-called second possessives have a regular system in which all forms end in *-n*:

That's mine	That's ourn
That's yourn	That's theirn
That's hisn	
That's hern.	

8. Reflexive *hisself, theirselves*:

He hurt hisself.

Many non-standard dialects of English have a regularized system of reflexive pronouns in which all forms are based on the possessive pronouns + *self/selves*:

myself	ourselves
yourself	yourselves
hisself	theirselves
herself	

It is perhaps, however, the traditional dialects of the south-west of England, and their descendants in Newfoundland, which differ most strikingly from the pronoun system outlined above. The pronominal systems of these dialects are dealt with in this book by Paddock in Chapter 5 and by Ihalainen in Chapter 9.

There are two major characteristics to note. The first is what Ihalainen (p. 106) calls 'pronoun exchange'. This refers to the fact that pronouns that are nominative in mainstream dialects can function as objects, and vice versa, in the south-west of England.[1] We are not yet entirely sure how this operates, but it is perhaps at least sometimes the case that the 'nominative' pronouns occur stressed and the 'oblique' pronouns occur unstressed:

Give it to he, not they – her don't need it.

The second characteristic has to do with the gender system, discussed at length by Paddock. The striking thing to speakers of mainstream dialects is that *he* and *she* in the south-west may occur as pronominalizations of inanimate nouns. As Paddock explains, the basic noun-class distinction in these dialects has to do not only with masculine and feminine but also with count and mass nouns, as well as with the categories of mobile and non-mobile.

Note that the Newfoundland dialects discussed by Paddock are interesting in many other ways also. Newfoundland was settled in the first place mainly by people from the south-west of England and from Ireland. Newfoundland dialects therefore show, to varying degrees, characteristics from both these areas, at all linguistic levels, with the added complication that the dialects of south-west England also played an important role in the formation of Irish English.

In Chapter 5, Paddock uses the historical label 'Wessex' to describe the counties of south-western England with which he is concerned. Chapter 4 by Harris in this section is also concerned with a Wessex dialect, that of an area of the county of Devon. Harris deals in this chapter with demonstratives. The system of demonstratives in all forms of Standard English is, of course, as follows:

	Singular	Plural
Close	*this*	*these*
Distant	*that*	*those*

Differences between this Standard English system and those of the non-standard dialects include the use of *them* and *they* rather than *those;* and the use of *here* and *there* in combination with the demonstratives:

them books on the table
them there boys
they books over there
these here people

Particularly interesting, however, are those demonstrative systems which have a three-way distinction between close-distant-remote pronouns rather than the two-way system of the mainstream dialects. Some Scottish dialects, for instance, distinguish:

<blockquote>
this   that   *thon*
</blockquote>

or

<blockquote>
this   that   *yon*
</blockquote>

South-western English English dialects, such as the one discussed by Harris, may also have three-way systems:

Singular	*thease*	*that*	*thicky*
Plural:	*theys*	*they*	*thicky.*

These south-western systems, that is, differ markedly from that of the mainstream dialects in both form and function.

Similar three-way distinctions are very common in the languages of the world, and occurred in Old English, but the 'distant-remote' distinction began to disappear in Middle English.

Finally, we can note a further type of difference between English dialects as far as pronouns are concerned: differences in syntactic restrictions on pronoun usage. One example of this type of difference is provided by the traditional dialects of East Anglia, England, where the second person pronoun may co-occur with imperatives:

> *Come you on!*
> *Shut you up!*
> *Be you quiet!*

In the present book we include Christian's study of personal dative pronouns as found in the dialects of the Appalachian mountain range of the eastern United States (Ch. 3). As Christian illustrates, the usage in these dialects of forms such as

> *I'm going to get me some coffee.*

appear to contravene the syntactic rules concerning reflexives that are found in most other English dialects. Note that Wolfram's paper, Chapter 17, comes from the same research project and deals with the same dialect.

Note

1. Older traditional dialects in Essex, eastern England, also showed this phenomenon.

Chapter 3

The personal dative in Appalachian speech*

Donna Christian

In English, when the same referent is mentioned twice within a clause, the second occurrence typically takes on a reflexive form, that is, a form with *-self*, as in *myself, themselves*. This happens not only when both references show up in the same clause in the utterances [1a] and [1b], but also when they both are part of the underlying structure, with one deleted or raised into the matrix clause at some prior point [1c].

[1]　(a) Did you hurt *yourself*?
　　(b) They fixed *themselves* some soup for lunch.
　　(c) I was saving money to buy *myself* a new coat.

In some varieties of English, it is possible to use a non-reflexive pronoun (*you, me* and so on) in certain cases for the second occurrence of a single referent within the same clause. This usage is illustrated in [2].

[2]　(a) I'd go out and cut *me* a limb off of a tree, get *me* a good straight one. (7)[1]
　　(b) It was about these people moved out on the prairie and they built *'em* a house. (58)
　　(c) We had *us* a cabin, built *us* a log cabin back over there. (146)

* An earlier version of this chapter was presented at the 1982 meeting of the South Atlantic American Dialect Society. I would like to thank Michael Montgomery for supplying me with data from Tennessee which provided numerous examples of the personal dative structure from another set of Appalachian English speakers. I am also grateful to Walt Wolfram for offering helpful comments on several versions of this chapter.

(d) And then you'd get *you* a bowl of ice-water. (160)

This structure appears to be fairly common in southern-based varieties and is often represented in stereotypical characterizations of speakers of these varieties.

A clear example of the use of a personal dative to invoke a stereotype occurs in the popular comic strip, 'Dennis the Menace', by Hank Ketcham. In this example, an urban 'cowboy' plays the part by wearing appropriate cowboy clothes and reflects appropriate vernacular speech by saying in answer to Dennis' question, 'Do you have a home on the range?', 'Nope, I got *me* a condo in the city'. As a result, his speech pattern helps to maintain the illusion he is creating by his manner of dress, and the writer is able to convey an entire speech variety by using a few carefully selected language features.

I will refer to this structure as the 'personal dative'. This label is chosen because of the similarity between this structure and the internal indirect object construction which represents a dative relationship in sentences like [3a] and [3c], which are related to sentences like [3b] and [3d], respectively.

[3] (a) They built a cabin *for me*.
     (b) They built *me* a cabin.
     (c) You'd get a bowl of ice water *for yourself*.
     (d) You'd get *yourself* a bowl of ice-water.

The qualifier 'personal' reflects the close relationship (co-referentiality) between the subject and the pronoun that follows the verb.

My attention was drawn to this structure during a study of a large sample of Appalachian speech in which numerous instances of personal dative usage occurred. The following discussion is based on the instances observed in that data. The corpus consists of 129 tape-recorded interviews with residents of Monroe and Mercer counties in south-eastern West Virginia that were collected in 1974 and 1975 (Wolfram and Christian 1976). Local community members conducted the interviews and this practice promoted casual speech in the interview situation most of the time. Thus, many of the interviews contain vernacular features like the personal dative which are favoured in casual speech styles.

The personal dative surfaces in the internal indirect object position (immediately after the verb) when a direct object is also present (therefore, with transitive verbs). There are no cases like *I hurt me* or *We could see us in the mirror,* in the sense in question. (Some emphatic contexts might allow something like

We couldn't see them, but we could see us in the mirror, but in that case the pronoun is a direct object.)

The personal dative is not an 'ideal' indirect object although it fills that slot in the sentence. It can occur with verbs that do not normally allow internal indirect objects, a fact which will be discussed shortly. Like other indirect objects that are co-referential with the subject, it cannot become the subject in a passive version of a sentence. *I gave Sam a pencil* is related to *A pencil was given to Sam* or *Sam was given a pencil,* so that both the direct and indirect objects can take the surface subject slot. Looking at example [2] above, we can see that this does not work for personal datives, given the unacceptability of **I was cut a limb off a tree.* Likewise, sentences like *I gave myself a raise* do not appear to passivize well. (*?I was given a raise (by me)* does not convey the same sense as the active sentence.)

Some other features help to characterize this structure. The personal dative is a relatively unstressed element in the clause. It is restricted to animate referents, but not necessarily human ones. Instead, the pronoun form appears to be the crucial point; as long as the pronoun is not *it,* the usage is acceptable. So, for example, *The cat found her a comfortable chair to curl up in* might be found, but not **The cat found it a comfortable chair to curl up in* (where the pronoun is co-referential with the subject).[2] With the exception of *it,* however, the full range of pronouns was observed. There may be some differences in the frequencies with which the personal dative structure occurs for different nouns. The structure can be found much more frequently with first- and second-person subjects than with third-person, singular or plural, subjects. Further investigation is needed to determine if other factors (such as topic) might contribute to the distributional pattern, but it holds for the over 200 instances examined in this study.

There is a fairly strong resemblance between this usage and the dative construction involving *for* in English (in those cases where the subject and indirect object are co-referential). The dative relationship is expressed by either *to* or *for* phrases as in [4] where the 'internal' counterparts follow each example. This relationship is illustrated in [4d] when the subject and indirect object are co-referential.

[4] (a) We gave a present *to our uncle.*
    We gave *our uncle* a present.
  (b) John knitted a sweater *for Susan.*
    John knitted *Susan* a sweater.
  (c) They ordered a sandwich *for me.*
    They ordered *me* a sandwich.

(d) I bought a lawnmower *for myself.*
I bought *myself* a lawnmower.

The personal dative has been linked to sentences like [4d], with the suggestion that the non-reflexive constructions come from the same source as the internal *for*-dative. The Appalachian speech example given in [2a] then would be directly related to *I'd go out and cut a limb off of a tree for myself.* Green (1974) gives a lengthy discussion of the verbs and at one point notes (p. 190): 'All of the *for*-dative verbs, in contrast to the *to*-datives, may occur with non-reflexive co-referential indirect object pronouns, but only in certain colloquial, rural or sub-standard types of speech, and for no apparent reason, only if the indirect object is internal.' This observation is of course too simplistic, at least to cover this sample of Appalachian speech, since there is not a one-to-one correspondence between this non-reflexive pronoun usage, the personal dative and an internal *for*-dative counterpart in other varieties of English.

It also appears to be the case that this usage is not as stigmatized as Green implies. Rather, it seems to be a non-stigmatized variant structure of informal speech in those varieties where it is used. Its wide acceptability is suggested by the following lines from 'September Song' (lyrics by Maxwell Anderson, music by Kurt Weill):

[5] When I was a young man, courting the girls, I played *me* a waiting game . . .³

Although, as noted above, personal datives can be used to invoke vernacular stereotypes and are strongly associated with certain vernaculars, this example demonstrates that they can be used without stigma in a wider set of contexts. Song lyrics often incorporate language features for reasons peculiar to that genre, such as rhythm (*a*-prefixing is one such feature). Personal datives appear to be available for such uses without apparent negative associations.

Allerton (1978) discusses the so-called dative movement rule in English, which relates pairs of sentences like those in example [4] above. He outlines a set of factors to account for those cases in which the rule can and cannot apply. It applies uniformly in the case of *to*-datives (like [4a]), but not always in the case of *for*. Without going into all the details, we can note a useful distinction that Allerton makes between benefactive *for* and deputive *for*. The benefactive case is one like [4b] and [4c], where the indirect object is the recipient of the direct object (closer to the meaning associated with *to*). The opposite end of *for*-datives is the deputive use, where the action involved is done on behalf of the indirect object, as in

[6] Mary taught a class *for Sam*.

There is apparently a scale in between the two constructions where those structures closer to the benefactive end can have dative movement, as in [4b] and [4c], while those closer to the deputive end of the scale cannot. *Mary taught Sam a class* is not acceptable.[4]

Returning to the personal dative examples, we find a number of verbs with this structure in the sample which do not appear to have internal reflexive indirect object counterparts. Many, but' still not all, could be paired with a phrase of the form *for + reflexive pronoun*, but it is not clear whether these would all be considered datives, and even if they could, they cannot undergo dative movement. Some examples appear in:

[7] (a) We want *us* a black German police dog cause I had one once. (29)
    (b) He done had *him* a way figured out to get out. (146)
    (c) Lotta time, I take *me* a pound or two of butter and cut me off a chunk of butter. . . . (22)
    (d) She wanted *her* some liver pudding. (152)
    (e) We got us some logs, . . . put *us* four big poles around the side of it, and got us logs put over top. (10)

The context surrounding these personal datives might allow the use of a *for*-phrase, for example, in [7d]: *She wanted some liver pudding for herself*. The internal counterpart, however, is unacceptable: *She wanted herself some liver pudding*. Allerton's account of the dative movement rule may help here in that he differentiates between datives which may be moved into internal position and those which may not. Since all cases of personal dative appear internally, it represents a structural expansion of internal position with datives, whereas the *for*-datives involve subcategorization restrictions based on verb type.[5]

Where correspondences exist, we can examine the possible relationship between these personal datives and the other dative constructions. One parameter is meaning. For most of the examples found where a reflexive pronoun counterpart for a personal dative was acceptable, the two variants seem to be close paraphrases, as in [8]:

[8] (a) He wanted some straw to build *him* a house out of. (14)
    He wanted some straw to build *himself* a house out of.

    (b) I traded it, sold it for twenty-five dollars and bought
         me a pony. (10)
         I traded it, . . . and bought *myself* a pony.
    (c) We'd head out up in them trees and roll that stuff up
         and make *us* cigarettes, you know, and smoke that.
         (30)
         We'd head out . . . and make *ourselves* cigarettes
         . . .
    (d) I'm going to get *me* a German police dog. (29)
         I'm going to get *myself* a German police dog.

There may be at least some subtle differences in meaning, but
these are somewhat difficult to pinpoint. Such differences may be
more evident in the examples in [9]:

  [9] (a) I shot *me* a pheasant. (2)
         (?) I shot *myself* a pheasant.
      (b) That day when he had the party, he got *him* a bow
         and arrow set . . . and he got *him* some Stomper Guns
         and some guns that . . . (1)
         That day when he had the party, he got *himself* a bow
         and arrow set . . . and he got *himself* some . . .

The personal dative in [9a] seems to vary in meaning from the
dative phrase *for myself* (and the internal *myself*) in that the *me*
seems less the benefactor of the action than the *for*-phrase would
indicate. It is possible, though, that this is a more widespread
difference between the construction with the overt *for*-phrase and
the one with the internal indirect object. There also seems to be
a degree of emphasis difference, with *myself* slightly more emphatic. In [9b], the difference relates to who is responsible for
the result of the action of the verb. The context tells us that the
toys were received as gifts (from others), but the structure with
the reflexive forms signals that the giver and receiver were the
same person. The semantics of the verb *get* may make a difference.

Certain structural differences show up when the reflexive and
non-reflexive forms in the internal indirect object position are
compared as they combine with other dative phrases and these
might have implications for the meaning relationships. For example, the personal dative can be found in some instances with
a verb that takes *to*-datives, such as *write*:

  [10] I'm gonna write *me* a letter to my cousin.
      *I'm gonna write *myself* a letter to my cousin.[6]

The alternate form with a reflexive pronoun is strange and would not appear derivable from a *for*-dative. Similarly, although *I'm gonna write a letter to my cousin for Fred* is acceptable, the only internal indirect object possible is *my cousin*, not *Fred*, as in example [11]:

[11] I'm gonna write my cousin a letter for Fred.
*I'm gonna write Fred a letter to my cousin.

We need to consider these examples with some caution, since constructions which allow dative combinations may be unusual in other ways; for example, 'a letter to my cousin' may be interpretable as a unitary object rather than as a dative construction (S. Elgin, personal communication).

There is, in addition, the possibility of a personal dative co-occurring with an overt *for*-dative phrase. In these cases, the *for*-phrase clearly specifies the benefactor of the action, and its inclusion serves to reduce, if not eliminate, the benefactor aspect of the personal dative. For example:

[12] (a) He was looking to buy *him* a house for his family.
(b) I want to find *me* a pretty card for my mother.

Here, the presence of the personal dative blocks the possibility of the *for*-dative occurring internally, though it could otherwise, as in *buy his family a house*. This fact makes it look like the personal dative fills the indirect object slot, although it does not necessarily need to have the full meaning of an indirect object, as the reflexive would.

In this examination of Appalachian speech, we have seen that the personal dative bears a strong relationship to *for*-dative constructions in meaning, and a somewhat less strong one in form. It cannot occur with the pronoun *it*, while the *for*-dative does not have this limitation. It carries a lower stress than the internal reflexive. The distribution of the structures with respect to various verbs and other positional considerations differs to some extent. Finally, the indirect object meaning of the personal dative can, in effect, be cancelled, if another candidate occurs, as in [12]. The pronoun remains to fill the internal slot, though, precluding the indirect object from moving.

We can conclude then that the personal dative is a low-stressed indirect-object-like structure, which carries a 'light' benefactive meaning (the strength of which probably relates to other features of the context). It may stem from the *for*-dative but its usage has generalized to a wider variety of contexts with a concurrent shift in meaning. Certain pieces of evidence put forth above may suggest, in fact, that this structure is simply a 'pseudo-dative', a particle which is a pronoun copy of the subject and which has distributional privileges like those outlined in this discussion.

Finally, we can note that the personal dative occurs widely beyond the West Virginia area studied here, or even the Appalachian region. Specific examples can be found in Tennessee,[2] the Arkansas Ozarks (Christian, Wolfram and Dube 1988), Alabama (Feagin 1979), in popular songs (see example 5 above), and widely in southern-based (and perhaps other) vernacular varieties. The personal dative is a productive and stable vernacular feature of English. If anything, its use is expanding as part of a general southern-based variety.

Notes

1. The numbers in parentheses indicate the tape number from the corpus in which the cited instance occurs. This corpus of tapes will be described shortly.
2. Although no instances of non-human animate referents occurred in our sample, examples of this type do exist in real speech, as attested in speech samples collected by Michael Montgomery in Tennessee, *cf.* 'We'd have the grandest time a-trying to find that hen. We could hear the little fellers, but she'd have, she'd steal *her* a place and lay her eggs and hatch 'em back in under, these hay and different places about the barn, you know (70-year-old female, White Pine, Tennessee; Michael Montgomery, personal communication).
3. I am grateful to Jack Chambers for pointing out this occurrence to me as a perfect example of the point I was trying to make.
4. Not everyone would agree that these are dative constructions at all; others would consider this type of phrase to be an adverbial complement. In that case, the scale would range from those structures closer to *for*-datives to those closer to the adverbial complement end of the scale.
5. Allerton does not consider co-referential cases, where subject and indirect object have the same referent, however. There may well be other special considerations involved.
6. This type of example was suggested by Richard Smaby (personal communication).

References

ALLERTON, D. J. (1978) 'Generating indirect objects in English', *Journal of Linguistics* **14**: 21–33.
CHRISTIAN, DONNA, WOLFRAM, WALT and DUBE, NANJO (1988) *Variation and Change in Geographically Isolated Communities: Appalachian En-*

glish and Ozark English. Tuscaloosa, Ala: University of Alabama Press.

FEAGIN, CRAWFORD (1979) *Variation and Change in Alabama English: A Sociolinguistic Study of the White Community*. Washington, DC: Georgetown University Press.

GREEN, GEORGIA (1974) 'The function of form and the form of function', *Chicago Linguistic Society* 10: 186–97.

WOLFRAM, WALT and CHRISTIAN, DONNA (1976) *Appalachian Speech*. Washington, DC: Center for Applied Linguistics.

Chapter 4

Demonstrative adjectives and pronouns in a Devonshire dialect

Martin Harris

In this chapter, an attempt will be made to describe and discuss the system of demonstrative adjectives and pronouns found in the dialect of South Zeal, a village on the northern edge of Dartmoor. The analysis is based on a corpus of some twenty hours of tape-recorded conversation, collected in the course of work for a Ph.D. thesis, either in the form of a dialogue between two informants or of a monologue on the part of a single informant. The principal informant, Mr George Cooper, has lived for

TABLE 4.1

Singular adjective			
Simple	/ði:z/ /ðs/	/ðat/	/ðɪ-ki:/
First compound	/ðɪ:z/ ji:r/ /ðɪs ji:r/	/ðat ðɛr/	/ðɪ-ki: ðɛr/
Singular pronoun			
Simple	/ðɪs/ /ði:z/	/ðat/	/ðɪ-ki:/
First compound	/ðɪs ji:r/	/ðat ðɛr/	
Second compound	/ðɪs ji:r ji:r/	/ðat ðɛr ðɛr/	
Plural adjective			
Simple	/ðejz/ /ði:z/	/ðej/	/ðɪ-ki:/[a]
First compound	/ðejz ji:r/	/ðej ðɛr/	/ðɪ-ki: ðɛr/[a]
Plural pronoun			
Simple (only)		/ðej/	

[a]For the status of /ðɪ-ki:/ and /ðɪ-ki: oɛr/ as 'plurals', see below, p. 24.

some eighty-five years in the parish, and has only spent one night in his life outside the county of Devon.

For the purposes of this chapter, only one phonological point needs to be made. The /r/ phoneme is retroflex in final position, and induces a preceding weak central vowel [ə] when occurring in the environment /Vr/, (thus [Vəɻ]), when the /V/ in question is /iː/ or /ɛ/. (These are the only two vowels relevant within this work.) The transcription used for the actual forms should not give rise to any further problems. In the case of the illustrative examples, I have decided to use a quasi-orthographical representation, since the actual phonetic/phonemic realization is not directly relevant to the point under discussion. The prominent syllable(s) in each example are illustrated thus: ".

We may now proceed to look at the actual forms found in the dialect (Table 4.1). The relative frequency of these forms is shown in Table 4.2

TABLE 4.2

Adjectives

Singular	%	Plural	%
/ðiːz/	13	/ðejz/	23
/ðɪs/	11	/ðiːz/	2
/ðiːz jiːr/	9	/ðejz jiːr/	7
/ðɪs jiːr/	2	/ðiːz jiːr/	4
/ðat/	15	/ðej/	49[a]
/ðat ðɛr/	3	/ðej ðɛr/	2
/ðɪ-kiː/	43	/ðɪ-kiː/	10
/ðɪ-kiː ðɛr/	4	/ðɪ-kiː ðɛr/	3
	100		100

Pronouns

Singular	%	Plural	%
/ðɪs/	10		
/ðiːz/	4		
/ðɪs jiːr/	2		
/ðɪs jiːr jiːr/	25	/ðej/	100[b]
/ðat/	22		
/ðat ðɛr/	2		
/ðat ðɛr ðɛr/	34		
/ðɪ-kiː/	1		
	100		

[a] Greatly inflated by the constant recurrence of the phrase 'in they days'.
[b] For the status of this form as a demonstrative, see below, p. 27.

The paradigm as outlined in Tables 4.1, 4.2 presents few morphological problems. The two pairs of forms /ðiːz/ and /ðɪs/ and /ðejz/ and /ðiːz/ do, however, need examination. In the singular of the adjective, the two forms /ðiːz/ and /ðɪs/ are both frequent, being used mostly in unstressed and stressed position respectively. However, some 30 per cent of the occurrences of each form do not follow this tendency, so it does not seem profitable to set up a stressed:unstressed opposition, particularly since such a division would serve no purpose in the case of /ðat/ and /ðɪ-kiː/. With the 'first compounds', the form /ðiːz jiːr/ outnumbers /ðɪs jiːr/ in the ratio 4:1 in the adjective position.

When functioning as a pronoun, /ðiːz/ is rare as a simple form and never occurs at all either within a first compound (although 'first compounds' are so rare as pronouns that no generalization can usefully be made, see Table 4.2) or within a 'second compound', where only /ðɪs jiːr jiːr/, never /ðiːz jiːr jiːr/, is found. Thus /ðɪs/ seems to be more favoured as a pronoun. and /ðiːz/ as an adjective; this, of course, is only a tendency.

In the plural, the position is more clear-cut. The normal adjective plurals are /ðejz/ and /ðejz jiːr/, which outnumber /ðiːz/ and /ðiːz jiːr/ by a large margin (see Table 4.2). Such cases of the latter as do occur may perhaps be ascribed to Standard English influence, since /ðiːz/ is clearly used normally as a singular rather than a plural form. The absence of any reflex of /ðejz/ as a plural pronoun is discussed below.

The other forms present little morphological difficulty. There is only one occurrence of /ðɪ-kiː/ as a pronoun, although as an adjective it almost outnumbers /ðiːz/ and /ðat/ together, so it seems to belong primarily to the adjectival system. The normal singular pronouns are either the simple forms or the 'second compounds', the 'first compounds' being most unusual.

In the plural of the adjective, the simple forms are much more frequent than their equivalent 'first compounds', whereas in the plural of the pronoun, there is apparently only the one form /ðej/. The status of this form is discussed below.

The following are examples of those demonstatives which are not further discussed below. The uses of /ðat/ as a singular adjective, of /ðɪ-kiː/ as a singular or plural adjective, and of all the pronouns are fully exemplified in the syntactic section, and thus no examples are given here.

/ðiːz/

I come down "here to live in *this* little old "street.
Well; "*this* year, I done a bit "lighter.
Now "*this* season, tis "over.
This was coming "*this* way.

/ðɪs jiːr/
There's all *this here* sort of "jobs going on to "day.
I was down "there where *this here* "plough was up "here.

/ðejz/
These places be alright if you know where you'm "going to.
They got to pay the "wages to *these* people.
I do a bit of "gardening . . . and likes of all *these* things.

/ðej/
What makes all *they* "hills look so well?
Where "Jim was sent to, *they* two "met.
"They won't have all *they* sort of people up there.
Tell "Cooper to "shift "*they* "stones "there.

We may now turn to the functions of those forms whose uses
are identifiably different from those of Standard English.

The most striking feature of the demonstrative system is that,
in the singular adjective system at least, there is apparently a
three-term opposition /ðiːz : ðat : ðɪ-kiː/, in contrast with the two-
term system of Standard English. It seems fair to say that the role
of /ðiːz/ is similar to that of 'this' in Standard English (but see
note on /ðiːz jiːr/ below), but any attempt to differentiate /ðat/
and /ðɪ-kiː/ proves extremely difficult. There are a number of sentences of the type:

If you was to put "*that* stick in across "*thicky* pony . . .

where the two forms seem to fill the same function. The virtual
absence of /ðɪ-kiː/ from the pronoun system, together with the
fact that /ðɪ-kiː/ is three times as frequent as /ðat/ as an adjective,
would suggest that /ðɪ-kiː/ is the normal adjectival form in the
dialect, and that /ðat/ has a greater range, having a function which
is basically pronominal but in addition adjectival at times. This is
further supported by the fact that when presented with sentences
of the type:

He turned *that* "hare "three "times and "he caught it.

the informant claimed that /ðɪ-kiː/ would be equally acceptable
and could indicate no distinction. Thus there are pairs of sentences such as

I used to walk *that* there "two mile and "half.
You'd walk *thicky* "nine "mile.

or again

That finished "*that* job.
I wouldn't have "*thicky* job.

There are certain cases where either one form or the other seems to be required. In particular, /ðat/ is used when actually indicating a size with the hands:

Go up and see the stones "*that* length, "*that* thickness.

while /ðɪ-kiː/ is used in contrast with /tə-ðr/, where Standard English would normally use 'one' or 'the one'.

Soon as they got it "*thicky* hand, they'd thruck(?) it away with the "*tother*.

In the adjective plural, the contrast between /ðɪ-kiː/ and /ðej/ is not a real one, since /ðɪ-kiː/ is found only with numerals.

I had *thicky* "eighteen "bob a "week.
I expect *thicky* "nine was all "one "man's sheep.

When presented with /ðɪ-kiː/ before plural nominals, the informant rejected them. It would therefore be preferable to redefine 'singular' and 'plural' in the dialect to account for this, rather than to consider /ðɪ-kiː/ as a plural form; this would accordingly neutralize in the plural any /ðɪ-kiː/:/ðat/ opposition which may exist in the singular.

In the pronominal system, there is only one occurrence of /ðɪ-kiː/

My missis bought "*thicky* before her "died (a radio).

It is true that most of the occurrences of /ðat/ as a pronoun do not refer to a specific antecedent, *eg* I can't afford to do "*that*, but there are a number of cases where /ðat/ does play a role closely parallel to /ðɪ-kiː/ above.

As "I was passing "*that*, and "*that* was passing "me (a dog).

As there are no other examples of /ðɪ-kiː/ as a singular pronoun, either simply or as part of a 'first' or 'second compound', and no cases at all in the plural, it seems fair to say that any /ðat/:/ðɪ-kiː/ opposition is realized only in the singular adjective, and that here too it is difficult to see what the basis of any opposition might be. A list of representative examples of /ðat/, /ðat ðɛr/, /ðɪ-kiː/ and /ðɪ-ki ðɛr/ is given below, in their function as singular adjectives, so that they can easily be compared.

/ðat/
All they got to "do is steer *that* little "wheel a bit.
You'd put in "dynamite to blast *that* stone "off.
Us'd go "in *that* pub and have a pint of "beer.

/ðat ðɛr/

I used to walk *that there* "two mile and "half.

Good as "gold, *that there* "thing was.

/ðɪ-kiː/

All of us be in "*thicky* boat, you see.

'*Thicky* "dog', he said, 'been there all "day?'

Stairs went up "there, like, "*thicky* side, "*thicky* end of the wall.

Thicky place would be "black with people . . .

I travelled *thicky* old road "four " year . . .

What's "*thicky* "little "place called, before you get up "Yel-verton?

Thicky field, they'd "break it, they called it.

He was going to put me and Jan "up *thicky* night.

"Never been through *thicky* road " since.

/ðɪ-kiː ðɛr/

Jim Connell carted home *thicky there* jar of "cyder same as he carted it "up.

We got in *thicky there* "field . . .

The morphological status of /ðiːz/ and /ðɪs/ as singulars, and of /ðejz/ and /ðiːz/ as plurals has already been discussed. Syntactically, their use seems to correspond to Standard English closely, except in one important respect: the 'first compound' forms are used in a way similar to a non-standard usage which is fairly widespread, in the sense of 'a' or 'a certain'.

/ðiːz jiːr/

He'd got *this here* "dog.

You'd put *this here* great "crust on top.

The 'first compound' is never used as an equivalent to Standard English 'this', being reserved for uses of the type above, although there is another form /ðiːz . . . jiːr/,[1] which is occasionally used where Standard English would show 'this', eg Between here and *this* village "*here* like.

In the plural, an exactly parallel syntactic division occurs between /ðejz/ (cf Standard English 'these') and /ðejz jiːr/.

These here "maidens that was here . . .

I used to put them in front of *these here* "sheds.

They got *these here* "hay-turners . . .

In all the above examples, the 'first compounds', both singular and plural, refer to items which have not been mentioned before, and which are not adjacent to the speaker; they are thus referentially distinct from the normal use of Standard English 'this'.

Although we can fairly say that /ðiːz/ and /ðejz/ are syntactically distinct from their equivalent first compounds, what of the other adjective compounds /ðat ðɛr/, /ðɪ-kiː ðɛr/ and /ðej ðɛr/? There seems to be no syntactic division in these cases between them and their equivalent simple forms, so it is perhaps not surprising that Table 4.2 shows them to be without exception much less common than /ðiːz jiːr/ and /ðejz jiːr/, which have a distinct syntactic role. Forms such as

> Us got in *thicky there* "field

and

> Good as "gold, *that there* "thing was.

do not seem any different from

> Us "mowed *thicky* little plat . . .

and

> He turned *that* "hare "three "times . . .

There is certainly no apparent correlation with any notional degree of emphasis.

In the case of the singular pronouns, the 'first compounds' are extremely rare, *cf.*

> He done "well with *that there*. (/ðat ðɛr/.)
> He went out "broad, *this here* what's "dead now. (/ðiːz jiːr/.)

The basic opposition here is between the simple forms and the 'second compounds' /ðɪs jiːr jiːr/ and /ðat ðɛr ðɛr/. Here the syntactic division is fairly clear: the second compounds are used in certain adverbial phrases, particularly after 'like', where the demonstrative refers to no specific antecedent:

> Tis getting like *this here* "here.
> I've had to walk home "after *that there there*.

and also, with reference to a specific antecedent, when particular emphasis is drawn to the item in question.

> I've had the "wireless there, *this here* "here, for "good many years.
> One of *these here* "crocks, something like *that there* "there.

In all other cases, the simple forms are used.

"This was coming "*this* way.
Then he did meet with "*this*.
That's "one "bad "job, "*that* was.

/ðat/ is used particularly frequently in two phrases, 'likes of that' and 'and that'.

He doed a bit of "farmering and likes of "that.
I got a "jumper and *that* home "now.

The last question is one of the most interesting. Is there really only one form /ðej/ functioning as a plural pronoun? At first sight, this would seem improbable, given that there is a plural adjective form /ðejz/ and that the 'this':'that' opposition is maintained elsewhere in the system. However, all attempts to elicit such a form failed, and there is at least one spontaneous utterance where, if a form /ðejz/ did exist as a pronoun, it might be expected to appear:

There's "thousands of acres out there would grow it better than *they* in "*here* grow it.

Taking all these factors together, we tentatively suggest that the opposition 'this':'that' is neutralized in this position, even though this seems rather unlikely, given the adjectival system.

But there is another point. It is in fact difficult to identify occurrences of /ðej/ as demonstratives with any certainty, because the form is identical with that of the personal pronoun /ðej/ (Standard English 'they' or 'them').

We may observe at this point that in the dialect, the third plural personal pronoun forms are /ðej/ and /əm/. The first form is used in all stressed positions and as unstressed subject except in inverted Q-forms; the second is used as the unstressed non-subject, and as the unstressed subject in inverted Q-forms. Thus we find:

/ðej/

"I had to show the pony but "*they* winned the cups.
I could chuck "*they* about.
That's up to "*they*, they know what they'm a"bout of.
They'd take 'em back of your "door for half-a-crown.

/əm/

They expect to have a "name to the house, "don't *'em*?
Where do *'em* get the "tools to?
That was as far as "ever they paid *'em*.
I stayed there "long with *'em* for more than a "year.

When considering /ðej/, we find a series of utterances such as the following in which a division between personal and demonstrative pronouns would be largely arbitrary.

I could "throw 'em, chuck "they about.
"They in "towns, they go to concerts,
Us finished up with "they in . . .
They do seven acres a "day, now, with "they.
There is "they that take an "interest in it.
I could cut in so straight (as) some of "they that "never do it.

Although, following the system of Standard English, we have so far differentiated between /ðej/ as a stressed personal pronoun and /ðej/ as a demonstrative pronoun, it is clearly more economical, in terms of the dialectal material, to consider the two functions as coalescing within one system: STRESSED /ðej/; UN-STRESSED /əm/.[2] This system would operate in all positions where Standard English would show either a third person plural personal pronoun, or a plural demonstrative pronoun. Similarly, there is a dialectal system STRESSED /ðat/ UNSTRESSED /ɪt/ in the third person singular, where the referent is abstract or non-specific, in that /ðat/ never occurs unstressed nor /ɪt/ stressed. Thus in contrast to the last example above, we find:

I seed some of 'em that never walked a "mile in their "lives,

where the form /əm/ is unstressed. (Such unstressed examples are much rarer than stressed examples in positions where Standard English would show a demonstrative pronoun simply because 'those' is normally stressed in Standard English.)
We should note finally, however, that this analysis of the material does not in any way explain the absence of a plural pronoun /ðejz/, any more than the linking of /ðat/ with /ɪt/ precludes the existence of a singular demonstrative pronoun /ðiːz/. The non-existence of /ðejz/ as a pronoun seems best considered as an accidental gap in the corpus.

Notes

1. Except where specifically mentioned, as here, the compound forms are inseparable. Where 'here' and 'there' do come after the nominal, they normally bear a distinct nucleus, as a postposed adverb.
2. Not wholly valid in view of certain occurrences of /ðej/ as unstressed subject (see above).

Chapter 5

The actuation problem for gender change in Wessex versus Newfoundland

Harold Paddock

5.1 Introduction

It is assumed that some changes in a language have a mainly extralinguistic (*eg* social) motivation while others have a mainly intralinguistic (*eg* psychological) motivation. This chapter[*] proposes intralinguistic motivations for a grammatical change in Wessex Vernacular English. These motivations will be used to explain why an earlier three-gender system for nouns in Wessex has been well preserved in those varieties of Newfoundland Vernacular English which have mainly Wessex origins, while change towards a two-gender system has taken place in the source area of Wessex[1] itself in south-western England. This is the type of question that Weinreich, Labov and Herzog (1968:102) called the 'actuation problem'[2] which 'can be regarded as the very heart' of a theory of language change.

Intralinguistic motivation of language change may be better understood if we regard each lect (*ie* language, dialect or variety) as a system of systems or subsystems. This chapter will attempt to explain some grammatical differences between two closely related lects of Modern English, Wessex and Newfoundland Vernacular English, in terms of how linguistic subsystems tend to support or undermine one another within a given lect. It is assumed that speakers or learners of any lect are subject to (conscious or unconscious) psychological pressure towards a state of 'systemic congruency',[3] in which associated subsystems are maximally congruent with one another.

[*] The author gratefully acknowledges the generous financial support of the Canada Council and the Social Sciences and Humanities Research Council of Canada.

At the system (or macrosystem) level we can easily see the lack of one-to-one correspondence between distinctions made in the five main components of any lect, that is, in the phonology, morphology, syntax, lexicon and semantics. This situation produces an internal tension within any lect which is probably one of the main motivations for intralectal changes and variations. For example, not all semantic distinctions are reflected in the lexicon. Thus, in English the semantic distinction of <male/female> is realized in the lexicon for horses (*stallion/mare*) and sheep (*ram/ewe*) but not for camels. Similarly, not all syntactic distinctions are reflected in the morphology. For example, in English an -*ing* suffix occurs on a wide range of syntactic verbals, nominals and adjectivals.[4] A language with a very restricted inventory of phonemes and syllable types is naturally more likely to use reduplication as a morphological process. Homophony and polysemy are well-known phenomena (Samuels 1972:67–77) which reflect the common lack of one-to-one correspondence between sound and meaning.

A similar lack of one-to-one correspondence between distinctions is found at the subsystem or microsystem levels. For example, in the Wessex-type lects discussed below nouns that are semantically <mass> nouns are normally assigned to the syntactic category of NEUTER.[5] However, such <mass> nouns are sometimes reassigned to the syntactic category of FEMININE, especially when the speaker seems to be attributing to them such semantic features as <mobile> or <self-moving>. Hence, such mass nouns as *rain, snow, fog* or *ice* are normally referred to in Newfoundland by using the NEUTER pronoun *it;* but when rain showers, snow flurries, fog banks or ice-pans are seen approaching one often hears sentences such as 'Here she comes!' However, this reassignment of gender might be more apparent than real in Newfoundland. This is because the nouns *shower, flurry, bank* and *pan* are all <count> nouns in Newfoundland. Furthermore, all <count> nouns are either MASCULINE or FEMININE in Newfoundland and the only <inanimate> <count> nouns that are normally FEMININE in Newfoundland are those that are <self-moving>, such as *boat, ship, car* and *aeroplane*. For example, in Newfoundland *cheese* as a <mass> noun selects the NEUTER pronoun *it;* but a *slice of cheese* selects the usual Newfoundland <inanimate> <count> pronoun, the MASCULINE *he*.[6]

Further uncertainties or ambiguities in the above covert gender system derive from the fact that the same feature appears to function syntactically in one subsystem but semantically in a related subsystem. For example, the mass/count distinction appears to have underlying semantic implications in the pronominal subsystem but surface morphosyntactic manifestations in such adnominal subsystems as articles and demonstratives. Henning Andersen (1973) has cogently argued that structural ambiguities can 'internally motivate' changes within the phonology of a lect. This chapter will try to demonstrate that such ambiguities can also motivate changes within the morphology and syntax of a lect. Andersen notes the significant fact that language change involves both continuity and discreteness. The continuity is provided by public community norms which regulate the rate of overt change; the discreteness is provided by private internalized grammars which are re-created in covert language acquisition by children and revised in covert 'rule' changes by adults. In this way, Andersen throws light on the two major questions of 'constraints' and 'transition' raised by Weinreich, Labov and Herzog (1968).

5.2 Gender marking in Wessex-type English

It is usually claimed that English nouns lost their grammatical gender during the historical period called Middle English, roughly 1100–1500. But this claim needs some qualification. What actually happened during the Middle English period was that more overt gender marking of English nouns gave way to more covert marking. As in Lyons (1968:281–8), the term 'gender' is used here to refer to morphosyntactic classes of nouns. It is true that the loss of adjective concord in Middle English made gender marking less overt; but Modern English still retains some determiner concord which allows us to classify nouns (Christophersen and Sandved 1969). In addition, Modern English (ModE), like Old English (OE) and Middle English (ME), possesses pronominal distinctions which enable us to classify nouns.

We can distinguish at least three distinctly different types of gender marking along the continuum from most overt to most covert. The most overt involves the marking of gender in the morphology of the noun itself, as in Swahili (Lyons 1968:284–6). Near the middle of the overt-covert continuum we could place the marking of gender in adnominals such as adjectives and determiners. At or near the covert end[7] of the scale we find the marking of gender in pronominal systems.

During all three main historical stages of the English language (OE, ME, ModE) one has been able to assign nouns to three syntactic classes called MASCULINE, FEMININE and NEUTER. However, throughout the recorded history of English this three-way gender marking has become less and less overt. In OE all three types of gender marking were present. But even in OE the intrinsic marking (by noun inflections) was often ambiguous in that it gave more information about noun declension (*ie* paradigm class) than about gender (*ie* concord class). The least ambiguous marking of gender in OE was provided by the adnominals traditionally called demonstratives and definite articles. In addition, gender 'discord' sometimes occurred in OE, in that the intrinsic gender marking (if any) and the adnominal marking, on the one hand, did not always agree with the gender of the pronominal, on the other hand. Standard ME underwent the loss of a three-way gender distinction in the morphology of both the nominals and the adnominals. This meant that Standard ModE nouns were left with only the most covert type of three-way gender marking, that of the pronominals. Hence we can assign a Standard ModE noun to the gender class MASCULINE, FEMININE or NEUTER by depending only on whether it selects *he, she* or *it* respectively as its proform.

During the ME and Early ModE periods the south-western (here called Wessex-type) dialects of England diverged from Standard English in their developments of adnominal and pronominal subsystems. In particular, the demonstratives of Standard English lost all trace of gender marking, whereas in south-western dialects their OE three-way distinction of MASCULINE/FEMININE/NEUTER developed into a two-way MASS/COUNT distinction which has survived in some Wessex-type dialects of Late ModE.[8] The result in Wessex was that the two-way distinction in adnominals such as demonstratives and indefinites[9] came into partial conflict with the three-way distinction in pronominals.

5.3 The Hierarchy Principle

The Hierarchy Principle states that subordinate distinctions are likely to disappear or change before their superordinate distinctions do so. This principle is partially supported by the data from Wessex, in which the subordinate masculine/feminine distinction is sometimes lost or changed, but in which its superordinate neuter/non-neuter distinction is always preserved. However, this principle is not supported by the history of the animacy and mobility distinctions in Wessex English, for here we will see that the Reflection Principle has outweighed the Hierarchy Principle.

For purposes of exposition the following three assumptions are made:

1. Semantic distinctions underlie the covert system of gender found in varieties of Newfoundland English that derive mainly from south-western England.
2. The semantic distinctions form a hierarchy, rather than a matrix of features that intersect without restrictions.
3. The hierarchy defined for the 'daughter' lect called Newfoundland Vernacular English used to underlie at least some varieties of the 'mother' lect called Wessex Vernacular English in the Early ModE period.

We note in Figure 5.1 that each of the three genders occurs at the ends of two semantic branches in the gender hierarchy for Newfoundland. On the <−count> or <mass> side of the hierarchy the bifurcation of the NEUTER nouns may be omitted, since all mass nouns are normally assigned neuter gender. However,

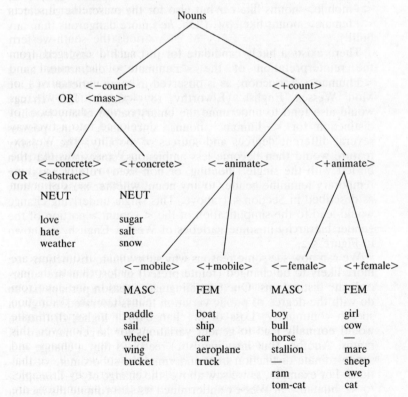

FIGURE 5.1   A gender hierarchy for Newfoundland Vernacular English.

on the $<+\text{count}>$ side of the hierarchy two levels of bifurcation below the $<+\text{count}>$ node seem necessary in order to semantically define the MASCULINE and FEMININE classes of nouns. Other things being equal, we would therefore expect that any simplification of the hierarchy would occur first on the $<+\text{count}>$ side; and that is exactly what is found in some varieties of Wessex English in the Late ModE period.

I will now try to deduce or, better, 'abduce' (Andersen 1973) the underlying changes in the hierarchy which could lead to the observed genders of count nouns in such varieties of Wessex English. When one observes[10] nouns such as *car* being assigned masculine gender ('You'll have to pay a lot for *hé*!') one might assume that the $<\pm\text{mobile}>$ distinction has been lost for all inanimate count nouns. But this assumption might be premature. It would be preferable if we could find a single underlying change that would account not only for the masculine gender of $<+\text{mobile}>$ nouns like *car* but also for the masculine gender of $<+\text{female}>$ nouns like *cow*. ('Oh, *he*'s more dangerous than any bull!').

There exists a likely candidate for just such a single change – the reinterpretation of the $<\pm\text{animate}>$ distinction as a $<\pm\text{human}>$ distinction, as is observed in some varieties of Late Mod Wessex English (Elworthy 1875–76:32). This change would also tend to undermine the binary nature of any mobility distinction for $<-\text{human}>$ nouns, since such nouns possess several different degrees and sources of mobility. The mobility feature would then become less ambiguous, since it would then be left with the single ('floating' or non-fixed) role of assigning temporary feminine gender to any noun, whether mass or count, as described in Section 5.1 above. This single underlying change would lead to the simplification of the $<+\text{count}>$ portion of the gender hierarchy in some varieties of Wessex English, as shown in Figure 5.2.

We can now see some reasons why subordinate distinctions are more likely to be changed (reinterpreted) or lost than are superordinate distinctions. One (extralinguistic) reason perhaps has to do with the degree of public variation that is tolerated in a given speech community. Loss of or change in a higher distinction would normally lead to gender variations for larger numbers of nouns. Another (but intralinguistic) reason is that a change in a superordinate distinction may undermine its subordinate distinctions. For example, as we saw above, the change of $<-\text{animate}>$ to $<-\text{human}>$ in Wessex undermined its subordinate distinction of $<\pm\text{mobile}>$. However, the change of $<+\text{animate}>$ to

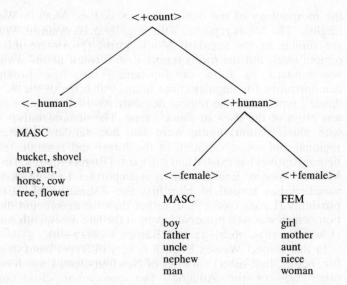

FIGURE 5.2   A gender hierarchy for count nouns in Wessex Vernacular English.

<+human> had exactly the opposite effect, for it conveniently eliminated the unwanted <±female> distinction from a whole group of non-human nouns of unspecified sex, such as *horse, dog, cat, sheep,* etc.

5.4 The Reflection Principle

The proposed Reflection Principle states that a distinction in one subsystem will be strengthened or weakened according to the extent to which it is reflected in analogous distinctions in other subsystems. When we compare gender marking in Newfoundland and Wessex we find two important differences. In Wessex, but not in Newfoundland, we find a mass/count distinction in an adnominal subsystem, the demonstratives, which would strongly reinforce the neuter/non-neuter distinction in the pronominals. Again in Wessex, but not in Newfoundland, we find extensive surface neutralization of the masculine/feminine distinction in the pronominals. This would tend to seriously undermine the masculine/feminine distinction, since this gender distinction surfaces only in the pronominals and never in the adnominals.

As was shown in the historical sketch of gender marking in Section 5.2 above, the mass/count distinction was preserved in the morphology of the demonstratives in Late Modern Wessex English. The forms reported with singular mass nouns in Wessex are similar to the standard ModE forms (proximate *this* and remote *that*), but the forms reported with count nouns are quite non-standard in form or function. Thus, the proximate demonstrative for singular count nouns was often of the *these* or *thease*[11] type, while the remote demonstrative for the same nouns was often of the *thick* or *thuck*[11] type. The demonstratives used with plural (count) nouns were also non-standard.[11] Extensive regional and social variation in the forms and functions of the demonstratives has existed and still exists (Rogers 1979: 32) in Late Modern Wessex English, but it is important to note that this variation has tended to blur first the distinction of deixis or proximity (Lyons 1968:278–9) rather than the mass/count distinction, which was well preserved even in the late nineteenth century (Elworthy 1875–76:29–32 and Barnes 1886:17–19).

In this respect Wessex English is very different from its sister (or, better, half-sister) varieties of Newfoundland English on the other side of the Atlantic. The mass/count distinction in demonstratives which was brought by most settlers from Wessex has not been preserved in Newfoundland. There are perhaps several reasons for this loss in Newfoundland. No doubt one of the main ones is the strong influence of Anglo-Irish or Hiberno-English on most varieties of Newfoundland English. Whatever the reasons for the loss of the mass/count distinction in the demonstratives in Newfoundland, the result was that the strong reinforcement of the neuter/non-neuter distinction in the pronouns by the mass/count distinction in the demonstratives continued in Wessex long after it was lost in Wessex-based varieties in Newfoundland.

Furthermore, the strengthening of the neuter/non-neuter distinction in Wessex has been accompanied by a weakening of the masculine/feminine distinction in Wessex, but not in Newfoundland. This weakening or undermining of the masculine/feminine distinction in Wessex English can be attributed to the homophony of some 'weak' forms of third person singular pronouns. This homophony consisted of the same phonological form, usually [ɚ], being often used in Wessex where more standard varieties of English would use either the distinctively masculine forms *he, him, 'im* or the distinctively feminine forms *she, her, 'er*. This homophony resulted from some rather radical functional and phonological changes in the pronouns.

A loss of morphological contrasts between subject forms and object forms of pronouns is commonly found in the whole south-western area of England. In addition, extensive parts of the region have replaced the former contrast between subject and object forms with a contrast between 'strong' and 'weak' forms. In some instances, the strong/weak difference is realized by using the former subjects as strong form and the former objects as weak forms. This yields variants such as the following.

FIRST PERSON PLURAL
[1] (a) *Wé* wouldn' do that, would *us*?
    (b) Give *us* the shovel.
    (c) Give the shovel to *wé*, not to *théy*.

THIRD PERSON PLURAL
[2] (a) *Théy* wouldn' do that, would *'um*?
    (b) Give *'um* the shovel.
    (c) Give the shovel to *théy*, not to *wé*.

The situation is complicated in the second person pronouns by the fact that some varieties of Wessex and conservative Newfoundland English appear to use parts of an earlier formal second person (*you, your, yours*) as its strong forms, but parts of an earlier informal second person (*thee, thy, thine*) as its weak forms. This yields variants such as the following.

SECOND PERSON
[3] (a) *Yóu* wouldn' do that, would *'ee*?[12]
    (b) I'll give *'ee* the shovel.
    (c) I'll give the shovel to *yóu*, not to he.

It should be noted here that the weak second person form *'ee* is not only from a formerly separate paradigm, that of the informal or familiar *thee*, but is also a phonologically reduced form without initial consonant.[13] In some cases the weak forms of pronouns originate mainly from phonologically reduced, unstressed forms. This yields variants such as the following.

THIRD PERSON SINGULAR MASCULINE
[4] (a) *Hé* wouldn' do that, would *'e*?[14]
    (b) *'a* wouldn' do that, would *uh* [ə]?[15]
    (c) *Uh* wouldn' do that, would *ur* [ɚ]?[16]

The retroflex r-colour added at the end of [4c] above is easily explained. In most of south-western England, except for Bristol,[17] r-colour was often added to unstressed, schwa-like vowels at the ends of phonological words or phrases. Hence words like *Martha, soda* and *shadda* 'shadow' came to be pronounced as *Marther, soder* and *shadder*. However, the r-colouring of the weak form of the feminine third person singular could represent a preservation of its Old English /r/.[18] Regardless of their sources, we find Wessex variants such as the following.

THIRD PERSON SINGULAR FEMININE

[5] (a) *Shé* wouldn' do that, would *'er*?
    (b) *Hér* wouldn' do that, would *'er*?
    (c) *'er* wouldn' do that, would *'er* [ɚ]?

One effect of the above variations is that [4c] and [5c] are almost totally homophonous. A stranger unacquainted with the dialect, and presumably a local child acquiring the dialect, must listen closely to detect any difference in retroflexion between the two initial schwa-type vowels in [4c] and [5c]. The result has sometimes been complete homophony for such pairs of sentences (Elworthy 1875–76: 33).

Wessex English differs from its sister, or half-sister, varieties in Newfoundland with respect to this neutralization of the masculine/feminine contrast in the third person singular pronouns. In Newfoundland this contrast has been rapidly re-established or reinforced in Wessex-based varieties so that sentences with masculine *ur*[ɚ] were likely to be heard only from older rural male informants by the middle of the twentieth century in Newfoundland. In addition, the use of feminine *'er*[ɚ] as subject apparently never flourished in Newfoundland.[19] Again, the strong influence of Anglo-Irish or Hiberno-English on the Newfoundland Regional Standard, especially until Newfoundland's confederation with Canada in 1949, has no doubt contributed to this situation.

With respect to the Reflection Principle for grammatical gender, then, Newfoundland English differs from Wessex in two important ways. On the one hand, the superordinate neuter/non-neuter distinction has been strongly reinforced by a mass/count distinction in the demonstratives in Wessex but not in Newfoundland. On the other hand, the subordinate masculine/feminine distinction has been undermined by frequent surface neutralization of this distinction in the third person singular pronouns in Wessex but not in Newfoundland. It is therefore not surprising that a change from a three-gender system towards a two-gender system developed in some varieties of Wessex English.[20] The neuter nouns were unaffected by this development, but most of the formerly feminine nouns have been reclassified with the formerly masculine nouns. It would be misleading, however, to say that they have become 'masculine', since the resulting binary gender distinction should be called neuter/non-neuter or mass/count rather than neuter/masculine. We should also note the strong parallels with gender changes in

North Germanic which have left a similar neuter/common distinction in many lects (Haugen 1976:73–9, 287–90, 370–1).

5.5 The Overtness Principle

The proposed Overtness Principle represents an attempt to assign a relative weighting[21] to different types of marking along the overt/covert gender marking continuum which has been outlined above in section 5.2. Our Overtness Principle states that, other things being equal, a more overt distinction is likely to outweigh a more covert distinction whenever two distinctions fail to mirror each other. This statement is of course only a crude first approximation to the actual psychological weighting, because other things are rarely equal. For example, on the internal causation side there is the question of relative frequency. Thus, a more overt distinction may occur with lower frequency than does a more covert one. This will tend to equalize their weights. On the external causation side a more overt distinction may be less standard or less prestigious while its more covert rival may be more standard or more prestigious.[22] Again, this will tend to equalize their weights.

However, for the grammatical gender data being considered in this paper we may disregard the above cautions with some confidence. On the question of relative frequency we may assume approximate equality, since both the demonstratives and the personal pronouns occur with very high frequencies in all varieties of spoken English. On the question of standardness or prestige we may also assume a crude equivalence, since our two crucial Wessex English features (i.e. the mass/count distinction in the demonstratives and the neutralization of the masculine/feminine distinction in the pronouns) are both non-standard and their prestige, if any, would be both covert and local in nature.

We can therefore with some assurance apply our Overtness Principle to the data under discussion, and claim that in Wessex English the more overt distinction (of mass/count) in the demonstratives should outweigh the more covert distinction (of masculine/feminine) in the third person singular pronouns, even if the latter distinction were not neutralized by homophony of sentences such as [4c] and [5c] (see section 5.4 above).

5.6 Conclusions

Because of the sociolinguistic movement pioneered in the 1960s by Labov, we now know a good deal about external (extralinguistic) motivations of language change and variation. These include such 'semi-permanent' features of speakers as their age, sex, socio-economic class and ethnic background, as well as the more 'temporary' stylistic features. Sociolinguists have also given us insights into certain internal (intralinguistic) motivations for change, especially the phonetic environments that condition certain sound changes. Attempts have been made by sociolinguists to quantify all the above types of conditioning. These attempts have been successful to the extent that the conditioners of variation were real rather than spurious and were also amenable to controlled 'scientific' observation.[23] Unfortunately, however, socio-linguistics cannot give us a complete picture of linguistic variation and change. This is because some of the main conditioners are not directly observable at all, but must be hypothesized after the fact. This unobservable psychological conditioning of language variation and change may be just as important as is the more observable social conditioning. We can therefore say that generativists such as Halle (1962) and King (1969) were justified in trying to find mentalistic or psychological explanations of certain changes in language. Of course, in specific cases we may be asked to choose between competing explanations. For example, Halle (1962) gives a psychological explanation of an apparent historical merger of English low vowels that later split to restore the surface contrast 'lost' in the merger. Samuels (1972:34) rejects Halle's explanation and states that, 'From a purely intrasystemic viewpoint, merger is irreversible'; but Samuels provides his own social explanation by saying that 'the old distribution can be "borrowed back" from a neighbouring system', that is, from a neighbouring social or regional dialect.

In this chapter, I have attempted to explain a change in grammatical gender of nouns in Wessex English in terms of unobservable psychological realities. To be more specific, I have tried to apply Henning Andersen's (1973) model of how learners or speakers of a language try to 'solve' by means of 'abductive reasoning' the structural ambiguities that always exist in the samples of the language that they experience. But how can we ever know that our assumed abductions are 'right' or 'correct', either in general terms or in any particular application? My own answer to this question would be very similar to Anttila's (1972: 202) given below:

> Abduction is certainly psychologically real, although we might get to know the particular cases only accidentally. It also explains why the actuation problem of change cannot be perfectly solved . . ., because

it is not a purely linguistic question, but a much wider one of human perception and reasoning. On the other hand, it explains the common core of change mechanisms . . . and analogy in analysis . . . Note that like folk etymology such analysis can be 'wrong' . . .

In any case, regardless of the uncertainties involved, we cannot afford to ignore the psychological realities of language, for it is only these that can provide insight into the genesis of variants which may have purely internal origins. Such variants must be psychologically created before they can be socially constrained. In this sense then, psychological explanation is prior to social explanation. However, both types of explanation are necessary. For example, in this chapter I have had to adduce external (extralectal and social) conditioning to explain why Newfoundland Vernacular English has retained a three-gender system, but internal (intralectal and psychological) conditioning to explain why Wessex English has moved towards a two-gender system.

In addition, neither type of explanation is ever likely to be complete or exhaustive. For example, sociolinguists do not claim to have investigated all the socially conditioned variation in a speech community by studying the apparent effects of a few (independent) social variables such as age, sex and class. Similarly, in this chapter I have not described all the relevant subsystems that covary with the gender differences between Wessex and Newfoundland. For example, I have not described their differences for the <±human> distinction as realized in the relative pronouns such as *who, which, that,* zero, etc.

Furthermore, both social and psychological explanations are alike in that they utilize the concept of covariation. Social explanations adduce covariations between extralinguistic and linguistic variables, while psychological explanations adduce covariations between linguistic subsystems. Both types of explanation are *post hoc* and inductive (or better, abductive) and they therefore cannot attain the certainties of true deductive reasoning. The main difference between the two is that social explanations now utilize statistical tests of covariation. This chapter proposes three principles by which we may more rigorously evaluate some of our psychological explanations of covariation. These three proposed principles should be tested on other cases of language change, and especially on gender changes in three branches of Indo-European (Indic, Romance and Celtic) in which three-gender systems (of neuter/masculine/feminine) have evolved into two-gender systems (of masculine/feminine or unmarked/marked).[24]

Finally, it seems to me that Labov has been wisely cautious, but perhaps overly pessimistic, about our ability to throw light on the actuation problem in language change. I believe in some cases that there is much rather than 'little that can be said about the particular social or linguistic events that trigger a particular change' (Labov 1972:317). For example, when two distinctive varieties of a language mix in a new location, as Hiberno-English and Wessex English have done in Newfoundland, it provides us with an opportunity 'to explain why some forms from the dialects contributing to the mixture survive and some not' (Trudgill 1985:6). It even allows us, as this chapter has shown, to explain why some features have survived better in the mixture than in the contributing dialects.

Notes

1. Here the term 'Wessex' is being used, as in Rogers (1979), as a convenient synonym for south-western England. It is also an appropriate term for the main English source area for Newfoundland English, since most English settlers in Newfoundland came from Dorset, the heartland of Wessex, and from adjacent areas of Devon, Somerset, Wiltshire and Hampshire (Handcock 1977:38).
2. Weinreich, Labov and Herzog (1968: 102) introduce the actuation problem as follows: 'In the light of answers to these, we can approach a fifth question, perhaps the most basic: What factors can account for the actuation of changes? Why do changes in a structural feature take place in a particular language at a given time, but not in other languages with the same feature, or in the same language at other times? This *actuation problem* can be regarded as the very heart of the matter.'
3. Compare and contrast the use of the term 'systemic regulation' by Samuels (1972: 64–87).
4. Compare the 'squishes' described by Ross (1973) and others.
5. Where it seems important to do so, I will distinguish semantic features from syntactic features by enclosing the former in angle brackets, <>, and writing the latter in capitals.
6. The masculine singular pronoun has a wide variety of forms in Wessex-type dialects. Some of these are described in the text below as well as in notes 14, 15 and 16.
7. Perhaps the most covert gender of all is that claimed for English by Joos (1964), who classifies the -s suffix on English verbs as a gender marker since the third person singular subjects (*he, she, it*) have marked gender whereas the other personal pronoun subjects (*I, you, we, they*) have unmarked gender.
8. See, for example, Barnes (1886:17–19) for the nineteenth century and Rogers (1979:32) for the twentieth century.

9. The binary mass/count distinction has not survived to the present day in the Newfoundland demonstratives, but it flourishes in the indefinites. See, for example, Kirwin (1968), Paddock (1981: 15) and Story *et al.* (1982: 162 under *e'er* and *either*), all of which describe the non-standard Newfoundland indefinites used with count nouns.

10. I spent eight months doing fieldwork in the Wessex area in 1978–79. The sentences cited, showing the use of *he* to refer to *car* and *cow*, were recorded in Dorset at that time. The *car* example is from a younger male informant, the *cow* example from an older male. Compare *sow* as *he* in Elworthy (1875–76: 32) for West Somerset about 100 years earlier.

11. For some nineteenth-century variants of Wessex demonstratives see Elworthy (1875–76: 29–32) and Barnes (1886: 17–19). For some twentieth-century ones see Rogers (1979: 32) and Orton and Wakelin (1967: vol. 4, part 3, *pp* 1159–67).

12. A phonologically reduced weak form *ya*, [jæ] and [jə], is also common in both Wessex and Newfoundland.

13. According to Wakelin (1972: 113), the weak second person form that I have written as *'ee* may derive from *ye* rather than *thee*. But see Rogers (1979: 35) on the unlikelihood of a *ye* origin.

14. Both Wessex and Newfoundland English possess another masculine singular weak form spelled variously as *en, un,* or *'n* which is commonly used as the weak object form rather than the weak subject form. As Wakelin (1972: 113) correctly observes, the strong form '*he* is used as object in emphatic cases only'. Since this alveolar nasal form is apparently from OE masculine accusative *hine* rather than from masculine dative *him*, its etymologically correct spelling would be *'in* rather than *en* or *un*.

15. The traditional Wessex spellings *a* or *'a* for masculine singular appear to represent full vowels such as [ei] and [e] as well as reduced schwa-like vowels (Elworthy 1875–6: 32–9). In this respect, the spelling parallels that of the indefinite article in Standard English.

16. The more traditional Wessex spellings in [4c] would be *'a* or *a* instead of *uh*, and *er* instead of *ur*.

17. In Bristol and some nearby areas an excrescent or intrusive lateral was added instead. Hence, words such as *Martha, soda* and *idea* became *Marthel, sodel* and *ideal*. See Wakelin (1972: 163, fn 17) and Wells (1982: 344–5) on the restricted regional and social distribution of this highly stigmatized feature.

18. But see Wakelin (1972: 164, fn 7) for another possible source of the /r/ in feminine singular *her* or *'er*.

19. This was due to regional and ethno-social factors arising from the patterns of settlement in Newfoundland. The earlier English settlers were mainly from further west (and especially from Devon) and often settled with or near the Irish on the Avalon Peninsula, whereas the later English settlers were mainly from further east (and especially from Dorset) and rarely settled near the Irish. The result was that the Devon-type or West Wessex settlers, with their more fre-

quent use of feminine *'er* as subject (Rogers 1979: 35, fn 3), were quickly exposed to Hiberno-English and to some standardization in the more ethnically mixed and more urbanized Avalon Peninsula. The Dorset-type or East Wessex settlers, with their less frequent use of feminine *'er* as subject, dominated nearly all of the island of Newfoundland outside of the Avalon Peninsula (Handcock 1977: 28)

20. Our proposed Reflection Principle is also supported within Wessex itself by the fact that more of the feminine nouns became masculine in precisely those regions, such as West Somerset (Elworthy 1875–76: 32–9), where surface neutralization of the masculine/feminine pronouns was most common.

21. Compare Bailey's (1973) attempt to assign weightings to feature marking in phonology in order to better describe and explain some aspects of variation and change in sound.

22. Prestige itself may be either covert or overt. See, for example, Trudgill (1974: 95–101) based on Labov (1972: 243 and elsewhere).

23. See, for example, Fasold's (1975) reply to Bickerton (1971 and 1973) on such questions.

24. Germanic languages should also be compared with Wessex-type dialects of English. For example, a comparison of the historical developments of gender marking in Wessex English and Dutch would be particularly interesting and instructive. See Dekeyser (1980) for a model. For North Germanic parallels see Haugen (1976).

References

ANDERSEN, HENNING (1973) 'Abductive and deductive change', *Language* **49**: 765–93.

ANTTILA, RAIMO (1972) *An Introduction to Historical and Comparative Linguistics*. New York: Macmillan.

BAILEY, CHARLES-JAMES N. (1973) *Variation and Linguistic Theory*. Arlington, Va.: Center for Applied Linguistics.

BARNES, WILLIAM (1886) *A Glossary of the Dorset Dialect with a Grammar . . .* Dorchester: M. & E. Case; London: Trubner.

BICKERTON, DEREK (1971) 'Inherent variability and variable rules', *Foundations of Language* **7**: 457–92.

BICKERTON, DEREK (1973) 'Quantitative versus dynamic paradigms: the case of Montreal *que*.' In Charles-James N. Bailey and Roger W. Shuy (eds) *New ways of Analyzing Variation in English* Washington DC: Georgetown University Press, *pp* 23–43

CHRISTOPHERSEN, PAUL and SANDVED, ARTHUR O. (1969) *An Advanced English Grammar*. London: Macmillan.

DEKEYSER, XAVIER (1980) 'The diachrony of the gender systems in English and Dutch.' In Jacek Fisiak (ed.) *Historical Morphology*. The Hague: Mouton, *pp* 97–111.

ELWORTHY, FREDERIC THOMAS (1875–76) *The Dialect of West Somerset.* English Dialect Society, vol. 17. London: Trubner.

FASOLD, RALPH W. (1975) 'The Bailey wave model: a dynamic quantitative paradigm.' In Ralph W. Fasold and Roger W. Shuy (eds) *Analyzing Variation in Language,* Washington DC: Georgetown University Press, *pp* 27–58.

HALLE, MORRIS (1962) 'Phonology in generative grammar', *Word* **18**: 54–72.

HANDCOCK, WALTER GORDON (1977) 'English migration to Newfoundland.' In John J. Mannion (ed.) *The Peopling of Newfoundland.* St John's: Institute of Social and Economic Research, Memorial University of Newfoundland, *pp* 15–48.

HAUGEN, EINAR (1976) *The Scandinavian Languages: An Introduction to their History.* London: Faber and Faber.

JOOS, MARTIN (1964) *The English Verb: Form and Meaning.* Madison: University of Wisconsin Press.

KING, ROBERT D. (1969) *Historical Linguistics and Generative Grammar.* Englewood Cliffs, NJ: Prentice-Hall.

KIRWIN, WILLIAM J. (1968) *Either* for *any* in Newfoundland,' *Regional Language Studies . . . Newfoundland* **1**: 8–10.

LABOV, WILLIAM (1972) *Sociolinguistic Patterns.* Philadelphia: University of Pennsylvania Press.

LYONS, JOHN (1968) *Introduction to Theoretical Linguistics.* Cambridge: Cambridge University Press.

ORTON, HAROLD and WAKELIN, MARTYN F. (1967) *Survey of English Dialects* (B) *The Basic Material,* vol. IV; *The Southern Counties* (in three parts). Leeds: E. J. Arnold.

PADDOCK, HAROLD (1981) *A Dialect Survey of Carbonear, Newfoundland.* Publication of the American Dialect Society, No. 68. University: University of Alabama Press.

ROGERS, NORMAN (1979) *Wessex Dialect.* Bradford-on-Avon, Wilts.: Moonraker Press.

ROSS, JOHN ROBERT (1973) 'A fake NP squish.' In Charles-James N. Bailey and Roger W. Shuy (eds) *New Ways of Analyzing Variation in English,* Washington DC: Georgetown University Press, *pp* 96–140.

SAMUELS, MICHAEL L. (1972) *Linguistic Evolution, with Special Reference to English.* London: Cambridge University Press.

STORY, GEORGE M., KIRWIN, WILLIAM J. and WIDDOWSON, JOHN D.A. (1982) *Dictionary of Newfoundland English.* Toronto: University of Toronto Press.

TRUDGILL, PETER (1974) *Sociolinguistics: an Introduction.* Penguin Books.

TRUDGILL, PETER (1985) 'Dialect contact, dialect mixture and new-dialect formation.' Quotation from abstract of Trudgill's keynote paper at the First Symposium on Hiberno-English, 16–17 Sept. 1985, *Programme and Abstracts, p* 6. Dublin: Trinity College, Centre for Language and Communication Studies.

WAKELIN, MARTYN F. (1972) *English Dialects: an Introduction.* London: Athlone Press.

WEINREICH, URIEL, LABOV, WILLIAM, and HERZOG, MARVIN I. (1968) 'Empirical foundations for a theory of language change.' In Winfred P. Lehmann and Yakov Malkiel (eds) *Directions for Historical Linguistics,* Austin and London: University of Texas Press, *pp* 95–195.

WELLS, JOHN C. (1982) *Accents of English 2: The British Isles.* London, etc.: Cambridge University Press.

Part two

Verb systems

Chapter 6

Verb systems in English dialects

Peter Trudgill and J. K. Chambers

A majority of chapters in this book deal in some way with the verb forms of English dialects, with the auxiliaries particularly well represented. In the two sections of the book following this one, we will present chapters that are concerned with, respectively, verbal aspect in English dialects and non-finite verb forms. In the present section we include, first of all, Cheshire's chapter on the use of *ain't* in working-class adolescent speech in the town of Reading, England. Details of the original and thorough fieldwork methodology which produced Cheshire's data can be found in Cheshire (1982).

Negation in dialects of English shows a considerable amount of variation, with even Standard English having variant forms:

you're not	you aren't
he's not	he isn't
we'd not	we hadn't
they'd not	they wouldn't
I'll not	I won't

Non-standard dialects show a wide range of forms, such as those involving Scots and north-eastern England *nae/na*:

I dinnae ken = 'I don't know'
I canna come

and north-western England enclitic *no*:

I shanno = 'I shan't'.

Within the non-standard dialects we also find, as is well known, multiple negation, the syntactic and lexical constraints on which vary from dialect to dialect:

I don't want none.
I haven't got only one.

We also find, as Cheshire herself has discussed elsewhere, *never* used as a negative preterite marker, particularly in British dialects:

I never seen him last night.
It was never me what broke it.

The form *ain't* itself has an interesting and not entirely agreed-upon history, as Cheshire relates. In very many English dialects it functions as the present tense negative form of *be* for all persons:

I ain't stupid.
She ain't coming.

And it also operates as the negative present tense of auxiliary *have*:

We ain't seen him.

but not of full verb *have*:

*We ain't our lunch at 12 = We don't have our lunch at 12.

Ain't occurs in very many areas of the English-speaking world, and comes in a number of different phonological forms: *ain't, en't, in't,* etc. Like the other authors in this section, Cheshire examines variation within the dialect under study, and examines constraints on the usage of the different variants.

Brown's chapter deals with a very difficult problem for syntacticians of English, the presence in a number of dialects of English – in Scotland, the north-east of England and parts of the southern United States – of double modals such as

I might could do it.
He may can come.

The problem of course is that it is well known to be the case that English permits only one modal to occur in this position in the verb phrase. So do these dialects have different rules concerning the structure of the verb phrase? Or is one of the modals 'really' an adverb? In a very detailed analysis based on work with informants from Hawick in the south of Scotland, Brown looks at constraints governing which modal combinations are and are not possible, and at both the syntax and semantics of these constructions.

Readers will also notice that he treats at some length the Scottish tag-form /e/ *eh*? It is sometimes believed by North Americans that this form is exclusively Canadian, presumably because it is more common in Canada than in the USA, but in fact it occurs in very many varieties of English, including Scots as here. Cheshire, too, examines non-standard tag-forms and usage.

The chapter by Ihalainen again takes up the theme of constraints on variation, but this time with the additional claim, which reminds us in particular of the work on variation of C. J. Bailey (see Bailey 1973), that some of the characteristics of variability are due to the diachronic spreading of linguistic innovations from one linguistic context to another. Even more specifically, Ihalainen claims that new forms are introduced first into non-prominent contexts, and only later spread into more salient environments. Ihalainen deals both with the south-west of England pronominal system, also discussed by Paddock (Ch. 5), and more especially with dialect forms of the present tense of *be*.

As Cheshire's chapter indicates, the form *ain't* in non-standard dialects represents not only a neutralization in the negative between auxiliary *have* and *be*, but also a neutralization of the person distinctions of the standard dialect:

	Standard English		Non-standard dialect	
	be	*have*	*be*	*have*
1.	I'm not	I haven't	I ain't	I ain't
2.	you aren't	you haven't	you ain't	you ain't
3.	he isn't	he hasn't	he ain't	he ain't

It is also the case, however, that many non-standard dialects, particularly the traditional dialects, also have no person distinctions in the case of affirmative *have* and *be*. Thus, in many west-of-England dialects, auxiliary *have* occurs as *have* with all persons (while main verb *have* is *has* for all persons, just as lexical verbs take present tense *-s* in all persons: *I has, I goes*). For *be*, some dialects in the north of England have *is* generalized to all persons, while others, in the West Midlands for instance, have generalized *am*. In the Somerset dialect which Ihalainen investigates, the undifferentiated present tense form of *be* appears formerly to have been *be* for all persons, with the possible exception of the second person singular. Ihalainen plots the intrusion into this original system of newer, but not necessarily standard, forms:

Standard English		Original East Somerset	
I *am*	we *are*	I *be*	we *be*
you *are*	you *are*	thou *art*	you *be*
she/he *is*	they *are*	she/he *be*	they *be*

The chapter by Eisikovits is the only one in this volume from the Southern Hemisphere, and the only one to deal exclusively with finite lexical verb forms as opposed to modals, auxiliaries and copulas. Many of the non-standard verb forms she discusses are common to very many English dialects in the Northern Hemisphere also, and her findings are of importance for the study of English far beyond inner-city Sydney.

It is clear that in particular the irregular lexical verb forms of English are subject to considerable variation and change, with both coined forms and regularization featuring. The process of regularization of irregular verbs takes the form for some verbs in some dialects of total regularization:

Standard English			Non-Standard dialects		
draw	drew	drawn	draw	drawed	drawed

This process, of course, has already affected many verbs in Standard English (such as *help,* past tense formerly *holp*), and is in the process of affecting others:

Older standard			Newer standard		
burn	burnt	burnt	burn	burned	burned
lean	leant	leant	lean	leaned	leaned

For other verbs it may occur as a reduction of three forms to two, as for the regular verbs, with past tense and past participle identical, but without the introduction of regular *-ed* forms:

	Standard English (three forms)			Nonstandard Dialects (two forms)		
	see	saw	seen	see	seen	seen
	do	did	done	do	done	done
	write	wrote	written	write	writ	writ
	take	took	taken	take	took	took
cf	love	loved	loved	love	loved	loved
	want	wanted	wanted	want	wanted	wanted

Eisikovits shows, however, that the process is much more complicated than this. Like Cheshire and Brown, she looks at constraints on variation in verb forms, and her results are of particular importance for the thesis advanced by Ihalainen in Chapter 9. Eisikovits shows that standard verb forms have infiltrated Sydney English much more in subordinate clauses, which Ihalainen might well want to claim are lower in prominence, than in main clauses. She also shows that passive and perfective verb forms behave differently, as do past and present perfectives.

References

BAILEY, C-J (1973) *Variation and Linguistic Theory*. Washington DC: Center for Applied Linguistics.

CHESHIRE, J. (1982) *Variation in an English Dialect*. Cambridge: Cambridge University Press.

Chapter 7

Variation in the use of *ain't* in an urban British English dialect

Jenny Cheshire

7.1 Introduction

This paper analyses variation in the occurrence of the grammatical variable *ain't,* using empirical data from a long-term study of the speech of three working-class adolescent peer groups in the town of Reading, England.[1] It describes the syntactic and semantic functions that *ain't* fulfils in the speech of the peer groups and shows how these may be linked to the vernacular subculture to which the groups belong. It also considers the etymology of *ain't* and the linguistic changes that the feature has undergone and that may still be in progress.

7.2 *Ain't* in non-standard Reading English

Ain't is a widespread feature of non-standard English dialects, both in Great Britain and in the United States. The non-standard form corresponds to several standard English verb forms. It occurs as the negative present tense contracted form of *be,* both as the copula:

[1] We've got a park near us, but there ain't nothing over there.[2]

and as the auxiliary:

[2] How come that ain't working?

It is also used as the negative present tense contracted form of the auxiliary *have*:

[3] I ain't got one single flea in my hair, they're all married.

It does not occur as the full verb *have* (this is usually replaced in colloquial speech by *have* + *got*). In some American Black

English dialects it is also used as a past tense auxiliary, where Standard English has *didn't*:

[4] I ain't see the fight, and I ain't hear the fight (from Labov *et al.* 1968).

Whereas the Standard English negative contracted forms are marked for person and number, *ain't* is not. Thus the one non-standard form has five Standard English equivalents: *haven't, hasn't, (a)m not, aren't,* and *isn't.*

7.3 Derivation of *ain't*

It is not unusual for the paradigms in non-standard English dialects to contain fewer forms than the corresponding Standard English paradigms. For example, the present tense verb system in Standard English consists of two forms: a suffixed form, used with third person singular subjects (*eg he goes*), and a suffixless form, used throughout the rest of the paradigm (*eg I go, you go, we go, they go*). Non-standard dialects in Britain and in the United States typically have a simpler present tense system. In the English spoken in south-western Britain, the suffixed form is used throughout the paradigm (Hughes and Trudgill 1979). In Appalachian English the suffixed form is used with third person plural subjects as well as with third person singular subjects (Wolfram and Fasold 1974). Other dialects, notably the Black English Vernacular, and the English spoken in East Anglia, Britain, use the suffixless form throughout the paradigm. Thus the fact that the single form *ain't* occurs for Standard English *(a)m not, aren't.* and *isn't,* on the one hand, and for Standard English *hasn't* and *haven't,* on the other hand, can be seen as typifying a general trend in non-standard dialects towards the simplification of linguistic systems. The fact that the one form, *ain't,* is used for two verbs that are quite distinct in meaning and in syntactic function, though, is an unusual phenomenon and one that requires some explanation.

There has been some discussion in the literature concerning the derivation of *ain't.* In the past this discussion has centred on whether the form derives originally from the Standard English contracted forms of *be,* or the Standard English contracted forms of *have* (see, for example, Willard 1936; Stevens 1954). In fact, however, the evidence that is available suggests that *ain't* derived by regular sound change from the negative present tense contracted forms of both *have* and *be,* so that the fact that the one form is used for both verbs is the result of a diachronic coincidence.

Both Jespersen (1940) and Stevens (1954) describe the route by which *ain't* could have derived from *hasn't* and *haven't*. In the Middle English period many of the irregular verb forms had two pronunciations, of which one predominated in positive sentences and the other in negative sentences. This meant that the contracted negative forms were clearly distinguished from the positive forms, and there could be no confusion of meaning (as in the case, for example, of *can* [kæn] and *can't* [kɑːnt] in British English today). The verb *have,* then, would have had two forms: one with a short vowel, used in positive sentences, and one with a long vowel, used in negative sentences. By the eighteenth century the fricative had been dropped in some contracted verb forms (in *isn't, wasn't* and *doesn't,* for example, as well as in *hasn't* and *haven't*), and also in some words used frequently in poetry (*cf e'er, se'en*). This is attested to in the literature of the time: Swift, for example, objected to the use of the form *hadn't* as early as 1710 (in *The Tatler,* No. 230). The initial aspirate would have been lost quite regularly in unstressed occurrences, and the long vowel would have diphthongized, via [æ]~[ɛ]~[e] to [eɪ], as it did, for example, in the compound verb form *behave* (Brook 1958).

Ain't, then, can be shown to derive regularly from *haven't* and *hasn't.* However, the derivation of the form from the negative present tense contracted forms of *be* is not so straightforward, though there is evidence to suggest that it derives from at least one of the contracted forms.

The most probable ancestor of *ain't* is the first person singular form *am not.* The first nasal would have assimilated to the second, giving the form *ann't* (Jespersen 1940), possibly via an intermediary syncopated form *amn't* (*cf* Stevens 1954), which occurs today in some Scottish English dialects. Simplification of the long consonant may then have been accompanied by a lengthening of the vowel to Early Modern [æ], which diphthongized to [eɪ], thus yielding the form [eɪnt].[3]

Jespersen suggests that *ain't* could also have derived independently from *aren't* and *isn't.* Loss of the [r] from *aren't* and subsequent diphthongization of the vowel would result in the form [eɪnt]. Loss of the fricative in *isn't* and a lowering and lengthening of the 'unstable' vowel (as in *don't* and *can't*), followed by its subsequent diphthongization would also give the form [eɪnt]. However, there is little evidence to substantiate these last suggestions, and the more likely explanation is that extension of the form [eɪnt] throughout the paradigm took place by analogy with the other negative present tense contracted forms (*eg can't* and *won't*), which have a single form throughout the paradigm.

In some dialects the form [ɪnt] occurs as a phonetic variant of [eɪnt]. It would seem reasonable to assume that the [ɪnt] variant is a survival of an earlier form and to expect it, therefore, to occur with third person singular forms of the verb *be* (*ie* to correspond to Standard English *isn't*). In Reading English, however, the form [ɪnt] has a specific syntactic function. This will become clear in the analysis that follows.

7.4 *Ain't* as a sociolinguistic variable in Reading English

The analysis of *ain't* in working-class Reading English is based on the occurrence of the form in the informal, vernacular speech of three adolescent peer groups. Members of the peer groups were recorded over an eight-month period in naturally occurring groups in the adventure playgrounds that they used as meeting-places. Care was taken to ensure that the recordings were natural, spontaneous and relaxed (see Cheshire 1982). In addition, recordings of a more formal speech style were obtained for some speakers by asking teachers to record members of the peer groups at school, in the presence of the teacher. Thirteen boys and twelve girls were recorded at the playgrounds; they ranged in age from 9 to 17, though most were aged between 11 and 15. A total of 331 occurrences of *ain't* in the speech of the groups was analysed, out of a potential 439 occurrences of the form.

TABLE 7.1 Frequency indices for *ain't*

Group	ain't = aux. have + not	ain't = copula be + not	ain't = aux. be + not
Orts Road boys	91.18	84.16	79.07
Shinfield boys	100.00	94.74	63.16
Shinfield girls	65.58	61.18	42.11

Table 7.1 shows the frequency of occurrence of non-standard *ain't* in the vernacular speech of the three groups of speakers. The non-standard form occurs with a high frequency, and its distribution shows regular patterning with both the linguistic and the non-linguistic context: all groups use *ain't* most frequently as the auxiliary *have,* and least frequently as the auxiliary *be,* and the girls use *ain't* less often than the boys, in all cases.

Ain't does not, however, show regular patterning with stylistic context. Table 7.2 shows the frequency indices for *ain't* as the negative auxiliary *have* and for *ain't* as the negative copula, in the vernacular style and the 'school' style of seven of the boys.

(The frequency of occurrence of the negative auxiliary *be* in 'school' style was too low to be included here.) Table 7.2 gives a clear indication of the absence of style shifting; in both cases the use of *ain't* actually increases in the more formal style.

TABLE 7.2 Frequency indices for *ain't* in vernacular style and in 'school' style

	Group frequency index: vernacular style	Group frequency index: 'school' style
Ain't = neg. aux. *have*	93.02	100.00
Ain't = neg. copula	74.47	77.78

7.4.1 Linguistic constraints on *ain't*

Wolfram (1973) found that the occurrence of *ain't* in the non-standard English of Puerto Ricans in New York City was constrained by the effect of multiple negation within the sentence and by the Standard English form to which *ain't* corresponded in the sentence. *Ain't* occurred more often when it corresponded to standard English *are* + *not* and *is* + *not* than when it corresponded to *am* + *not*. Neither of these constraints, however, has a significant effect on the use of *ain't* in vernacular speech in Reading. Of far more significance in Reading English is the syntactic context in which *ain't* occurs.

In the recordings, *ain't* occurs in declarative sentences, in interrogative sentences and in tag questions:

[5] I ain't in the bloody guest house now.
[6] Oh, ain't you going?
[7] I'm going out with my bird now, ain't I?

Interrogative sentences occurred only eleven times in the data, and therefore could not be included in the analysis.

Table 7.3 shows the frequency of occurrence of *ain't* in declarative sentences and in tag questions. Bracketed figures indicate that the number of occurrences from which the index was calculated is low, so that in these instances the indices are not statistically significant. Despite gaps caused by low numbers, it is clear from Table 7.3 that the occurrence of *ain't* is consistently higher in tag questions than it is in declarative sentences. This is particularly evident in the speech of the girls. Tag questions, then, act as a strong constraint here, favouring the use of the non-standard form.

TABLE 7.3 Frequency indices for *ain't* in declarative sentences and in tag questions

	Declarative sentences	*Tag questions*
Aux. *have*		
Orts Road	88.68.	100.00
Shinfield boys	100.00	(100.00)
Shinfield girls	62.50	80.00
All speakers	78.57	95.00
Main verb *be*		
Orts Road	68.00	100.00
Shinfield boys	92.31	100.00
Shinfield girls	44.44	89.66
All speakers	59.83	96.30
Aux. *be*		
Orts Road	76.67	100.00
Shinfield boys	60.00	(75.00)
Shinfield girls	31.25	(66.67)
All speakers	60.66	88.89

7.4.2 Phonetic realizations of *ain't*

The discussion so far has used the general term *ain't* to refer to all the non-standard realizations of the negative present tense contracted forms of the copula and of the auxiliaries *be* and *have*. In reality, however, the non-standard form has a range of phonetic realizations. The *Survey of English Dialects* shows *ain't* as being variously realized as [eɪnt] and [ɛnt] in Berkshire (Orton *et al.* 1968). The informants used in this survey, however, were all from rural areas, and there are no observations of the English spoken in urban centres in Berkshire. In the data obtained for the present study the realizations of *ain't* fall into two groups: those that can be said to approach *ain't* (including [eɪnt], [eɪn], [eɪʔ], [ẽɪ], [ɛnt] and [æn]), and those that can be said to approach *in't* (including [ɪnt], [ɪn], and [ɪ],). In addition, there were three occurrences in the data of the form [ənt], and three of the form [ən], all in tag questions. Two of these occur as the negative auxiliary *be*, and four as the negative copula, and all persons of the verb are involved, with the exception of the first person singular. However, these [ənt] forms are too low in number to allow further analysis.

If we take the traditional view that *ain't* derives from the Standard English forms, then it would be reasonable to expect that a phonetic realization approaching *in't* would occur with third person singular subjects of the copula, or of the auxiliary *be* – in other words, that non-standard *in't* would correspond to Standard English *isn't*, and non-standard *ain't* to Standard English *(a)m not, aren't, hasn't,* and *haven't.*

Table 7.4 shows the distribution of *in't* (i.e. of those phonetic realizations that contain the vowel [ɪ]), with third person singular subjects and with non-third person singular subjects, for all verbs. The indices for the Shinfield boys' group show the distribution that would be expected if non-standard *in't* corresponds to standard *isn't: in't* does not occur as the negative auxiliary *have,* nor does it occur with non-third person singular subjects of the negative copula and of the negative auxiliary *be.* However, this group of speakers is small, consisting of only three boys. The other, larger, groups do not confine their use of *ain't* to this environment. The Shinfield girls use *in't* for the negative copula and for the negative auxiliary *be* with subjects that are not third person singular, and the Orts Road boys use *in't* not only with non-third person singular subjects of the copula and auxiliary *be* but also as the auxiliary *have,* with all subjects.

TABLE 7.4 Frequency indices for *in't*:

$$\frac{\text{No. of } in't \text{ forms}}{\text{no. of } in't + \text{no. of } ain't \text{ forms}} \times 100$$

	Auxiliary have		Copula be		Auxiliary be	
Group	3rd pers. sing.	Other subjects	3rd pers. sing.	Other subjects	3rd pers. sing.	Other subjects
Orts Road	24.00	8.33	63.24	41.67	50.00	15.38
Shinfield boys	(0.00)	(0.00)	33.33	0.00	(66.67)	0.00
Shinfield girls	0.00	0.00	61.54	10.00	(50.00)	(25.00)
All speakers	16.22	5.17	60.34	19.35	53.85	12.82

The most favourable environment for the occurrence of *in't* for all groups of speakers is with third person singular forms of the verb *to be,* as we would expect. However, in Reading English the use of *in't* is not confined to this environment, as we have seen, and the non-standard forms *ain't* and *in't,* as a result, do not correspond exactly to their supposed Standard English equivalents. This becomes clearer when we consider the phonetic realizations of *ain't* in the syntactic contexts in which it occurs most often.

Table 7.5 and Table 7.6 show the frequency indices for the main phonetic realizations of the non-standard form in declarative sentences and in tag questions. Table 7.5 shows the frequency indices with third person singular subjects, and Table 7.6 shows

TABLE 7.5 Frequency indices for *ain't, in't,* and standard forms, with third person singular subjects

3rd pers. sing. subjects	Declarative sentences			Tag questions		
	ain't	*in't*	*hasn't*	*ain't*	*in't*	*hasn't*
Aux. *have*	82.35	0.00	17.65	33.33	66.67	0.00
	ain't	*in't*	*isn't*	*ain't*	*in't*	*isn't*
Copula *be*	54.32	6.17	39.51	2.86	92.86	4.28
Aux. *be*	50.00	8.33	41.67	0.00	85.71	14.29

the frequency indices with non-third person singular subjects. In both tables the figures represent the total use of each form by all speakers in the study. (A full version of Table 7.5 and Table 7.6, showing the breakdown for each of the three peer groups, can be seen in the Appendix. The group figures show the same distribution of forms, except that the Shinfield girls use the Standard English contracted form more often than *ain't* or *in't,* with third person singular subjects.)

Table 7.5 shows that although *in't* forms do occur more often with third person singular subjects and the verb *be,* as we would expect if *in't* corresponds to Standard English *isn't,* these occurrences of *in't* are almost entirely in tag questions. In declarative sentences the form *ain't* predominates, for all verbs, and *in't* occurs only rarely (as the copula and the auxiliary *be,* and never as the auxiliary *have*). In tag questions, the distribution is reversed: *in't* predominates here, for all verbs, and *ain't* occurs much less often as auxiliary *have,* and rarely or never as the auxiliary *be* or as the copula.

TABLE 7.6 Frequency indices for *in't, ain't* and standard forms, with non-third person singular subjects

Non-3rd pers. sing. subjects	Declarative sentences			Tag questions		
	ain't	*in't*	*haven't*	*ain't*	*in't*	*haven't*
Aux. *have*	76.56	0.00	23.44	72.73	27.27	0.00
	ain't	*in't*	*aren't*	*ain't*	*in't*	*aren't*
Main verb *be*	58.33	0.00	41.67	40.00	60.00	0.00
Aux. *be*	61.22	0.00	38.78	44.44	55.56	0.00

Table 7.6 shows that these tendencies persist when the subject is non-third person singular. If the non-standard forms corresponded to the Standard English forms, then *in't* would not be expected to occur at all in this table. Yet *in't* is again the predominant form in tag questions when the verb is the auxiliary *be* or the copula, and it also occurs, though to a more limited extent, when the verb is the auxiliary *have*. In declarative sentences, *ain't* is the only non-standard form that is used, for all verbs.

It is clear, then, that the non-standard forms *in't* and *ain't* do not stand in a simple relationship to the Standard English forms *isn't* and *aren't*. That they do bear some relationship to the Standard English verb forms is shown by the fact that *in't* forms occur with the verb *have* less frequently than with the auxiliary *be* or with the copula. And in the environment that is, so to speak, the furthest removed from *isn't* (*ie* non-third person singular subjects and the verb *have*), *ain't* is the preferred form in tag questions, rather than *in't*, although *in't* does, even here, occur 27.27 per cent of the time. In all other environments, the main constraint on the non-standard variants is the syntactic context in which they occur: *ain't* is the preferred form in declarative sentences, and *in't* is the predominant form in tag questions.

The tendency to use *in't* as an invariant form in tag questions is not confined to Reading English. Brown and Millar (1978) report that in Edinburgh Scots *in't* also occurs with all subjects of the verb *be*. An invariant past tense form, *win't,* also occurs, with all subjects, in some varieties of Scottish English.[4]

7.5 Standard English forms

Although the Standard English forms are not of central interest here, it is worth noting the forms that are preferred in vernacular speech. In colloquial Standard English, contracted negatives are abbreviated in one of two ways. The verb may be assimilated to the preceding subject.

[8] You're not making room for me.

or the particle may be reduced and assimilated to the preceding verb:

[9] You aren't a virgin.

In the data, the former, uncontracted negative form predominates when the verb is the auxiliary *be* or the copula. It occurs 100 per cent of the time with the auxiliary *be* and 74 per cent of the time with the copula. With the exception of *isn't*, however, and one isolated occurrence of *haven't*, the Standard English forms occur only in declarative sentences. Possibly the use of the full negative particle here emphasizes the negation of the verb. With auxiliary *have*, however, the general tendency of southern English dialects to prefer the contracted negative form is followed:

[10] No, you've had one. I haven't even had one, so shut up.

Where the Standard English forms are used in vernacular speech, they are used in the same way as they are in the standard language; that is, *isn't* occurs only with third person singular subjects of the verb *be, haven't* only with non-third person singular subjects of the verb *have* and so on.

7.6 The semantic functions of tag questions

It is instructive at this point to look at the semantic properties of the tag questions that are used by the speakers. The syntactic and semantic structure of tag questions has been discussed in some detail (*eg* Palmer 1965; Arbini 1969; Huddleston 1970; Quirk *et al.* 1972; Cattell 1973; Millar and Brown 1979). For our purposes the most relevant analysis is that given by Hudson (1975). This will be described in some detail here in order to show how it applies to the data from the speech of the peer groups.

Hudson analyses polar questions (considering tag questions as reduced polar interrogatives) in terms of their syntactic, semantic and pragmatic properties. The pragmatic analysis is based on the concept of 'illocutionary force', as conceived by Austin (1962), and on Grice's rules of social interaction (Grice 1975). Hudson shows that the illocutionary meaning of an utterance is related to the syntactic properties of the sentence via an intermediary set of semantic properties that are concerned with the situation of the speaker and the listener, and with their beliefs regarding the 'truth' of the proposition expressed in the sentence. He points out, for example, that although sentences [11] and [12] below have different syntactic properties, they both can have the 'illocutionary force' (in the sense used by Austin 1962) of WARNING, in certain circumstances:

[11] That kind of lock isn't safe. (from Hudson 1975)
[12] Is that kind of lock safe? (from Hudson 1975)

Sentence [11] will serve as a warning only if the hearer is in danger because of the lock and not if said, for example, by A to

B while they are looking at a catalogue of locks. For sentence [12] to serve as a warning, not only must the hearer be in danger because of the lock, but he or she must also *believe* that the lock is dangerous. It would be inappropriate for A to use sentence [12] to B if B knew nothing about locks, and if A knew that B knew nothing, although sentence [11] would be perfectly appropriate in these circumstances.

Conversely, sentence [13] can be used both as a challenge and as a kind of apology, depending partly on the intonation contours of the main clause and partly on the circumstances in which it is uttered. When spoken with a falling intonation on the main clause and a rising intonation on the tag, the sentence acts as a challenge. When spoken with a rising intonation on the main clause, the sentence acts as an apology.

[13] This is your seat, is it? (from Hudson 1975)

Here the syntactic properties of the sentence are identical in both cases (although the intonation is different), but the beliefs of the speaker concerning his or her relationship to the hearer (and of the hearer to the seat!) are different.

Hudson draws a distinction between the 'illocutionary force' of a sentence, which may vary on the different occasions on which it is uttered, and the 'permanent' properties of the sentence that are relevant to the syntactic distinctions of mood (*eg* declarative, interrogative, imperative) and that apply at the level of semantic structure. These 'permanent properties' of sentences can be specified in terms of 'sincerity conditions'. Declarative sentences, for example, are subject to the sincerity condition below.

The speaker believes that the proposition is true.

And interrogative sentences are subject to the sincerity condition:

The speaker believes that the hearer knows at least as well as the speaker does whether the proposition is true or false.

Hudson's discussion of the meaning of questions, then, involves the following separate categories: syntactic categories (*eg* interrogative, declarative), semantic categories (*eg* question, statement) and sincerity conditions on the semantic categories. The total meaning of the question, of course, also involves general pragmatic principles (*eg* Gricean rules of conversation) and illocutionary force ('whatever conclusions the hearer may draw from a particular utterance on a particular occasion' [Hudson 1975: p. 30]

Sentences that contain tag questions are subject both to the sincerity condition on declarative sentences and to the sincerity condition on interrogative sentences, since they contain both a statement (in the main sentence) and a question (in the tag). The majority of the tag questions used by the peer groups in the data do conform to both these sincerity conditions. Tag questions are most often used to seek confirmation of an offered fact:

[14] He lives here, doesn't he?

to seek corroboration of a statement:

[15] My brother carried him all the way down the hospital, didn't he?

and to seek support for an opinion:

[16] Well, it is rude, isn't it?

In all of these examples, the tag is spoken with a falling intonation. The function of these tag questions corresponds to what is generally considered to be the central function of tags: to seek confirmation or corroboration for the hopes or suppositions expressed in the sentence to which they are attached (*cf* Stockwell, Schachter and Partee 1973).

As noted above, the sincerity conditions on both declarative sentences and interrogative sentences are fulfilled in these tags; the speaker believes that the statement in the main sentence is true, and that the hearer knows 'at least as well as the speaker does' whether it is true or false. In addition, he or she expects the hearer to confirm the proposition of the main sentence.

There are a number of tag questions in the data, however, that do not expect the hearer to confirm the proposition of the main sentence, and that do not conform to the sincerity conditions on interrogative sentences. The interchange below provides one example:

Mick: Any intruder that comes down here, they gets beat.
Jenny: Why didn't you beat me, then?
Mick: 'Cos you're a girl, in't you?

Here the proposition in Mick's main sentence, *you are a girl,* is obviously true, and the function of the tag is not to ask for confirmation, but rather to show that the question Mick had been asked was in his opinion a foolish one. The tag carries overtones of sarcasm and of slight hostility; no answer is required here. The sincerity condition on interrogative sentences does not apply; the speaker is fully committed to the truth of the proposition, and he assumes, in addition, that the hearer also knows that the proposition is true.

A further example is Cathy's tag in the conversational fragment below:

Jacky: We're going to Southsea on the seventeenth of next month. And on Sunday they . . .
Cathy: Yeah, and I can't bloody go.
Jenny: Why not?
Cathy: 'Cos I'm going on fucking holiday, in I?

Again, no answer is expected, and it would in any case have been impossible to provide one, since I had no way of knowing when Cathy was going on holiday, and she knew that I did not know. The sincerity condition on interrogative sentences cannot apply here. The speaker believes that the proposition in the main sentence is true, but she does not believe that the hearer knows whether it is true or false.

Tag questions of this kind occur regularly in working-class speech. They occur in Reading, as we have seen, and they have been noted in Edinburgh (Millar and Brown 1979) and in London (Hudson 1975). Hudson suggests that it is because the sincerity conditions are not fulfilled that tags of this type strike outsiders as odd. Millar and Brown suggest further that the aggressive and hostile overtones that these tags possess result from the fact that they play 'on the conventional meaning' associated with tag questions that have the same syntactic structure. They 'mimic the presentation of an analytic truth, such that the hearer is made to feel that he really should have known either by intuition, perception, or deduction that the proposition was true' (Miller and Brown 1979: p. 35)

A further type of tag question, whose occurrence is not confined to working-class speech, occurs in the data, and again no answer is required from the hearer:

[17]   You're a fucking hard nut, in't you?

This tag question was used provocatively, with the intention of starting a fight. Although no verbal answer was expected, a physical response may well have been; in this case, the hearer immediately jumped on the speaker and threw him to the ground. It is difficult to establish whether the sincerity conditions are fulfilled here or not; the speaker may not really believe that his friend is a 'hard nut', but may believe it only temporarily, or may be pretending to believe it in order to start a fight, and his assumptions about the hearer's beliefs are equally unclear.

Broadly speaking, then, the tag questions that are used by the speakers fall into two groups: a larger group, where tags have the 'regular' function of requiring confirmation or corroboration and where Hudson's sincerity conditions are fulfilled, and a smaller group, consisting of tags that do not require an answer and that do not fulfil Hudson's sincerity conditions.[5]

These groups turn out to be extremely relevant to our analysis of the phonetic realizations of *ain't*. Table 7.7 shows the number of times that *ain't*, *in't* and the Standard English verb forms occur in the vernacular style of all speakers in the two groups (or types) of tags. Group 1 consists of those 'conventional' tags that require an answer and that fulfil the sincerity conditions. Group 2 consists of what may be termed 'non-conventional' tags: tags that do not require an answer and that do not fulfil the sincerity conditions. Both groups of tags are spoken with a falling intonation.

Table 7.7 shows clearly that, whereas *in't* occurs in both conventional and non-conventional tags, *ain't* and the Standard English contracted verb forms occur only in conventional tags. The use of *in't*, in other words, is categorical in non-conventional tags, but is variable in conventional tags.

TABLE 7.7 Number of occurrences of *in't*, *ain't* and Standard English forms in 'conventional' tags and in 'non-conventional' tags

Tag type	*in't*		*ain't*		Standard English form	
	1	2	1	2	1	2
Non-3rd pers sing subjects						
Copula	5	1	1	0	0	0
Aux. *be*	1	4	4	0	0	0
Aux. *have*	1	2	7	0	1	0
Total	7	7	12	0	1	0
3rd pers sing subjects						
Copula	59	5	2	0	3	0
Aux. *be*	3	3	0	0	1	0
Aux. *have*	6	0	3	0	0	0
Total	68	8	5	0	4	0
Combined total (all subjects)	75	15	17	0	5	0

There is an interesting link here between the categorical use of *in't* in non-conventional tags and the vernacular culture in which the speakers participate. Non-conventional tags, as we have seen, have certain semantic properties in common: they are non-conducive, and they do not conform to Hudson's sincerity conditions. In addition, they all convey overtones of aggression, assertion or hostility to the hearer.

Almost all the members of the peer groups were involved in a street-corner vernacular culture, which is in many respects directly opposed to the mainstream culture in society. Dominant themes within the culture are aggression, violence and hostility. These can be seen as underlying features of the shoplifting, fighting, arson and vandalism that the peer groups enjoy. Prestige within the peer groups is achieved through success in these activities, by carrying weapons, and by generally 'acting tough'.

The extent to which speakers participate in the vernacular culture is reflected in their language by the frequency with which they use certain non-standard linguistic features (Cheshire 1982). Interestingly, *ain't* is one feature whose frequency of occurrence is not directly correlated with the degree to which speakers adhere to the vernacular culture. It seems that there is a more indirect link between *ain't* and the vernacular culture: when the feature occurs in a non-conventional tag, carrying overtones of aggression or hostility, then the form *in't* is categorical; when it occurs elsewhere, then any of the variable forms may occur. We can say, then, that when tag questions overtly specify the dominant themes of the vernacular culture, *in't* is used as an invariant negative form of *be* and auxiliary *have* (other auxiliaries, such as *can* or *will,* may also occur in non-conventional tags).

This kind of phenomenon is not unknown in language. In his discussion of negative concord in the Black English vernacular, Labov (1972) gives an example of a cultural feature [–book learning] coinciding with the use of non-standard grammar. And Hudson (1975) argues that the -*n't* that occurs in exclamations of this kind,

[19]   Hasn't he gone a long way?

is not a reflex of the deep formative NEG, as it is in questions such as this:

[20]   Hasn't he finished yet?

(though it presumably was at one stage of English), but is instead a marker of 'exclamation', related to the negative form -*n't* only at the level of morphology. Hudson points to other 'syntactic splits' that have occurred in English – for example, the split between *use* and the modal auxiliary *used* or the split between *owe* and *ought* (*ought* was at one time the past tense form of *owe*). It could be similarly argued that the *in't* that occurs as an invariant form in non-conventional tag questions is not related to the third person singular present tense form *in't* other than historically and that it is now a marker of the vernacular themes of aggression and hostility (a 'force marker'; Hudson 1975).[6]

7.7 Ongoing linguistic change in the form of *ain't*

As we have seen, the phonetic variants of *ain't* are best explained as the result of the combined effects of linguistic change and morphological analogy. The data suggest that these processes are still at work on the phonetic realizations of *ain't*.

It is reasonable to assume that the form *in't* derived by regular sound change from Standard English *isn't*. In the tag questions in the data, the verb *be* occurs more often than the verb *have* (105 times, as compared to 22 times), and third person singular subjects occur more often than other subjects (82 times with *be* and 10 times with *have*). This means that third person singular forms of *be* account for 78 per cent of the verbs in tag questions. If this is typical of vernacular speech in Reading, and there is no reason to suppose that it is not, then this means that the form *in't* occurs more often in tag questions than elsewhere. It seems highly plausible that, as a result of its widespread occurrence in tag questions, it is becoming used, by morphological analogy, with subjects other than third person singular subjects, and with auxiliary *have* as well as with *be* in tags. In other words, what may be happening here is precisely what is presumed to have happened at an earlier stage of English to the form *ain't*: a form that occurs frequently in one morphological environment in colloquial speech is spreading throughout the paradigm, though here it is happening, at present, only in tag questions. In addition, the form *in't* appears to have become a marker of an overt vernacular norm in non-conventional tag questions, so that here it occurs categorically.

We can use the figures for the frequency of occurrence of *in't* in the data to guess at the state of progress of the change. Table 7.5 suggests that the change is further advanced with third person singular forms of the verb *have*: *in't* occurs 66.7 per cent of the time. Again, this could be due to the fact that third person singular subjects occur more often than other subjects. Table 7.6 indicates that the change is also spreading to non-third person singular forms of *be*, and that it is beginning to affect non-third person singular forms of *have* also.

7.8 Conclusion

This analysis of the use of *ain't* in working-class speech in Reading has shown that, whereas in Standard English the negative present tense contracted forms of *have* and *be* are marked for subject and for the verb, in non-standard Reading speech they are marked instead for syntactic function: *ain't* is used predominantly in declarative sentences, and *in't* is used predominantly in tag questions. In non-conventional tag questions the use of *in't* is categorical, and this may be due to the fact that here it is a marker of an overt vernacular norm [+aggression]. In conventional tag questions the use of *in't* is variable, but there is some indication that a linguistic change is in progress here, towards the use of *in't* with all subjects and with both *have* and *be*.

Notes

1. I am very grateful to Richard Hudson and Peter Trudgill for their comments on an earlier version of this paper.
2. Unless otherwise stated, all sentences used as examples are from the speech of members of the peer groups.
3. Alternatively, in some British English, eastern New England, and coastal southern American English dialects, Early Modern [æ] before a following [nt] may have developed a schwa glide, or lengthened to produce the form [ɑːnt]. This would account for the hitherto unexplained occurrence of the form [ɑːnt] with first person singular subjects in interrogative sentences in Standard British English and also in declarative sentences in some non-standard dialects. The orthography *aren't* would be explained as dialect borrowing or as analogy with other members of the paradigm (McDavid 1941).
   A simpler explanation would see the occurrence of [ɑːnt] with first person singular subjects as the result of analogical extension of other forms in the paradigm.
4. This is confirmed by the research of John Kirk of Queens University, Belfast.
5. For a more rigorous description of the syntactic and semantic structure of tag questions, which includes their functions in working-class speech, see Millar and Brown (1979).
6. It could be further argued that non-conventional tags of the type described here are not tags in either a semantic or a syntactic sense. They do not have the semantic properties of tag questions (in that they are not conducive and do not conform to Hudson's sincerity conditions), nor do they have the syntactic structure of tag questions, which normally repeat the NP and the VP of the main sentence.

References

ARBINI, R. (1969) 'Tag-questions and tag-imperatives in English', *Journal of Linguistics* **5**: 205–14.

AUSTIN, J. L. (1962) *How to do Things with Words*. Cambridge, Mass.: Harvard University Press.

BROOK, G. L. (1958) *A History of the English Language*. London: André Deutsch.

BROWN, K., and MILLAR, B. (1978) 'Auxiliary verbs in Edinburgh speech', *Work in Progress* **11**. Department of Linguistics, Edinburgh University.

CATTELL, R. (1973) 'Negative transportation and tag questions', *Language* **49** (3): 612–39.

CHESHIRE, J. (1982). *Variation in an English Dialect: A Sociolinguistic Study*. Cambridge: Cambridge University Press.

GRICE, M. P. (1975) 'Logic and conversation'. In P. Cole and J. Morgan (eds) *Syntax and Semantics* 3: *Speech Acts*. London: Academic Press.

HUDDLESTON, R. (1970) 'Two approaches to the analysis of tags', *Journal of Linguistics* **6**: 215–21.

HUDSON, R. A. (1975) 'The meaning of questions', *Language* **51**(1): 1–31.

HUGHES, G. A., and TRUDGILL, P. J. (1979) *English Accents and Dialects: An Introduction to Regional and Social Varieties of British English*. London: Edward Arnold.

JESPERSEN, O. (1940) *A modern English Grammar on Historical Principles*. Part V. Copenhagen: Ejnar Munksgaard.

LABOV, W. (1972) 'Negative attraction and negative concord in English grammar', *Language* **48**: 773–818.

LABOV, W., COHEN, P., ROBINS, C., and LEWIS, J. (1968) *A Study of the Nonstandard English of Negro and Puerto Rican Speakers in New York City*, I & II. Final report, Co-operative Research Project 3288. Washington, DC: US Office of Health, Education and Welfare.

MCDAVID, R. I. (1941) 'Ain't I and aren't I', *Language* **17**: 57–9.

MILLAR, M., and BROWN, K. (1979) 'Tag questions in Edinburgh speech', *Linguistische Berichte* **60**: 24–45.

ORTON, H., *et al.* (1968) *Survey of English Dialects*, vol. IV, part 3. Leeds: E. J. Arnold.

PALMER, F. R. (1965) *A Linguistic Study of the English Verb*. London: Longman.

QUIRK, R., GREENBAUM, S., LEECH, G., and SVARTVIK, J. (1972) *A Grammar of Contemporary English*. London: Longman.

STEVENS, M. (1954) 'The derivation of *ain't*', *American Speech* **29**: 196–201.

STOCKWELL, R. P., SCHACHTER, P., and PARTEE, B. M. (1973) *The Major Syntactic Structures of English*. New York: Holt, Rinehart & Winston.

WILLARD, E. P. (1936) 'The Origin of *ain't*', *Word Study* **11**(2).

WOLFRAM, W. (1973) *Sociolinguistic Aspects of Assimilation: Puerto Rican English in New York City*. Arlington. Va.: Center for Applied Linguistics.

WOLFRAM, W., and FASOLD, R. (1974) *The Study of Social Dialects in American English*. Englewood Cliffs, N.J.: Prentice-Hall.

Appendix

Full version of Table 7.5 and 7.6 (frequency indices for realizations of *ain't*)

	Declarative sentences			Tag questions		
3rd person singular	*ain't*	*in't*	*hasn't*	*ain't*	*in't*	*hasn't*
Have						
Orts Road	100.00	0.00	0.00	14.29	85.71	0.00
Shinfield boys	(100.00)	(0.00)	(0.00)	—	—	—
Shinfield girls	60.00	0.00	40.00	(100.00)	(0.00)	(0.00)
All speakers	82.35	0.00	17.65	33.33	66.67	0.00
	ain't	*in't*	*isn't*	*ain't*	*in't*	*hasn't*
Main verb be						
Orts Road	62.50	7.50	30.00	0.00	100.00	0.00
Shinfield boys	83.33	0.00	16.67	(25.00)	(75.00)	(0.00)
Shinfield girls	40.00	5.71	54.29	3.85	84.62	11.54
All speakers	54.32	6.17	39.51	2.86	92.86	4.29
Auxiliary be						
Orts Road	80.00	(0.00)	20.00	(0.00)	(100.00)	(0.00)
Shinfield boys	(50.00)	(0.00)	(50.00)	(0.00)	(66.67)	(33.33)
Shinfield girls	20.00	20.00	60.00	—	—	—
All speakers	50.00	8.33	41.67	0.00	85.71	14.29

Non-3rd person singular	ain't	in't	haven't	ain't	in't	hasn't
Have						
Orts Road	82.86	0.00	17.14	57.14	42.86	0.00
Shinfield boys	(100.00)	(0.00)	(0.00)	(100.00)	0.00	0.00
Shinfield girls	64.00	0.00	36.00	(66.67)	(0.00)	(33.33)
All speakers	76.56	0.00	23.44	72.73	27.27	0.00

	ain't	in't	aren't	ain't	in't	hasn't
Main verb be						
Orts Road	60.00	0.00	40.00	16.67	83.33	0.00
Shinfield boys	100.00	0.00	0.00	(100.00)	(0.00)	(0.00)
Shinfield girls	42.11	0.00	57.89	(50.00)	(50.00)	0.00
All speakers	58.33	0.00	41.67	40.00	60.00	0.00
Auxiliary be						
Orts Road	76.00	0.00	24.00	42.86	57.14	0.00
Shinfield boys	61.54	0.00	38.46	(100.00)	(0.00)	(0.00)
Shinfield girls	27.27	0.00	72.73	(0.00)	(0.00)	(0.00)
All speakers	61.22	0.00	38.78	44.44	55.56	0.00

Chapter 8

Double modals in Hawick Scots

Keith Brown

'Double modal' constructions are reported from a variety of regional forms of Scots: see, for example, Murray (1873), Anderson (1976), Brown and Millar (1980), the *Scottish National Dictionary* and, for a historical perspective on double modal constructions with *can,* see Scur (1968). They are also reported from other regional forms of English, see, for example Pampell, (1975), Boertien (1979), Di Paolo *et al.* (1979), Butters (1973), McDonald and Beal (1985). This chapter is concerned with such constructions in the Scots spoken in Hawick.* It is mainly concerned to describe their occurrence rather than to follow the many theoretical issues they raise.

Let us assume that the 'modals' at issue are those listed in Figure 8.1, which sets out the combinatory possibilities. For expository purposes I shall assume that the constructions fall into three broad groups, each of which has syntactic characteristics of its own. At the end of the chapter we will return to consider all the constructions together.

  1. 'Double modal auxiliary constructions': *can* or *could* follows a modal auxiliary in what appears to be the same 'verb group':

> He should can go tomorrow.
>> (= 'he ought to be able to go tomorrow')
> He would could do it if he tried.
>> (= 'he would be able to do it if he tried')

*This work was originally carried out under SSRC Grant No 5152/1. I am grateful to those who acted as informants and to Jim Miller for comments on an earlier version of the chapter.

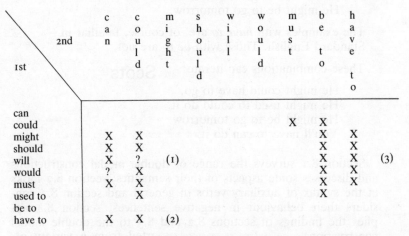

1st \ 2nd	can	could	might	should	will	would	must	be to	have to
can									
could					X	X			
might	X	X				X	X		
should	X	X				X	X		
will	X	?		(1)		X	X		(3)
would	?	X				X	X		
must	X	X				X	X		
used to		X				X			
be to									
have to	X	X	(2)						

FIGURE 8.1   (1) Double modal auxiliaries; (2) 'embedded modal auxiliaries'; (3) 'modal + main verb'.

Will can occur first and *can* second.

> He'll can get you one.
>   (= 'He will be able to get you one')

Will can also precede the other combinations, yielding a 'triple modal auxiliary' construction with *will* as first auxiliary and *can* or *could* as third:

> He'll might could do it for you.
>   (= 'he might be able in the future to do it for you')

2. 'Embedded modal auxiliary constructions': *can* or *could* occurs after the complementizer *to* in an embedded construction (constructions with *have to* are used as an example in Figure 8.1):

> You'll have to can do it whether you like it or not.
>   (= 'you'll have to be able to do it . . .)
> I would like to could swim.
>   (= 'I would like to be able to swim')

3. 'Modal + main verb constructions': *have to* and *be to* as the sole verb in a verb group can have the syntax of an auxiliary verb. Both can, however, be preceded by a modal auxiliary:

We'll have to get the roof mended.
He might be to go tomorrow.

The examples with *have to* are, of course, familiar in
Standard English. Those with *be to* are not.

These combinations can iterate:

He might could have to go.
He might used to could do it.
He might be to go tomorrow.
You'll have to can do it.

Section 8.1 surveys the range of double modal constructions
and discusses some aspects of their semantics; section 8.2 looks
at the syntax of auxiliary verbs in general and section 8.3 considers their behaviour in negative sentences; section 8.4 applies the findings of sections 8.2 and 8.3 to the double modal
constructions.

8.1 Double modal constructions

The number and distribution of auxiliary verbs in spoken Scots
is somewhat different from Standard English. A brief description
of the system follows in section 8.2: for fuller details see Brown
and Miller (1975) and Brown and Millar (1980). There seems
no reason, however, to believe that the semantics of modality in
general in Scots is different from that of Standard English, and
in particular that the standard distinction between 'epistemic' and
'root' modality is not drawn as in Standard English, though its
realization may be different. The pragmatics of modality is different, but is not our concern here.

As already noted, for expository purposes we will consider
double modal constructions in three groups. The first involves
constructions with *can* or *could* as second modal, preceded by one
of the other modal auxiliaries. Examples are:

He might can (could) do it, if he tried.
He must can (could) do it.
He should can (could) do it.
He'll can do it.
He would could do it, if he tried.

The first modal is restricted to an 'epistemic' sense: 'it is
possible that . . .). 'I conclude that . . .', etc. With *might* and
must this is not surprising since in spoken Scots these two modals

are used only in this sense. As a single modal *should* can be used with either an epistemic (*that should be enough*) or a root sense (*you should go and see your granny*), though the distinction tends to neutralize. As first modal in this construction *should* seems to be restricted to an epistemic sense. *Would* is typically used in an epistemic sense indicating a hypothetical state of affairs, as in the example. *Will* can be used epistemically, with a sense of 'prediction', though it seems often to be best interpreted as a simple marker of futurity, a point I return to below.

The second modal, *can* or *could*, has a 'root' sense. Many descriptions (e.g. Palmer, 1965, 1979; Quirk *et al.* 1986) distinguish a variety of senses for root *can* and *could* – 'possibility', 'ability', 'permission' and so forth – but these distinctions often merge with one another as they do in the examples above (*cf* Coates 1983). So *he will can do it* might be glossed in an 'ability' sense (*'he will be able to do it . . . if he tries'*) or a 'possibility' sense (*'it will be possible for him to do it . . . if he wants to'*), etc. For our purposes it will be sufficient to identify this as root modality.

It seems then that in all these cases the two modals are 'non-harmonic' in the sense of Lyons (1977): the first of the two modals having an epistemic and the second a root sense.

In glossing the examples above Standard English paraphrases (*be able to* or *possible*) have been used for the second, root, modal. In Hawick Scots it seems that the double modal constructions are as acceptable as these particular alternatives. It is also usually possible to paraphrase the first, epistemic, modal:

He might could do it; He could maybe do it.
He must can do it; He can surely do it.
He should can do it; He can likely do it.

The use of modal adverbs instead of modal auxiliaries is, of course, a common feature of all dialects of English, and, in the case of *maybe,* is particularly common in Scots. Standard English *He may go tomorrow* is likely to be rendered as *He's maybe going tomorrow* or *He'll maybe go tomorrow,* where the 'futurity' implied by *may* is spelt out with either *will* or the progressive, and the 'possibility' is spelt out in the adverb *maybe.* In this connection, note that **can could* or **could can* are impossible. So if *can* or *could* is used in a root sense and an epistemic sense is also required, an epistemic adverb must be used:

Maybe he could do it for you.
He could maybe do it for you.

There is no adverbial substitute for *will* as a simple future marker, though temporal adverbs, *the morn* (*tomorrow*), *next week,* etc., frequently co-occur with *will.* In this use *will* can also co-occur with epistemic adverbs

> He'll maybe come the morn.
>   (It is possible that he will . . .)

and in 'triple modal' constructions:

> He'll might can come the morn.
>   (It is possible that he will be able to . . .)
> He'll should can come the morn.
>   (It is likely that he will be able to . . .)

Will does not co-occur with epistemic *must* or *would*:

> *He'll must be rich
> *He'll would go.

The second group of double modal constructions involves the use of *can* or *could* after the complementizer *to:*

> He'll have to can do it whether he likes it or not.
> He used to could do it when he was younger.

This construction is quite impossible in Standard English, but seems to be quite general in Hawick Scots:

> I want to can do that.
> I'd like to could do that.
> He's bound to could do that.

Here it seems that *have to* and *used to* are simply main verbs. As before, *can* and *could* typically have a root, 'ability', sense here, and paraphrase with *be able to*. In Hawick Scots *can* and *could* seem to be the only modals to participate in this construction. In other varieties other modals occur. Thus MacAfee (1980), quotes:

> He used to widnae let me up the brae.
>   ('it used to be the case that he wouldn't let me go up the hill)

(note the enclitic negative in the embedded sentence). Miller (1980) cites examples from Prestonpans of *would* as second modal in this construction.

The third group of constructions seems best analysed as involving a main verb and needs no further comment at this stage.

8.2 The syntax of auxiliary verbs

This section briefly reviews the syntax of auxiliaries in affirmative sentences involving a single modal. In most forms of non-standard Scots, and Hawick Scots is no exception, the class of auxiliary verbs is: *do* (supportive), *have* (perfective), *be* (progressive and passive), *can, could, might, should, will, would* and *must. Be (to)* and *have (to)* can behave either like main or auxiliary verbs. *Be* always behaves like an auxiliary when it is the sole verb and *have*, as a 'possessive', sometimes behaves like an auxiliary. *Used (to)* shows a few similarities with the auxiliaries. *Shall, may* and *ought (to)* do not typically occur. For a discussion of auxiliaries in Edinburgh speech, most of which applies also to Hawick Scots, see Brown and Millar (1980). Comparable lists of criteria for Standard English are Quirk *et al.* (1986) and Pullum and Wilson (1977).

8.2.1 Morphology

All the auxiliaries have 'strong' and 'weak' forms – the 'strong' forms occurring under 'stress', typically realized as high pitch in spoken Scots. The weak forms of finite *have, be, will* and *would*, when they are operators,[1] are much reduced and are usually phonologically enclitic to an immediately preceding form, typically the subject: They've gone; He's coming; He'll tell you; He'd do it if you asked him, etc. In addition 'perfective' *have* is enclitic even when it is non-finite and cliticizes to a preceding auxiliary, enclitic or not, and to the isolate negative particle: *He'll 've gone; He could've told you; He'll no've gone.*

Finite *have* and *be* show a full range of forms under number agreement, both as auxiliaries and in *have (to)* and *be (to)*. None of the other auxiliaries show number agreement. If the alternations *can/could* and *will/would* are alternations of 'tense', then note that *might* and *should* have no 'non-past' alternants and *must* has no 'past' alternant.

8.2.2 Subject–operator inversion

As in Standard English, subject and operator invert in interrogative sentences: Is he coming? *Will he tell you,* etc.

8.2.3 Negative morphology

Negative sentences are discussed in more detail in the next section. In declarative sentences, the negative is either enclitic to the operator or an isolate. The enclitic negative has a variety of phonological forms but is represented here as *-nae: He isnae com-*

ing; He willnae tell you; He cannae come, etc. The Standard English enclitic negative, *-n't*, is also occasionally found in simple sentences, but is not preferred.

The isolate negative is *no* (*cf* Standard English *not*). In many cases the clitic and isolate negative seem to be in free variation (*He's not coming, He isnae coming, etc.*), except that the isolate is preferred when the negative itself is stressed. With the modal auxiliaries the choice of the enclitic rather than the isolate negative can indicate a difference in scope: this is discussed in section 8.3 below. Note that operator and negative cannot both be enclitic **he'llnae come,* etc. The enclitic *-nae* never inverts. In negative interrogative sentences the operator inverts with the subject leaving the negative marker, which must be the isolate form, behind: *He's no coming; He isnae coming; Is he no coming? *isnae he coming?*

8.2.4 The morphology of reversed polarity tags
Tags are discussed in more detail in section 8.3. Auxiliaries occur in 'reversed polarity' tags: *John isnae coming, is he?, John's no coming, is he?, John's coming, is he no?, John's coming, isn't he?*. We noted above that the clitic *-nae* does not participate in subject–operator inversion: hence it is not available in tags: **John's coming isnae he?* It is curious that *-n't*, which is not usually available in main clause negatives (*cf* section 8.2.3), seems to occur freely in tags. There is no such restriction on the isolate negative. The tag form with *-n't* is typically associated with 'falling' intonation, and that with the isolate negative *no* with rising intonation, with implications similar to those for Standard English (the generalizations in Millar and Brown (1979), a discussion of tags in Edinburgh speech, hold good in the type of speech discussed here).

8.2.5 VP deletion
Auxiliaries occur in constructions like *he hasnae done it yet, but he will.*

8.2.6 Quantifier floating
'An *all* which follows an auxiliary may be semantically associated with the subject of a sentence: an *all* which follows a main verb cannot be' (Pullum and Wilson 1977: 743). (*All the boys are coming = the boys are all coming; *the boys came all.*)

8.2.7 DO support
Auxiliaries do not take 'DO support'. Main verbs in the construc-

tions discussed in sections 8.2.2–8.2.5 require it (*Did he come? he didnae come, did he no come?* etc.).

The behaviour of the various items listed at the head of this section in terms of these criteria is not absolutely uniform, but all the items noted meet most of the criteria set out above. *Have to* sometimes does and sometimes does not behave like an auxiliary. So, for example:

> You dinnae have to go.
>   (= you are not obliged to go)
> You've no to go.
>   (= you are obliged not to go)

with the wide scope negative *have to* operates typically like other main verbs, with narrow scope negative it may operate like an auxiliary. *Used to* is even more marginal in that it does not straightforwardly fulfil any of the criteria noted above. It has been included for reasons which will appear in the discussion in section 8.4.

8.3 Negative sentences

Negation is a notoriously complicated subject and I cannot hope to exhaust it here. Some aspects of negation are, however, relevant to our topic. We shall be interested in three types of negation, referred to as sentence, or wide scope, negation; VP, or narrow scope, negation; and main verb negation. The first two are familiar in modalized sentences such as

> Sentence, wide scope, negation:
>   She couldnae have told him.
>   ('it is not possible for her to have told him')

> VP, narrow scope, negation:
>   She could no have told him.
>   ('it was possible for her not to have told him')

The paraphrases are intended to make it clear that in the first case the modal falls within the scope of the negation and in the second it does not. Main verb negation is less familiar: as the name implies, the scope of the negative is the main verb alone:

> Main verb negation:
>   He's still no working.
>   ('it is the case that he is still out of work')

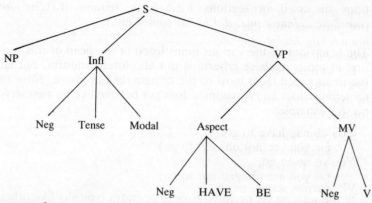

FIGURE 8.2

For expository purposes let us suppose that the three negatives are distributed in phrase markers as in Figure 8.2.[2] The negative dominated by 'infl' is the wide scope, sentence, negation, that dominated by 'aspect' is narrow scope, VP, negation, and the negative that is sister of the verb is main verb negation.

Let us consider main verb negation first. The negative marker must be the isolate negative, it cannot cliticize and it must immediately precede the verb over which it has scope. In the example above, the position of the negative after the adverb *still* unambiguously indicates that the scope is the main verb. By contrast, neither:

He isnae still working.
He's no still working.
    ('It isn't the case that he is still working')

can be interpreted as involving main verb negation. Main verb negation can co-occur with sentence negation:

He isnae still no working.
    ('It isn't the case that he is still out of work')
He hasnae been no working.
    ('It isn't the case that he has been out of work')

Main verb negation seems a sensible analysis in at least two circumstances. One is in cases like that illustrated above where there is no antonym for a particular lexical verb: it is for this reason that *no working* has been glossed as 'out of work'. The situation is parallel with adjectives, for example, but in this case there is often a morphological process involving a prefix like *un-*, as in *unhappy (cf* McAfee 1980). The other is when for contrastive purposes only the verb is negated, as for example *he's been not working but playing:* compare the parallel *Pillar boxes are not yellow but red.*

Let us now consider sentence and VP negation in negative sentences with a single modal auxiliary. We will start the description by considering *could:* the examples quoted above are repeated for convenience:

> Sentence, wide scope, negation:
> > She couldnae have told him.
> > > ('it is impossible for her to have told him')

> VP, narrow scope, negation:
> > She could no have told him.
> > > ('it was possible for her not to have told him')

With *could,* the enclitic negative, as in the first example, invariably shows wide scope negation, and the isolate negative, as in the second example, normally shows narrow scope negation. Thus:

> ? She couldnae have told him, but she did.
> > (? 'It was impossible for her to have told him, but she did (tell him)')

is anomalous since it has an apparently contradictory reading. By contrast

> She could no have told him, but she did.
> > ('It was possible for her not to have told him, but she did (tell him)')

is interpretable, with the reading given. We should immediately note a small complication. With *could* the enclitic negative:

> She couldnae have told him.

unambiguously shows wide scope. The isolate form is obligatory with the VP negative, but it can also be found with the wide scope negative, particularly if a speaker wishes to put stress on the negative itself. Thus

> She could no have told him.

is potentially ambiguous between a narrow scope reading and a negative stressed wide scope reading.

Both wide and narrow scope negations are possible:

> She couldnae no have told him.
> > ('it is not possible that she didn't tell him').

Let us now consider what happens when we have an aspectual auxiliary in addition to the modal. As already observed, sentence negation with *could* typically involves the enclitic negative:

He couldnae have been working.

With VP negation, however, it seems that the negative, which must be the isolate form, can be positioned either before the first auxiliary, after the last auxiliary or between two auxiliaries:

He could no have been working.
He could've no been working.
He could've been no working.

can all have the same interpretation. The only example which is unambiguously verb negation is the second. The first, as we have already seen, could be sentence negation with the isolate negative and the third might be main verb negation.

We have seen that a sentence may have both wide and narrow scope negation. So, avoiding the structure that could be interpreted as main verb negation we can have

He couldnae no have been working.
He couldnae have no been working.

with the VP negative (*no*) either initial to, or between the aspectual auxiliaries. It seems that we cannot find a sentence with the two VP negations:

*He couldnae no have no been working.

This suggests that the configuration shown in Figure 8.2 which allows for only one VP negation is correct, though the negative particle itself has a variety of possible sites.

If we further complicate the position by introducing main verb negation as well, we can have sentence and main verb negation:

He couldnae have been no working.
('It is impossible that he has been out of work')

and VP and main verb negation

He could've no been no working.
He could no have been no working.
('It is possible that he has not been out of work')

It is indeed possible to interpret sentences with three negations:

He couldnae no have been no working.
He couldnae have no been no working.
('It is impossible that he has not been out of work')

though they are normally only interpretable in an appropriate context! Four negatives

*He couldnae no have no been no working.

seem uninterpretable.

We now turn to negative interrogative sentences, and to simplify the exposition disregard main verb negation. It will be recalled that in an interrogative sentence the first auxiliary inverts with the subject NP, leaving behind the negative marker, which is always in the isolate form. This means that an interrogative sentence like:

Could he no have come?
('Is it impossible that he has come?')
('Is is possible that he hasn't come?')

is potentially ambiguous, involving either sentence or VP negation. These two interpretations may be distinguished in speech:

^{1}Could ^{1}he ^{1}no ^{1}have ^{3}come?
(sentence negation: 'Is it impossible that he has come')
^{1}Could ^{1}he ^{3}no ^{2}have ^{2}come?
(VP negation: 'Is it possible that he hasn't come)

(N.B. The superscript numerals indicate pitch: 1 is relatively low in pitch and 3 relatively high. In the first example, the intonation nucleus is on *come;* in the second example it is on *no.*

As expected:

Could he have no come?
(VP negation: 'Is it possible that he hasn't come')

can only be VP negation (if we leave aside the possibility of main verb negation) since the negative particle follows *have.*

To summarize the situation with *could*:

Sentence negation:
He *couldnae* have been working (preferred)
He *could no* have been working.

VP negation:
He could *no have been* working.
He could *have no been* working.
He could *have been no* working.

Main verb negation:
He could have been *no working.*

With sentence negation the negative must immediately follow the modal and is usually enclitic; with VP negation the negative may either precede or follow the aspectual auxiliaries or come between them, but is never enclitic; with main verb negation the negative always immediately precedes the main verb and is invariable isolate.

Let us now consider *might*. This also expresses 'epistemic possibility' and has a rather restricted distribution. In negative sentences it seems that it is restricted to VP negation. Surprisingly *might* permits the negative marker to cliticize. Thus:

He might no have come.
He might have no come.
He mightnae have come.

are all interpreted as 'it is possible that he hasn't come'. Perhaps this is possible because wide scope negation is not possible with *might* so there can be no confusion. Since *might* is restricted to VP negation we would expect double negation (disregarding main verb negation) to be impossible, and this is indeed the case – we do not find:

*He mightnae no have come.
*He mightnae have no been working.

We have noted that *might* has a restricted distribution in that it does not occur with sentence negation nor in interrogative sentences. In both cases appropriate forms involving *could* are used, as illustrated above. This interaction between *might* and *could* is exploited to avoid ambiguity.

Affirmative declarative:
   He could have come (preferred form).
   He might have come.

Negative declarative, sentence negation:
   He couldnae have come (preferred form).
   He could no have come.

Negative declarative, VP negation:
   He might no have come (preferred form).
   He might have no come.
   He mightnae have come.
   He could have no come.
   He could no have come.

Affirmative interrogative:

Could he have come (preferred form).
*Might he have come.

Negative interrogative, sentence negation:
Could he ^{1}no have come.

Negative interrogative, VP negation:
Could he ^{4}no have come.
Could he have ^{4}no come.

After this extensive discussion we can deal with the other modals more rapidly. *Can* operates like *could*. Both sentence and VP negations are possible, the sentence negative normally being enclitic:

You cannae do it, even if you want to.
(you can no do it, even if you want to)

and the VP negative always being the isolate form:

You can no do it, if you dinnae want to.
*You cannae do it, if you dinnae want to.

(though under emphasis, as we have observed, the wide scope negative may also occur in the isolate form). Double negation is again possible:

You cannae no do it.

Should, will and *would* all show the same syntactic behaviour, with one qualification. In declarative sentences when there is no other auxiliary, sentence and VP negations seem to be indistinguishable. Thus pairs like

You shouldnae do that.
You should no do that.

He'll no tell you.
He willnae tell you.

do not seem to differ in meaning. This is perhaps best treated as a case of semantic neutralization. The distinction begins to surface again, however, when other auxiliaries are involved, thus

You shouldnae have told her.
('what you shouldn't have done is told her')
You should have no told her.
('what you should have done is not told her')

In negative interrogative sentences the distinction is fully alive again:

Should he no have told her?
  ('wasn't it his duty, etc. to tell her?')
Should he have no told her?
  ('Was it his duty, etc. not to tell her?')

Would you no do that?
  (equivalent in wide scope to 'won't you do it')
  (equivalent in narrow scope to 'please stop doing it')

The salutation:

Will you no come back again

encountered at the border driving south from Scotland to
England is, perhaps intentionally, ambiguous as between the wide
scope reading, equivalent to 'won't you return', and the narrow
scope reading, equivalent to 'will you stay away'. In speech, typically, but not invariably, the narrow scope reading would be
marked by high pitch on the negative and wide scope by lower
pitch on the negative.

Must, like *might,* is only found in an epistemic sense: 'from the
available evidence I conclude that . . .'. Root necessity is
rendered by *have to,* to which we return. It seems that only a
narrow scope negation is possible, and this makes semantic sense,
since whereas a reading 'I conclude that X is not the case' is interpretable, it is not clear how to interpret 'I do not conclude that
X is the case'. Two negations seem inconceivable. This may explain why

He mustnae've gone.
He must no have gone.
He must've no gone.

all have the reading 'I conclude that he didn't go' and why sentences with two negatives:

*He mustnae no have gone.
*He mustnae have no gone.

are impossible.

We have already remarked that *have to* is marginal as an
auxiliary. The situation is further complicated by the fact that
have got to is usually preferred to simple *have to.* We restrict
ourselves, however, to *have to.* As remarked above, it typically
has a root necessity sense ('obligation' and the like). When it is
the only verb in a sentence, then it will usually behave like an
auxiliary:

You've to go.
Have you to go.

though, as has been remarked:

You've got to go.
Have you got to go.

are preferred.

In negative sentences under wide scope negation *have to* normally behaves as a main verb:

You dinnae have to go.

whereas under narrow scope negation it behaves like an auxiliary:

You've no to go.

Confusingly, however, it seems that

You havenae to go.

is interpretable as either wide or narrow scope negation. Under wide scope negation this causes no surprise since cliticization seems to be regular in this sense. It is, however, unusual to find cliticization under narrow scope negation when there is a possibility of confusion. Double negation is not possible:

*You dinnae have no to go.

The conclusion is that *have to* takes either wide or narrow scope negation, but not both.

Be to also poses some difficulties. The most usual negation is narrow scope:

You're no to do that.

This sense can also be expressed, though it is less usual, by the enclitic

You arenae to do that.

A point which is not entirely clear is whether wide scope negation is also possible with *be to*. The problem partly lies with the semantics of *be to*, which are not well understood. *Be to* seems to have a general root sense of 'arrangement' rather than the 'obligation', 'necessity' or the like typical of *have to*. The 'obligation' sense of *be to*, which is undeniably present in some instances, seems to spring from the fact that in appropriate circumstances if something is 'arranged' then a speaker may feel an obligation to conform to the arrangement. So *be to* and *have to* are often interchangeable:

I'm to be there by six.
I have to be there by six.

This is not always the case. Thus

> I feel I've got to go because she would be disappointed if I
> didnae.
> (= 'I feel under an obligation to go . . .')

is well formed but

> *?I feel I'm to go because she would be disappointed if I
> didnae.
> (= *?'I feel that I have an arrangement to go . . .')

seems anomalous: perhaps individuals can, as it were, 'put themselves under an obligation', but cannot themselves 'put
themselves into an arrangement'. Similarly,

> You have to be over six foot to join the police.
> ('you are obliged to be . . .')
> You have to be under fourteen to travel half price on the
> buses.

are well formed but *be to* cannot be substituted in these cases.
Further investigation is clearly needed here, and for the present
we will suppose that *be to* only accommodates narrow scope
negation. Double negation is not possible:

> *He isnae no to do that.

Used to behaves like a main verb in negative sentences, except
that with narrow scope negation the negative marker may either
precede or follow *to*.

> Wide scope negation:
> He didnae used to do that.

> Narrow scope negation:
> He used to no do that.
> He used no to do that.

> Both wide and narrow scope negations:
> He didnae used to no do that.
> He didnae used no to do that.

This might suggest that *used to* is treated in these cases like a
unit, and that *to* does not here have quite the force of a complementizer, as it does with other main verbs.

Figure 8.3 summarizes these observations.

8.3.1 Reversed polarity tag questions

The distribution of negatives in 'reversed polarity' tag questions

	Sentence	*VP*
Either or both negations		
COULD (epistemic: possibility)	op-nae (op no)	op no
WILL (epistemic: future)	op-nae (op no)	op no
WOULD (epistemic: hypothetical)	op-nae (op no)	op no
SHOULD (epistemic: likelihood)	op-nae (op no)	op no
CAN (root: ability, etc.)	op-nea (op no)	op no
COULD (root: possibility, etc.)	op-nea (op no)	op no
SHOULD (root: duty, etc.)	op-nae (op no)	op no
Only VP		
MIGHT (epistemic: possibility)	—	op no/op-nae
MUST (epistemic: conclusion)	—	op no/op-nae
BE TO (root: 'arrangement')	?	op no/op-nae
Either but not both		
HAVE TO (root: obligation)	DO/op-nae	op no/op-nae

('op' = operator)

FIGURE 8.3

is also relevant to our main theme: for an extended discussion of tags in Edinburgh Scots see Millar and Brown 1979. In section 8.2.4 above we have described tags for sentences involving the aspectual auxiliaries *have* and *be*. Recall in particular the forms

He's coming, isn't he?
He's coming, is he no?

He isnae coming, is he?
He's no coming, is he?

(and parallel forms with *have*). The first example, a conducive tag, is associated with falling intonation, and the second with rising intonation. In the second set of examples it seems that the negative involved is a wide scope, sentence, negative.

We should now also note the tag particle *e*, which alternates freely with reversed polarity tags:

He's coming, e? (*cf* He's coming isn't he?)
He'd gone, e? (*cf* He had gone, hadn't he?)

He isnae coming, e? (*cf* He isn't coming, is he?)
He hadnae gone, e? (*cf* He hadn't gone, had he?)

He isnae coming, e no? (*cf* He isn't coming is he?)
He hadnae gone, e no? (*cf* He hadn't gone, had he?)

Note that *e* does not involve 'pronoun repetition', and that it occurs with both *be* and *have* (and with other items as we will see). The most satisfactory analysis seems to be that *e* is a conducive tag particle, unmarked for polarity, that seeks agreement to the proposition to which it is attached. If that proposition is negative, then *no* is optionally copied after *e*: *e no* then seeks concurrence with a negative proposition. This alternative account is supported by the fact that both *e* and *e no* are associated with a falling tone, just like the conducive *isn't he* or *is he*. This is the analysis that we will adopt. Given this analysis, note two things. First, the *no* that occurs in the tag *is he no,* etc. is derived from a reversal of the polarity value of the sentence, and is obligatory; whereas the *no* that occurs in the tag *e no* derives by copying the polarity value, and is optional. Second, *e* tagged to an affirmative sentence is distributionally equivalent to negative tag forms like *isn't he* rather than to forms like *is he no* and conversely that *e (no)* tagged to a negative sentence is distributionally equivalent to affirmative tag forms like *is he*.

The distribution of the tag forms, together with a schematic representation of what is at issue is thus:

> He's coming,   is he no?
> He's coming,   isn't he?
> aff S   neg Tag
> └────── reversal ──────┘

> He's coming,   e?
> aff S   con Tag
> └────── conducive ┘

> He isnae coming, is he
> neg S   aff Tag
> └────── reversal ──────┘

> He isnae coming,   e (no)
> ┌────── (copying) ──────┐
> neg S   con Tag *no*
> └────── conducive ┘

It will be no surprise that the form with *e* is preferred to that with the -'*nt* tag.

Consider now the modal auxiliaries. *Could, would, should* and *be to* will all take reversed polarity tags on the lines of:

> He couldnae do it, could he?
> He couldnae do it, e (no)?

> He could do it, e (couldn't he)?
> He could do it, could he no?

and so on. Note that *couldn't, wouldn't,* etc. which are not found in simple interrogative negatives, are available in tags, though tags with *e* are preferred. The tag forms with the isolate negative, *could he no,* etc. are fully acceptable.

Can, will and *must* also occur in tagged sentences, except that the verbs themselves do not have *-n't* forms. Thus we find:

He can come, e (*can't he)?
He can come, can he no?

He'll come, e (*won't he)?
He'll come, will he no?

We have seen that *might* does not occur in interrogative forms. It does not occur in tags either, though *e* can occur:

He might come, e (*mightn't he)?
He might come, *might he no?

Have to works like a main verb

He had to come, e (didn't he)?
He had to come, *had he no?
He had to come, *hadn't he?

Thus far the situation is fairly straightforward, apart from the distributional restrictions on negative forms. The situation becomes more interesting when we consider VP negation. Consider:

He could have no done it

with VP negation. This is tagged:

He could have no done it, couldn't he?
He could have no done it, could he no?

rather than

*He could have no done it, could he?

The polarity of the tag (*couldn't he/could he no*) derives from reversing the polarity value of the sentence as shown on the first auxiliary (*could*). The polarity of the VP negation is ignored.

The *e* tag now becomes interesting since we can find both

He could have no done it, e?
He could have no done it, e no?

If *e* is a conducive tag particle distributionally equivalent to *couldn't,* etc. as argued above, then in the second example *no* must be an optional copy of the VP negation. Let us represent this schematically as

He could have no done it, e no?

```
            ┌────── copying ──────┐
    aff S    neg VP          con Tag no
            └───── conducive ─────┘
```

That this is a plausible analysis is revealed when we discover that alongside:

He could have no done it, couldn't he?

there is an alternative with a double negative tag:

He could have no done it, couldn't he no?

In both cases *couldn't he* must be a reversed polarity tag deriving from *could*. It seems then, as with the account of *e no* above that the additional *no* is an optional copy of the VP negation:

He could have no done it, couldn't he (no)?

```
            ┌──── (copying) ────┐
    aff S    neg VP        neg Tag   no
            └───── reversal ─────┘
```

It will be clear that double negative tags are only possible in a restricted range of circumstances. They require an affirmative sentence, to yield a negative tag, together with VP negation, to yield the additional *no*, as in the example above. The following are impossible:

*He could have done it, couldn't he no?
    (no source for the additional no)
*He couldnae have done it, couldn't he no?
    (negative sentence requires reversed tag)

They also require the *-n't* negative to be available. This means that they do not occur with the isolate negative form of tag.

He could have no done it, could he no?

```
    aff S    neg VP        neg tag
            └───── reversal ─────┘
```

is possible, where *no* is part of a regular negative interrogative, but there is no sentence:

*He could have no done it, could he no no?

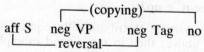

```
            ┌──── (copying) ────┐
    aff S    neg VP        neg Tag   no
            └───── reversal ─────┘
```

It seems that here the sequence *no no* is not permitted.

8.4 The syntax of double modals

We now come to apply the findings of the previous sections to double modal constructions. The description follows the taxonomy of section 8.2 above.

8.4.1 Morphology

Let us first consider *have to* and *be to*. These can operate syntactically like either main verbs or like auxiliaries. Like other forms of *have* and *be*, when they are the only verb in a predication they have clitic forms (*I've to, he's to*, etc.), co-occur with the clitic negative and invert with the subject in interrogative sentences (*Have I to, Is he to*, etc.). *Have to* also occurs with 'DO support', (*Do I have to*, etc.), but *be to*, does not (**Does he be to*, etc.). They also agree in number with the subject NP (*I have to, he has to, I am to, He is to*, etc.) and, unlike the other modal auxiliaries, the 'tense' alternation (*I have to, I had to: I am to, I was to*, etc.) typically corresponds to a 'past' 'non-past' time reference as with main verbs. *Have to* can, like any main verb, be preceded by the perfect and progressive auxiliaries (*I have had to, I am having to*, etc.). *Be to* cannot. Both can, however, themselves be preceded by other modals (*I might have to, I'll have to, I might be to*, etc.). In Standard English *have to* has this behaviour, but not *be to*. The obvious conclusion is that both of these items operate syntactically like 'main verbs', except that they share with *have* and *be* the ability to cliticize, etc.

We now turn to *can* and *could*. The obvious problem here is that both forms can occur as second modal auxiliary (*will can*, etc.) and embedded after *to* (*used to could*, etc.). The alternation between forms like *can* and *could* is usually described as involving the category of 'tense', though it has long been recognized that this is not an entirely satisfactory account. Its 'double' occurrence in a single sentence presents obvious difficulties. It is not our intention in this chapter to attempt to resolve this problem, but to discuss some of the data that will need to be accounted for in an eventual description.

Before considering 'tense' in double modal constructions, we should briefly review the applicability of a category of tense to modal verbs in general. The tense alternation does not typically correlate with a temporal distinction except in a few cases such as the use of *can* in an 'ability' sense (*I can (could) lift a hundredweight*). Temporal distinctions are usually shown in other ways, typically involving the auxiliary *have*: 'permission': (*I can (could) go tonight/I could have gone yesterday; 'possibility': That could* (*can) be the postman/That could have been the postman. The distinction is sometimes said to correlate with 'remoteness', etc. in some non-temporal sense (eg I can go tonight, definitely, I could go tonight, I suppose). There is, however, more to the matter than this, since some uses typically require could in any circumstances – for example the 'epistemic' use of could (That could be the postman, *?That can be the postman).

The same sort of situation holds with the alternation will/would, though here the temporal relationship, and indeed the semantic relationship between the forms, is even more remote. Will has usages involving 'willingness' and the like, but it is most frequently used as a simple marker of futurity. Would is characteristically used in a hypothetical sense.

May is not typically found in vernacular Scots, as we have already noted in section 8.1. Might, however, does occur, though this form has no obvious connection with 'past time'. As with other forms, past time is typically indicated by a form of have: he might have come, etc.

Similarly, though shall is hardly ever found, the form should is common, both in a 'duty' or 'obligation' sense and in an 'epistemic' sense. Should has no obvious relationship to past time either.

To summarize, can/could and will/would could be morphologically paired as 'non-past' and 'past' forms, though distributionally they do not operate like other 'past' and 'non-past' verb pairs; should and might are 'past' forms with no 'non-past' congener; must has no 'past' alternate. A description involving a morphological category of 'tense' does not seem particularly helpful since only a minority of forms exploit the alternation. Nor does it seem particularly insightful to relate the alternation to 'tense' since few of the forms have clear temporal correlations.

We should at this point briefly consider the status of maybe. This is usually described as a 'modal adverb', and we have already noted that it appears to have taken over many of the functions of Standard English may. However, as Miller (1980) has shown, it seems to have retained some syntactic properties of the modal auxiliaries. So the sentence:

I maybe better answer questions

(Miller 1980: example 1f) has no auxiliary, and in:

He maybe no can do it

the negative particle follows maybe as though it were an auxiliary. The negative cannot, however, cliticize: *He maybenae can do it. It seems that maybe has some 'auxiliary like' characteristics. Conversely, Miller (1980) has suggested that the restricted distribution of some modal auxiliaries, especially *might*, suggests that not only do some adverbs have 'auxiliary like' characteristics, but some modal verbs may have some of the characteristics of modal adverbs! It might be better simply to consider them all as individual items in their own right.

When we come to consider the behaviour of *could/can*, either in double modal constructions or as an embedded modal, we meet the same sort of problems as we meet with simple modal constructions. To begin with we find the following typical co-occurrence restrictions between *can/could* and a preceding form:

have to can	but not typically	?have to could
had to could	but not typically	?had to can
will can	but not typically	?will could
would could	but not typically	?would can
used to could	but not typically	?used to can

In these cases there appears to be a 'sequence of tenses' kind of relation between the forms. Interestingly, when the initial modal has no 'past': 'non-past' alternation, then either form can follow:

might can	and also	might could
should can	and also	should could
must can	and also	must could

The alternation suggests that there is at least a residual category of some description attached to the second modal.

However, if the alternation is one of 'tense' then it seems that a sentence can then be 'doubly tensed', on condition that it contains two modals the second of which is *can,* and that a complement structure can be tensed on condition it contains the modal *can.* Such a description should surely be avoided!

8.4.2 Subject auxiliary inversion
Under this heading there is little to say. In double modal auxiliary constructions only the first of the modals inverts with the subject NP. Thus we find:

He will can do it.
Will he can do it?

but not

*Will can he do it?

This pattern is general for all the double modal constructions noted. Negative particles do not invert along with the subject. Subject–auxiliary inversion is not possible in embedded constructions.

8.4.3 Negative forms

In section 8.3 above we established that, disregarding the possibility of main verb negation, sentences could take two negations – a wide scope, sentence, negation and a narrow scope, VP, negation. We further found that *should, will* and *would* can take either or both such negations and that *might* and *must* only occur with narrow scope, VP, negation. In double modal constructions the possibilities for negation are the same: a sentence negation and a VP negation taking the second modal and the other auxiliaries in its scope.

With *might* and *must,* which only take narrow scope negation, the following sets of examples are synonymous:

He might no could have done it.
He might could no have done it.
He mightnae could have done it.
('it is possible that he was unable to do it')

He must no can do it.
He must can no do it.
He mustnae can do it.
('I conclude he is unable to do it)

Note that with only the narrow scope interpretation possible, the negative can float towards the main verb (the second examples) or cliticize to the first modal (the third examples)

The position is different with *would* and *should,* both of which accommodate either wide or narrow scope negation. Here we find that the clitic and non-clitic negatives typically indicate a different scope of negation.

He shouldnae can come.
('it should not be possible for him to come')
He should no can come.
('it should be impossible for him to come')

Once again the narrow scope negative can float towards the main verb:

He should no could have come.
He should could no have come.

Double negation is possible:

He shouldnae no could have come.
He shouldnae could no have come.

The same pattern is observable with *would* and *will*, though it seems that the scope distinction is neutralized in declarative sentences:

He willnae can come.
He'll no can come.

are synonymous. In interrogative sentences, however, the scope distinction emerges as before:

Will he no can come?

is ambiguous as between 'Won't he be able to come?' and 'Will he be unable to come?'.

8.4.4 Reversed polarity tags

In double modal constructions with *can* or *could* either, but not both, of the modals can occur in a tag. With an affirmative main sentence we expect to find a negative tag and both of

He'll can do it, will he no?
   └─ reverse ─┘
He'll can do it, can he no?
   └─reverse─┘

are found. The difference between them is tenuous, but it seems that when *can* is tagged the emphasis is on 'ability' and when *will* is tagged the emphasis is on 'futurity'. Thus the second of the examples would be appropriate if asked of a task currently in hand: suppose A were currently mending a piece of machinery and B wished to enquire whether a successful outcome was likely, B might enquire *you'll can do it, can you no?* On the other hand if B were asking whether the task could be performed in the future, he might enquire *you'll can do it, will you no?*

This pattern of tagging generalizes across all the constructions labelled as 'double auxiliaries', and it is interesting to find that it also occurs with *used to*:

He used to could go, didn't he?
   └─ reverse ─────┘
He used to could go, couldn't he?
    └──── reverse ─┘

In this respect, however, *have to* operates like a main verb:

He has to can swim, doesn't he?
   └reverse ────────┘
*He has to can swim, couldn't he?
    └── reverse ─┘

He'd like to can swim wouldn't he?
└─reverse ─────────────────┘

*He'd like to can swim, couldn't he?
└─reverse──┘

8.4.5 VP deletion

Double modals operate just like other auxiliaries with respect to VP deletion:

I didnae think he'll dae it, but I suppose he might could.
I cannae dae it the now, but I would could next week.
He disnae want to dae it, but he might have to.
He cannae do it these days, but he used to could.

8.4.6 Quantifier floating

In a sentence like

(all) the boys (all) will (all) can (all) go

all can occur in any one, but only in one, of the positions indicated in brackets and it will be semantically associated with the subject of the sentence. This behaviour is parallel to that of *all* when 'floated' in sentences with only a single modal. This behaviour can be generalized across all the double modal constructions discussed earlier, thus:

(all) the boys (all) should (all) could (all) go
(all) the boys (all) might (all) could (all) have (all) done it

All will also float across *used to*:

(all) the boys (all) used to (all) could (all) go

and when it does it floats to a position after *to* as shown; thus we find

The boys used to all could go.

but not

*the boys used all to could go.

All will not float across *to* in other constructions

(all) the boys are (all) bound to could go
*the boys are bound to all could go
*the boys are bound all to could go

Have to does not permit floating over *to*:

(all) the boys (all) have to go
*the boys have all to can swim
*the boys have to all can swim

8.5 Some conclusions

Let us now return to the taxonomy we started with and summarize our main findings. A few remarks are made on the
theoretical implications, but it is not the purpose of this chapter
to follow these through.

The first and second groups share the idiosyncrasy of permitting *can* and *could* to occur directly after another modal ('double
modal auxiliary constructions') or to occur in an embedded sentence after the complementizer *to* ('embedded modal auxiliary
constructions'). In Hawick these two environments seem to show
the same syntax; in other dialects the two groups differ. The problem here can be defined in a number of ways, all of which offend
the syntax of Standard English. One way is this: a finite verb
group can only exhibit the category of tense once, on its initial
member, and cannot occur in a non-finite complement clause
after *to*. If the alternation *can/could* shows a category of tense,
then both restrictions are offended. A further problem attends a
phrase marker configuration like that of Figure 8.2, if, as is stan-
dardly assumed, modals are inserted to the 'infl' node. If both
modals are inserted here then this represents the facts of negative
scope incorrectly.

A variety of solutions suggest themselves, a couple of which
we will adumbrate. Each has difficulties. We might, for example,
suppose that CAN has finite, tensed, forms (*can* and *could*)
which, like other verbs, occur initially in the verb group (*He is
(was)* . . .; *he can (could)* . . .); and that it also has non-finite
forms (*can* and *could*) which occur in the appropriate environments – eg after a modal (*He might be* . . .; *He might could*
. . .) or embedded after to (*He used to be* . . .; *He used to
could* . . .). This would accommodate the residual 'sequence of
tenses' phenomenon noted above, but CAN would then be the
only verb with alternate non-finite forms. Or again, we might
abandon any pairing related to 'tense' and suppose that each of
the modals is unique. The distributional peculiarities of each
could then be accommodated separately in the lexicon. The parallelism between some of the modals and some epistemic adverbs
could then be brought out, but at the expense of the 'verb'-like
behaviour that they undoubtedly still retain, and there would then
be a problem of what to do with 'tense'. The reader can easily

envisage other solutions: all seem to raise as many problems as they solve.

Thankfully the third group we identified ('modal + main verb constructions') presents few problems. They only differ from Standard English in that *be to* can, like *have to* in Standard English, itself be preceded by a modal auxiliary. *Used to* has a few auxiliary-like features.

Notes

1. Following Quirk *et al.* (1986) the first auxiliary in the verb group is termed the 'operator'. It is the operator to which negatives cliticize (*He hasn't been talking*) and which inverts with the subject in interrogative sentences (*Has he been talking?*).
2. The tree is intended to indicate scope distinctions rather than to make a particular theoretical point. It could, obviously, be elaborated along the lines of several contemporary models.

References

ANDERSON, J. A. (1976) *On Serialization in English Syntax. Ludwigsburg Studies in Language and Linguistics*. 1. Ludwigsburg.

BOERTIEN, H. S. (1979) 'The double modal construction in Texas', *Texas Linguistic Forum* 13: 14–33. University of Houston, Houston, Texas.

BROWN, K. and MILLER, J. (1975) 'Modal verbs in Scottish English, *Work in Progress* 8: 99–115. Dept. of Linguistics, University of Edinburgh.

BROWN, K. and MILLAR, M. (1980) 'Auxiliary verbs in Edinburgh speech', *Transactions of the Philological Society* 78: 81–133.

BUTTERS, R. R. (1973) 'Acceptability judgments for double modals in Southern English'. In C-J. N. Bailey and R. Shuy (eds) *New Ways of Analyzing Variation in English*. Washington DC: Georgetown University Press.

COATES, J. (1983) *The Semantics of the Modal Auxiliaries*. London: Croom Helm.

DI PAOLO, M. *et al.* 'A survey of double modals in Texas', *Texas Linguistic Forum* 13.

JACKENDOFF, R. (1972) *Semantic Interpretation in Generative Grammar* Massachusetts: MIT Press.

LAKOFF, R. (1969) 'A syntactic argument for negative transportation', *CLS* 5: 40–8.

LEECH, G. (1978) 'A corpus based semantic analysis of modal auxiliary verbs in British and American English.' Final report on SSRC grant HR3792.

LYONS, J. (1977) *Semantics*. Cambridge: Cambridge University Press.

MCAFEE, C. (1980) 'Characteristics of non-standard grammar in Scotland', MS.

MCDONALD, C. and BEAL, J. C. (1985) 'Modal verbs in Tyneside English', Dept of English, University of Newcastle, MS.

MILLER, J. (1980) 'The expression of possibility and permission in Scottish English.' Working paper in final report in SSRC grant 5152/1.

MILLAR, M. and BROWN, K. (1979) 'Tag Questions in Edinburgh Speech.' *Linguistische Berichte* 60: 24–45.

MURRAY, J. (1873) *The Dialect of the Southern Counties of Scotland.* London

PALMER, F. (1965) *A Linguistic Study of the English Verb.* London: Longman.

PALMER, F. (1979) *Modality and the English Modals.* London: Longman.

PAMPNELL, J. R. (1975) 'More on double modals', *Texas Linguistic Forum,* 2.

PULLUM, G. and WILSON, D. (1977) *Autonomous Syntax and the Analysis of Auxiliaries, Language* 53: 741–88.

QUIRK, R. *et al.* (1986) *A Comprehensive Grammar of English.* London: Longman.

SCUR, G. S. (1968) 'On the non-finite forms of the verb *can* in Scottish', *Linguistica Hafniensia* 11: 211–18.

Chapter 9

On grammatical diffusion in Somerset folk speech*

Ossi Ihalainen

9.1 Introduction

This chapter examines two cases of grammatical variation in present-day Somerset English.[1] Analysis of the evidence shows that certain contexts have old dialectal forms more frequently than others. Assuming that the dialect is in a state of change, with older dialectal forms being replaced by standard forms, or in some cases by new dialectal forms, the obvious conclusion to draw is that the changes concerned arose in those contexts where older dialectal forms have become rare (or non-existent) and are spreading from them to more conservative contexts.

This does not mean that the change is necessarily towards the standard. For example, invariant *be* with noun subjects, as in *Foxes be witty* or *Here be thee clothes,* seems to have practically disappeared. However, the usual form in casual speech is not necessarily *Foxes are witty*; instead, forms like *Foxes is witty* are frequently used. In cases where the subject follows the verb, *is* with plural noun subjects is almost the rule: *Here's your clothes, There's two houses 'pon the hill.* To establish the direction of change (for example, that *I am* is replacing *I be* rather than vice versa), the present-day data will be compared with data from Elworthy's *Grammar of West Somerset* (1877) and *West Somerset Word-Book* (1886).

I shall start by looking at some general characteristics of Somerset folk speech and comment on the development of those features. Then I shall concentrate on the following two

---

*A version of this chapter was read at the Third English Historical Linguistics Conference in Sheffield on 30 March 1983.

phenomena: the alternation between invariant *be,* as in *I be so tired,* and the standard forms; and the alternation between the dialectal subject and object pronominal forms *he/un* 'it' and their Standard English equivalents.

I shall argue that in both cases the principle regulating the variation is the same: the most prominent linguistic contexts are also the most favourable to dialectal forms. Interpreted diachronically, this means that the changes concerned arose in non-prominent contexts and are spreading to more salient ones.

9.2 General characteristics of Somerset dialect

In Alexander Ellis's *Early English Pronunciation* (1889: 1476), which seems to rely heavily on Bonaparte (1875–76) and Elworthy (1877), Ellis lists the following features as being characteristic of the dialect area to which Somerset belongs (Ellis's area D4).

In grammatical construction, that which strikes a stranger most is:

1. *I be* for *I am;*
2. The prefix *a-* before past participles (*I have a-done*);
3. The periphrastic form *I do go* for the simple form *I go;*
4. [ən] for the object pronoun *him;*[2]
5. The use of *he* and [ən] 'him' for inanimate objects;
6. The use of the nominative form for the objective, and sometimes the converse;[3]
7. *Utch, utchy* 'I'.

With the exception of (2) and (7), my tape-recordings from the 1970's show that the characteristics listed by Ellis are still commonly found in Somerset, as evidenced by the following examples:

[1] He's older than what I be.
[2] (Not attested.)
[3] We did always salt it, see.
[4] I looked up to un and said, 'What's say? I had thee rabbits?'
[5] He (= the spade) were like that, see, a long handle on un.
[6] I likes everybody. Well, not everybody, but a lot don't like I.
     We don't know, do us?
[7] (Not attested)

The Survey of English Dialects (*SED,* Orton *et al.,* 1962–71), based on field-work done in the 1950s, has occasional instances

of the participial prefix a-; that is, forms like *We've a-got one.*
My recordings do not show a single instance of this. Nor have I
ever heard it when talking to my informants.

Judging from Bonaparte's comments (1875–76: 579), the
pronoun *utch* 'I' was already very rare well before the end of the
nineteenth century. According to him, *utch* was found in two
small, isolated areas of Somerset and was used only by elderly
speakers. The *ees* [is] that Elworthy attests in cases like *bae·ŭn
ees?* 'aren't I?' probably derives from *us* rather than *ich*, as he
convincingly argues (Elworthy 1887: 34–5). Examples from the
1970s recordings, like *I showed it to ee, didn's,* suggest that the
derivation of this enclitic subject from *us* is justified.

9.2.1 Pronoun exchange
As for pronoun exchange, the use of object forms in subject position is very restricted in declaratives: only *her* can occur in
declarative main clauses, as in *Her do live by the pub, don' er?*[4]
Sentences like **Him do know it* or **Us be ready* do not occur. I
specifically checked the use of *us* as a subject in declaratives because it seems to be common in Devon. However, all my informants violently rejected sentences like *Us be thirsty* (cf SED
VIII.9.5, Devon).

In questions, on the other hand, object forms like *her, us* and
em 'them' are almost the rule. The question clitic [ər] corresponding to the full form *he*, as in *He do live in Latcham, don' er?*
probably derives from the unstressed from [ə] of *he* with final
r-colouring (Wakelin 1977: 113) and has nothing to do with the
feminine pronoun *her*.[5]

I and *thee* seem to be the only pronouns that do not have a
distinctively different enclitic form, although, as was pointed out
above, *us* may be used as the question pronoun of *I* (*I showed it
to ee, didn's?*). Also, there is a tendency for some speakers to
replace *thee* by *ee* in questions and object position, but this *ee*
probably derives from *thee* by *th*-dropping rather than being the
second person plural pronoun form *ee* of *you*. This view is supported by the fact that speakers themselves regard *ee* and *thee* in
sentences like *I'll let ee have some tools/I'll let thee have some
tools* as different forms of the same word, the latter being more
'emphatic'.

The use of nominative objects is quite frequent and in casual
speech almost the rule: *You got to take he right out of your herd.
You got to send he in, have'm slaughtered. He is no good.* (Tape
SB 1977). Elworthy (1877: 36) and, following him, Wakelin
(1977: 113) claim that the use of nominative objects is restricted

to 'emphatic' contexts. It is true that nominative objects often occur in emphatic contexts like *I likes everybody. Well, not everybody, but a lot don't like I*, where *I* occurs under contrastive stress, but, as the example above shows, nominative objects do not necessarily have to be emphatic. In fact, most nominative objects attested in the recordings are not 'emphatic' at all.[6]

The analysis of pronoun exchange, then, shows that the distinction between full and enclitic subject pronouns (which in some cases are the same as the object forms) is still operative in Somerset English. As for the use of the nominative in object position, if we were to take Elworthy's description literally (*ie* 'nominative objects are emphatic'), we would have to accept that the usage has spread, because today nominative objects occur in both emphatic and non-emphatic contexts. However, this does not seem to me a very likely development. Since contrastive stress is even today one of the factors that favours nominative objects, and since it is a very prominent feature, it is possible that Elworthy overlooked the less striking contexts where nominative objects occurred and over-generalized on the basis of one context.

9.3 Invariant *be*

I shall now look in detail at one specific development, namely the apparent replacement of invariant *be* by standard forms: that is, the replacement of forms like *ben em*? for *aren't they*?

My interest in this particular development was aroused when I noticed that invariant *be* was rare in the recordings and that it showed a curious distributional pattern.

Today the dialectal present tense positive and negative forms of *to be* in declarative sentences are the following:

1 sg.	be	ben't, ain't
2 sg.	art	ardn
	([ət] unstressed)	
3 sg.	is, 's	idn, ain't
1 pl.	be, 'm	ben't, ain't
2 pl.	be, 'm	ben't, ain't
3 pl.	be, 'm	ben't, ain't

These forms were recorded in 1982 from J.M. (born in 1892 in Brompton Ralph, Somerset), but interviews with two informants in Wedmore (in the north-east of Somerset) show that the same forms are used there. None of my informants had *be'st* (2 sg.),

which occurs in some eastern villages in Somerset (*SED* IX.7.2
So 1; 4, 11). The pronunciation of *ben't* varies a lot. The following varieties are attested: [baːn, bɛn, bɪən, beɪn], with a *t* present
when the informants gave isolated forms but always omitted in
actual speech, as in *ben em?* 'aren't they?'.

Also, it is interesting to note that, although all the informants
readily gave examples like *I be tired* 'I am tired' when they were
asked to illustrate the use of *be,* only *I'm* occurred in the actual
recordings (information on invariant *be* was elicited only from
those informants whose speech had been recorded earlier). The
implications of the observation that forms like *I be tired* did not
occur in the actual interviews while forms like *Where be I to?* and
I ben't taking her down there did, will be discussed later.

The enclitic *'m,* as in *we'm, you'm,* and *they'm,* only occurs in
unstressed position in declaratives. There are no sentences like
Am they all right? or *Yes, they am.*

The singular form *is* is frequently used with plural noun subjects, as in *These here is spars* and *All horses is gone.* However,
it does not seem to occur with personal pronouns, not even with
speakers who use a singular past tense form with plural subjects
(*we was, you was, they was*). The only exception may be *they* in
questions (*Is they all right?*).

In the recordings, 'pure' dialectal forms are typically inter-
spersed with other forms (either standard or non-standard), so
that a speaker may say *I said to un, 'I ben't taking her down there'*
when he quotes his own speech, but *I ain't sure* when he talks to
the interviewer. The difference between *ain't* and *ben't,* according
to J.M., is that the former is 'more polite'. It is perhaps worth
pointing out here that when J.M. was asked about the difference
between *you* and *thee,* he explained that *thee* is only used when
you talk to someone who you are 'pally with'. This suggests that
the selection of a particular form in the recordings is conditioned
by stylistic as well as purely linguistic factors.

The negative form *ain't* has several variants: [eɪnt, ɛnt, ənt, nt].
However, it seems to me that the negative form *i'n,* which often
occurs in questions like *I'n it?, I'n er?,* derives from *idn,* precisely
the way *wa'n* derives from *wadn* 'wasn't'.

Elworthy's paradigms (1877: 55) of the verb *to be* suggest
that invariant *be* could occur irrespective of syntactic context. His
contemporaries writing on other south-western dialects also give
the impression that invariant *be* was evenly distributed over all
grammatical persons and sentence types (Barnes 1863: 24;
Hewett 1892: 3; Wilson 1913: 30). The only authority who gives
a standard form as an alternative is Hewett. In the case of *I,* she

lists both *I be* and *I'm,* but unfortunately she gives no further details. Nevertheless, it seems significant to me that in an early grammar a standard form occurs as an alternative in the context that shows the greatest amount of standard agreement today and which in terms of grammatical diffusion has advanced further than the other grammatical contexts involved. This point will be discussed in some detail below.

9.3.1 Distribution of *be* in the recordings

There were only 26 instances of invariant *be* in a corpus of some 12 hours of speech, although the estimated total number of the present tense forms of *to be* was 550. The distribution of the attested instances of invariant *be* was curious in that they tended to occur in the least frequent syntactic contexts. For example, very few instances were found in unemphatic declaratives, that is, in sentences like *They're ready,* although this is the commonest context. In fact, with *I* no instances at all of invariant *be* were attested in this context. The syntactic contexts where *I be* did occur are exemplified below:

[8] Where be I to? (='Where am I?')
[9] I'm not under no obligation about this, be I?
[10] I says, 'I ben't taking her down there'.
[11] He's a bit older than what I be.

In other words, invariant *be* with the first person singular pronoun occurs only in questions (including tag questions), negatives and in sentence-final position in declaratives. There were no attested contexts of the sort *I be seventy now.*

To determine the role of syntactic context in the possible implementation of new forms, the attested instances of invariant *be* were classified into the categories given below:

Weak affirmative (*He's ready*)
Strong affirmative (*He IS ready; Yes, he is*)
Negative (*He isn't ready*)
Question (*Is he ready?; When's he going?*)

Weak affirmatives are sentences where the verb can freely contract,[7] whereas strong affirmatives are sentences where a full form must be used. Strong affirmatives, then, are sentences with a heavily stressed verb or a verb in sentence-final position, as in *Yes, I am.*

The relative frequencies of contexts having invariant *be* were compared with the relative frequencies of contexts having any present tense form of *to be,* either standard or dialectal. By comparing these two distributions, we should be able to tell which contexts favour the dialectal form. That is, we shall try to find out whether certain contexts are statistically over-represented in the invariant *be* corpus. If certain contexts are less favourable to invariant *be* than others, we might interpret the situation diachronically by concluding that the replacement of invariant *be* originally arose in contexts where this verb form is now rare or non-existent and is spreading to more conservative contexts. The frequencies of the present tense forms of *to be* in the corpus are given below:

Relative frequencies of contexts having a present tense form of *be*, either standard or dialectal		Relative frequencies of contexts having invariant *be*	
Weak affirm	88.0%	Weak affirm	19.23%
Strong affirm	1.5%	Strong affirm	23.08%
Negation	4.5%	Negation	15.38%
Question	6.0%	Question	42.31%

The most striking feature about these frequencies is that, although about 88 per cent of the sentences containing a present tense form of the verb *to be* are weak affirmatives, only 19 per cent of the sentences with an invariant *be* are of this type. This is to say, weak affirmatives are vastly under-represented in the invariant *be* corpus.[8] On the other hand, questions seem to be over-represented. The percentage of negatives does not give a good picture of the frequency of dialectal forms in negation in general because the form *ain't* (*ent*, *en*) is not included in the invariant *be* corpus. Had *ain't* been included, the figures would have shown the striking fact that negative sentences have dialectal forms far more frequently than do weak affirmatives.

Another striking feature of the invariant *be* corpus is the number of strong affirmatives. They account for 23 per cent of the contexts, although in the total corpus they amount to only 1.5 per cent.

On the evidence provided by the tape-recordings, we might hypothesize then that the distribution of the dialectal forms is regulated by the following factors:

1. *Syntactic position and stress:* Positions where contracted forms cannot occur are conservative, whereas unstressed sentence-medial position in affirmatives is favourable to new forms.

2. *Sentence modality:* Questions and negatives seem to be less favourable to standard forms than are weak affirmatives.

9.3.2 Distribution of *be* in the SED data

To test the hypothesis that the above factors are relevant to the implementation of new forms, data from the SED were also analysed. These data come from seven south-western counties (Cornwall, Devon, Somerset, Dorset, Wiltshire, Hampshire, Berkshire). These seven counties were chosen because – besides the obvious requirement that they show invariant *be* – they share a great number of grammatical features. Also, there is some recent evidence that from the viewpoint of lexicon, too, these seven counties (with parts of Gloucestershire and Oxfordshire) form a unified dialect area (Viereck 1980).

On the basis of the tape-recordings, we would hypothesize that *be*-forms would be more frequent in questions, negatives and stressed affirmatives than they are in weak affirmatives. We might also assume that these contexts form an implicational hierarchy, so that if a speaker says *Am I right?*, he will also say *I'm right*, and if he says *I be right*, he will also say *Be I right?*, and so on. Beyond this, the evidence of our recordings is inconclusive. For example, we do not know if stress overrides sentence modality as a constraint. We have seen that questions show invariant *be* about twice as often as strong affirmatives do, but of course questions are about twice as frequent as strong affirmatives.

To work out the order of implementation of the standard forms, the *SED* data were arranged in terms of possible grammars.[9] The following example will illustrate the notion of 'possible grammar'. The grouping shows that there are speakers who say *I'm thirsty* and *Be I right?* (type 2 below). On the other hand, there are no speakers who say both *I be thirsty* and *Am I right?* (after hapax legomena were eliminated). The grammar *I'm thirsty/Be I right?* is said to be a possible grammar, whereas the grammar *I be thirsty/Am I right?* is said to be an impossible grammar.

Grammars that occurred only once were discarded. In the end, the grammars of thirty-three informants were included.[10] The following types were attested with the subject *I* (with *I*, there were no fully standard grammars, i.e. *am* in all contexts):

Type 1: I be thirsty.
             Be I right?
             Oh no, I ben't/ain't.
             Oh yes, I be.

Type 1 accounts for 82 per cent of the total number of grammars.

Type 2: I'm thirsty.
             Be I right?

Oh no, I ben't.
Oh yes I be.

Type 2 accounts for 12 per cent of the total number of grammars.

Type 3:   I'm thirsty.
Am I right?
Oh no, I ben't.
Oh yes, I be.

Type 3 accounts for 6 per cent of the total number of grammars.

With *They*, all the grammars analysed except one (thirty-three in all) were of the type 1 (full dialectal kind)

They'm/be thirsty.
Be they married?
Oh no, they ben't.
They be.

There was one type 2 grammar (So 3) showing the standard form *'re* in the weak affirmative sentence and dialectal forms elsewhere:

They're thirsty.
Is they married?
Oh no, they ben't.
They be.

The occurrence of the standard form in the weak affirmative context is, of course, in accordance with what was said about the distribution of standard forms on the basis of the tape-recordings, but naturally one should not draw far-reaching conclusions on the basis of a single occurrence.

The grammars constructed on the basis of the SED thus support the view that weak affirmatives are the most favourable to standard forms. But beyond this the evidence is less clear-cut. If we go back to the statistics provided by the tape-recordings (p. 110), the number of strong affirmatives is considerable. It accounts for 23 per cent of the cases, although we would expect it to account for only 1.5 per cent. Therefore, strong affirmatives might be the most conservative environment.

As for questions and negatives, the *SED* data suggest that negatives are more conservative than questions, but it should be borne in mind that the negative forms in *SED* are strong negatives, so that it is impossible to say whether the decisive factor involved is stress or sentence modality. On the basis of the tape-recordings, nothing can be said about the relative order of questions and negatives. They are over-represented in the invariant *be* corpus, but whether it is the questions or negatives that are over-represented is not clear. In any case, the following order may be established: assuming that invariant *be* was formerly evenly distributed over all contexts, it is replaced by the standard form in weak affirmatives first, then in questions, and finally in the so-called strong contexts, either positive or negative.

9.3.3 Animacy

A further factor that ought to be considered here as having possible relevance to the implementation of standard forms is animacy. According to the animacy principle, we would expect first and second person pronouns to develop standard agreement before third person pronouns and nouns (Comrie 1981: Chs 6 and 9). Since the traditional Somerset English third person singular verb with pronoun subjects shows standard agreement to start with, nothing can be said about the significance of the animacy principle on the basis of the third person singular pronoun.[11] But does the third person plural show less agreement than the other persons? The possible grammars discussed above suggest that there might be a difference: with *I*, the spread of standard forms has gone further than with *they*; *they* shows only one instance of type 2 grammars and none of type 3.

To study this question in greater detail, some further data from *SED* were analysed. The percentages of standard agreement with *I*, *we* and *they* (*SED* VIII.9.5) in weak affirmative position are given below. Since only one sentence frame was involved, this time all seventy-five responses could be used as evidence:

Percentages of standard agreement with *I*, *we* and *they*:[12]

I'm thirsty	28
We're thirsty	11
They're thirsty	11

Comparison of the contexts *We're thirsty* and *They're thirsty* shows that there is no difference as to the number of standard forms that occur in these sentences, both showing standard agreement 11 per cent of the time. The more advanced state of *I* (standard agreement 28 per cent of the time) is probably accounted for by the fact that Somerset already has an *'m* form, as in the dialectal *we'm, you'm* and *they'm*. It is therefore probably easier for *'m* to be accepted than the totally alien form *'re*.

Noun subjects were not studied in the *SED* at all. In my own tape-recordings there were no instances of invariant *be* with noun subjects. In the case of singular nouns, this is understandable because the dialectal form is the same as the standard form (*ie is*), so that it is the plural nouns that need commenting on.

The absence of invariant *be* with plural nouns does not mean that, in violation of the animacy principle, plural nouns have developed standard agreement before pronouns, for the verb form with plural nouns is frequently *is* rather than *are*, which is in fact consistent with the animacy principle. However, at the moment I am not in a position to say whether nouns show non-standard agreement substantially more often than pronouns in the case of the present tense. There is some evidence from past tense forms that pronouns might develop standard agreement before nouns: sentences like *They were nice* outnumber sentences like *Boots were dear* by four to one in the speech of people who occasionally use standard forms instead of the dialectal forms *They was nice* and *Boots was dear*.

The distribution of the standard forms of the verb *to be* thus very strongly suggests that the least salient environment is the most innovative. Since the pronominal system is also undergoing a change at the moment, it would be interesting to study whether the implementation of standard pronominal forms is actually regulated by the same principle as the implementation of standard verb forms. That is to say, we would like to know here too whether standard forms are more frequent in non-prominent environments than they are elsewhere.

9.4 Dialectal pronouns

Prominence and salience are, of course, complex notions which there is no space to discuss further here, but one would probably expect the preverbal subject position to be both psychologically and phonologically more prominent than the complement position. Therefore, we would expect the standard pronoun *it* to be more frequent in sentences like *Harry found it* than *It's on the desk*.

A sample of Somerset speech was specifically analysed to test this assumption, and it is indeed the case that standard forms in object position outnumber standard forms in preverbal subject position by a considerable margin. So in Somerset English, *He (=the river) got trout in it* is far more likely to occur than *It got trout in un*.

A sample drawn at random from the tape-recordings showed 106 contexts where the dialectal form *he* and its object forms could have occurred instead of the standard form *it*. (To simplify the matter slightly, in Somerset English a neuter *he* can only refer to countable things.) The distribution of *he*-forms as against the standard form *it* in subject and object position is given in the table below:[13]

	Subject (%)	Object (%)
He-form	88	70 ('n, 'm, him, he)
It	12	30

The table shows that the standard form is more likely to occur in object position, given a context where both standard and dialectal forms may occur (namely when the antecedent is not a mass noun).

That prominence might be a regulating factor is further suggested by the use of the second person singular pronoun *thee*. *Thee* is used only in intimate style and even there it is becoming rare. The pronouns *you* and *ee* are used instead. However, when a pronoun is emphatic, *thee* replaces *you,* as in the context below:

B.L.   What be you, Herb? Seventy-two?
H.T.   Gone seventy-five.
B.L.   Gone seventy-five! Thee!
W.B.   Thee! Thee! I didn't know you were gone seventy-five.
        (Tape BB 1975/2)

Unfortunately, the SED failed to elicit information about the second person pronoun in weak affirmatives. However, it is possible to compare *thee* in unemphatic questions (*Art thee married?*) with *thee* in heavily stressed contexts like *THEE art* (*SED* IX.7.2 and IX.7.7). The responses (fifty-two in all) show that *thee* is more frequent in stressed position (75 per cent) than in unstressed position (54 per cent).

I would like to add that, while stress and syntactic position go together, the decisive factor here is probably prominence; thus, we cannot automatically assume that subject positions are conservative and complement positions innovative. For example, I have attested sentences like *You taught theeself, didn't ee?,* where a conservative form occurs in object position. However, we can explain the occurrence of *theeself* here by the principle of prominence: in this sentence, *theeself* represents new information and is thus part of the information focus.

The development of the distribution of the pronoun *ee* 'you' does not lend itself to this kind of interpretation, though. According to Elworthy (1877: 36), unless special emphasis was required, *ee* could freely occur before and after the verb, as in *Ee didn say so, did ee?* Today, *you* (which originally then appears to have been a kind of emphatic form) has replaced *ee* in preverbal subject position, whether emphatic or not, but not in post-verbal position. Elworthy's sentences would now appear in the form *You didn say so, did ee?* In other words, unlike the case of *thee* and the neuter pronoun *he* 'it', the conservative form occurs in a less salient environment than the new form.

A plausible explanation for this 'exception' is paradigmatic pressure. Since *ee* was an object form on a par with forms like *us* and *em,* it gradually assumed their distributional pattern as well. That is, it can still be used as object and subject, but only in postverbal position. This principle may also explain why today *her* is much less frequent in preverbal subject position (*Her do live by the pub*) than it used to be, judging from Elworthy's description (1877: 33, 55; 1886: 336, '*Her* used as a nominative – nearly always: *Her gid'n to she*').

Observations like those above suggest, then, that grammatical diffusion is not simply conditioned by the immediate linguistic context of the forms involved (stress, syntactic position, sentence modality); it is also sensitive to larger patterns of the language into which the new forms are being integrated.

9.5 Summary

To summarize the main points, I have tried to present evidence to the effect that grammatical diffusion is regulated by stress, syntactic position and sentence modality. It may also be regulated by animacy, but that question must be left open at present.

These principles at least allow us to make certain predictions about possible dialect mixtures. For example, we should expect question-tags to be more conservative than the actual declarative that the tag is attached to. There is some evidence that this is in fact the case. This comes from experiments where informants had to manipulate various dialectal forms that they were found to be familiar with. Thus, when an informant was asked what kind of tag he would attach to the sentence *They ben't ready,* he changed it into *They're not ready, be em?* As such, pieces of evidence like this are not very impressive, but it will be remembered that the combination the informant produced is in fact one of the possible grammars attested above (p. 111). Furthermore, the same kind of mixture was shown within the data collected from the tape-recordings and referred to above: *I'm not under no obligation about this, be I?*

The extent to which these factors may affect other syntactic structures and dialects is a matter for further research. I hope that this chapter has generated at least some questions for further research to answer.

Notes

1. The data come from tape-recorded interviews with fourteen elderly natives of ten villages in rural Somerset. A total of some twelve hours of continuous speech was analysed. The recordings vary from proper interviews, where the informant talks to the interviewer, to small talk between two or more natives without the interviewer participating, or in some cases even being present.

   The dialectal spellings in this paper are basically those found in Elworthy (1886). However, my spellings are mainly 'morphological' and do not necessarily reflect phonological phenomena like consonant cluster simplification. Thus the spelling *don't* may represent a *t*-less or a *t*-full pronunciation.

2. Alexander Ellis, like many others, believes that *un* derives from Old English *hine*. Synchronically, however, *un* can be regarded as a variant of *him*: *un* tends to replace *him* in unstressed, non-labial contexts. Somerset speakers themselves characterize *un* as a 'slovenly' pronunciation of *him*.

3. This phenomenon will henceforth be referred to as 'pronoun exchange'.

4. Another object form that occasionally occurs in subject position in declaratives is *ee*, the object form of *you*, but its occurrence seems to be restricted to quite specific environments such as the phrase *ee know* 'you know'. There is a form *ee* that can be frequently heard in rapid speech in declarative subject positions, but that derives from *thee* by *th*-dropping, as in *If 'ee 's make a mistake, he'll put up wi it*, 'If thee shouldst make a mistake, he'll put up with it'.

5. Instead of the subject enclitic *er* 'he', a true object form may occasionally occur. Thus SED ix.7.5. shows forms like *idn him* [əm] (So 13) and *ent n* (W 3) for 'isn't he?' in the South-west.

   The enclitic subject *er* seems to have had a much wider distribution in the past. According to Elworthy (1877: 39), *did er?* could mean 'did I/he/she/we/you/one?'. Of these, then, only 'did he?' and 'did she?' have survived. I am not claiming that one could not hear isolated instances of the other types from conservative speakers. For instance, I have heard a sentence like *We saved them, didn't er?*, but since this is the only instance of *er* being used with a pronoun other than *he* or *she*, one can hardly call the pattern productive any more.

6. An interview with a blacksmith from Meare contained 41 object pronouns referring to 'things'. That is, the pronouns occurred in contexts where a dialect speaker might have chosen a *he*-form but speakers of Standard English would have used *it*. In these contexts, *he* occurred 20 times (*You take a V-iron and put he in the hole*), *un* 'him' 13 times, and *it* 8 times. Granted, I chose the passage to make a point. However, on the basis of my experience, I should be inclined

to say that this passage comes very close to being truely spontaneous speech.

7. The occurrence of contracted auxiliaries in questions like '*sthee found'n*? 'Hast thou found it/him?' and '*vee found'n*? 'Have you found it/him?' suggests that, besides affirmatives, at least some questions form a 'weak' context for verbs.

8. Actually the situation is somewhat more complicated than this because of the possibility of having '*m* besides *be* with plural pronominal subjects. Consequently, the figure 19.23 per cent does not include all dialectal forms. However, since the inclusion of '*m*-forms would not change the figures significantly, and since its distribution is highly idiosyncratic ('*m* can only occur with pronominal subjects in weak declarative positions), I thought it best to exclude it from the count and include only invariant *be*, which can occur in all syntactic contexts.

   Had '*m* been included, the number of dialectal forms in weak affirmatives would have been 29 per cent; that is, the distribution would still have been strikingly skewed, with weak affirmatives showing far fewer standard forms than expected.

9. The relevant *SED* questions are: VIII.9.5, IX.7.1, IX.7.2, IX.7.7, IX.7.9, IX.7.10. The data were grouped into possible grammars by doing a Ward's method cluster analysis on the contexts and verb forms involved. I am grateful to Mr Visa Rauste for writing the necessary computer programs for me.

10. Unfortunately, the negative sentences in the *SED* are all of the strong type (*No, I ben't* rather than *I ben't sure*), so in the case of negation it was not possible to differentiate between strong and weak contexts. Furthermore, the pronoun *you* could not be included because there were no sentences of the type *You're right;* that is, there were no sentences of the weak affirmative type with the subject pronoun *you*. Nor were there any questions of the type *Are we ready?*, so that first person plural forms could not be studied either.

   Also, in some cases the *SED* field-workers used different informants for questions and negatives. Naturally, these responses could not be used to construct individual grammars either. Furthermore, in some cases the informants gave alternatives and it is not clear whether they regarded a particular form as part of their own speech or as something they had heard.

11. If the verb is stressed or occurs in what I have called strong position, invariant *be* may replace *is* even with the third person singular subjects. Thus, *SED* IX.7.7 shows two instances of *be* in 'SHE is' and two instances in 'Oh yes, she IS'. It seems to me that this can be interpreted as further evidence that dialectal forms tend to occur in prominent positions.

12. The actual *SED* context is a subordinate clause ('We drink water when *we're* thirsty') rather than a main clause. There is some evidence from the tape-recordings that main clauses and subordinate clauses may behave differently with respect to subject-verb agree-

ment with the verb *to be*. However, this question cannot be studied on the basis of the *SED* data.

13. The chi-square value for the table is 4.58 (d.f. = 1). The difference between *it* and *he* is statistically significant at the 0.05 level.

References

BARNES, WILLIAM (1863) *A Grammar and Glossary of the Dorset Dialect with the History, Outspreading and Bearings of South-western English*. Berlin: Asher.

BONAPARTE, L.-L. (1875–76) 'On the dialects of Monmouthshire, Herefordshire, Worcestershire, Gloucestershire, Berkshire, Oxfordshire, South Warwickshire, South Northhhamptonshire, Buckinghamshire, Hertfordshire, Middlesex, and Surrey, with a new classification of the English dialects', *Transactions of the Philological Society* 1875–76: 570–81. London: Trübner.

COMRIE, BERNARD (1981) *Language Universals and Linguistic Typology*. Oxford: Basil Blackwell.

ELLIS, ALEXANDER J. (1889) *On Early English Pronunciation*, Part V. The Early English Text Society, E.S. LVI report. New York: Greenwood Press (1968).

ELWORTHY, THOMAS (1877) *An Outline of the Grammar of the Dialect of West Somerset*. (from *transactions of the Philological Society* (1877–79: 143–257. London: Trübner. Vaduz: Kraus Reprint, 1965.

ELWORTHY, THOMAS (1886) *The West Somerset Word-book: A Glossary of Dialectal and Archaic Words and Phrases Used in the West of Somerset and East Devon* (London: Trübner Co.). Vaduz: Kraus Reprint, (1965).

HEWETT, MARY (1892) *The Peasant Speech of Devon*. London: Elliot Stock.

ORTON, HAROLD *et al.* (1962–71) *Survey of English Dialects* (Introduction and 4 Vols). Leeds: E.J. Arnold.

VIERECK, WOLFGANG. (1980) 'The dialectal structure of British English: Lowman's evidence', *English World-Wide* I (1): 25–44.

WAKELIN, MARTYN (1977) *English Dialects: An Introduction*, 2nd edn. London: Athlone Press.

WILSON, JAMES (1913) *The Dialect of the New Forest in Hampshire (as Spoken in the Village of Burley)*. Publications of the Philological Society, IV. London: Oxford University Press.

Chapter 10

Variation in the lexical verb in Inner-Sydney English

Edina Eisikovits

Together with the use of double negatives, the use of non-standard verb forms is generally stigmatized in all varieties of English, including Australian English. But although we all know, for example, that some speakers use *done* for the past tense of *do,* or *went* for the past participle of *go,* we have little systematic knowledge regarding the nature or extent of this variation. Shnukal's (1978) study of Cessnock English is the only Australian study which attempts to quantify the occurrence of non-standard past tense and past participle verb forms, or to explore systematically the linguistic and non-linguistic factors which influence this variation, while Cheshire (1982) provides an investigation of variation in present tense verb forms in Reading English.

This chapter attempts to fill this gap by examining the variation in the lexical verb apparent in the speech of inner-Sydney adolescents. The focus of this chapter will be on variation in irregular past tense and past participle forms. Two main questions will be addressed in order to identify the system underlying the variation apparent, and where appropriate, some remarks relating this variation to historical patterns are also included:

1. What kinds of variation occur?
2. What linguistic/non-linguistic factors influence this variation?

10.1 Methodology of the present study

This study is based on the speech of forty adolescent residents of the inner-city area of Sydney. The informants were selected on the basis of the following criteria:

1. The informants should be Australian-born of Australian-born

parents. Given the high migrant population of the inner-city area of Sydney, this was important to eliminate the possibility of language interference;

2. The informants and their families should be long-term residents of the inner-city area;

3. The informants should adequately represent the age/sex groupings established for this study.

Social class was not a strict criterion of selection, but as this area of Sydney is to a large extent characterized as low status, the informants tended to be at the lower end of the social spectrum. Their parents were engaged in occupations relatively low in social status, for example, cleaner, truck driver, storeman.

No attempt was made to produce a random sample, instead there was a focus on natural groups since, as Labov (1972; 256–7) points out, 'The vernacular is the property of the group, not the individual [. . .] the group exerts its control over the vernacular in supervision so close that a single slip may be condemned and remembered for years [. . .]'. In all, forty children were selected: twenty from year 8 (average age 13 years, 11 months) and twenty from year 10 (average age 16 years, 1 month). Within each group, half were males and half females.

Contact with the informants was made through three inner-city high schools: Petersham Girls', Enmore Boys' and Dulwich High School. The feeder areas for these schools include the working-class suburbs of Marrickville, Leichhardt, Annandale and Glebe as well as Petersham and Enmore. Exploratory investigations established that these schools provided a rich source of language variation for further investigation.

Each interview was tape-recorded using a portable cassette-recorder. Such a portable recorder was used because of the need for manoeuvrability as many of the interviews were conducted in the school playground. Interviews lasted from one and a half to three hours depending on the involvement and interest of the informants. Many were spread over two sessions. In all a total data base of more than fifty hours of recorded conversation was collected.

Labov (1970) has stressed the need for good data, and it is clear that the quality of the results of any investigation of this type is dependent on the quality of the data on which they are based. As Labov (1970: 46) has pointed out, it is in the vernacular that the systematic patterning of language can most clearly be seen, since it is in this style that the least conscious attention is paid to speech:

Some styles show irregular phonological and grammatical patterns, with a great deal of 'hypercorrection'. In other styles, we find more systematic speech, where the fundamental relations which determine the course of linguistic evolution can be seen most clearly. This is the 'vernacular' – the style in which the minimum attention is given to the monitoring of speech. Observation of the vernacular gives us the most systematic data for our analysis of linguistic structure.

Yet any systematic observation, such as the interview situation, necessarily involves more than the minimum attention paid to speech – hence, we are left with the observer's paradox (Labov 1970: 47): '[. . .] the aim of linguistic research in the community must be to find out how people talk when they are not being systematically observed, yet we can only obtain this data by systematic observation'.

In this study, several methodological strategies were implemented in order to get as close to the informants' vernacular as possible:

1. Attempts were made to meet the respondents informally before the interview sessions. It was hoped that such prior familiarity would reduce the unnaturalness of the interview situation, creating instead a sense of 'renewed friendship' when the recording session actually took place.

2. The informants were interviewed in self-selected pairs (and occasionally in groups of three) rather than alone. It was anticipated that such a three-way conversation would involve peer-peer dialogue as well as interviewee-informant questioning, thereby detracting from the formal 'interview' nature of the situation. Such a group would also alter the power relationships within the interview situation.

   As a result of this approach, much of the discourse in this study was elicited by the informants themselves. Either the comments or narrative of one child would spark a response from the other, or one child would directly prompt the other for information or narrative. The interviews are thus conversational as well as questioning and are at times directed by the children as well as by the interviewer. Indeed, not only is the interviewer sometimes ignored as the two speakers converse between themselves, but also at times the roles are completely reversed so that one of the speakers takes over the role of the interviewer, seeking information from the adult interviewer herself, who thereby becomes the informant. As well, tangential comments by the informants dramatically shifting the direction of the conversation were not uncommon.

3. The topics chosen for discussion were largely determined by the informants who were encouraged to talk freely about subjects close to their own interests, to introduce their own topics if they chose and to abandon those they did not wish to pursue. Consequently, topics varied from interview to interview, although some obvious 'favourites' did emerge. For example, with the younger girls, the conversation invariably took on the quality of a 'confessional' as the girls complained at length of their problems with their families, especially their mothers. But while this proved a most fruitful source of extended discourse with the younger girls, with the older girls and even more so with the boys, questions about parents produced only the briefest responses. Instead, the older girls, in a similarly 'confessional' manner, chose to discuss their relationships with boyfriends, often seeking out the interviewer on successive visits to the school to continue these discussions.

10.2 Method of analysis

The data were analysed using the quantitative approach of variation theory pioneered by Labov (1966) in his study of social stratification in New York speech. Such an approach is based on the assumption that linguistic variation is not random or free but part of a coherent underlying system. It begins with the isolation of a linguistic variable. As Labov (1966: 15) points out, this concept is an abstraction which is realized in actual speech behaviour by variants, that is, individual items which are members of a class of variants constituting the variable: 'Whereas the linguistic variant is a particular item – a morph or a phone – the variable is a class of variants which are ordered along a continuous dimension and whose position is determined by an independent linguistic or extra-linguistic variable.' Its isolation is important because it acts as a basis against which extralinguistic factors can be correlated.

Having isolated the linguistic variable, a number of steps are required before counting may proceed. These steps may be delineated as follows:

1. First, it is necessary to delimit the number of variants which can reliably be identified and to select relevant categories of variants for tabulation.

2. Next, it is important to identify the total population of utterances in which an item may 'potentially' vary (Labov 1969: 723). It is then possible to state the proportion of cases in which a given variant has occurred out of all those cases in which it might have occurred;
3. Third, it is necessary to identify relevant linguistic environments which may affect the variation of items.

The influence of these linguistic environments may then be organized into a hierarchy and this hierarchical relationship may be formulated, either in the writing of linguistic rules or displayed in a table based on implicational scaling. In this study, the latter approach was adopted because, as Feagin (1979: 34) argues: 'implicational scales bring out the relationships within quantitative and qualitative data better than variable rules which can become nearly unreadable'.

In this approach the linguistic environments ordered according to degree of variability are displayed along one axis of a two-dimensional table, while along the other is an array of individual speakers, communities or varieties. From the pattern of application (indicated by 1), non-application (0) or variable application (X) of a particular rule displayed in the table, the dynamic nature of variation becomes apparent. The approach has been adopted in the work of Bailey (1973), Wolfram and Christian (1975) and Feagin (1979).

10.3 What kinds of variation occur in Inner-Sydney English?

In identifying the kinds of variation in the lexical verb in Inner-Sydney English (ISE), perhaps the first thing to note is those areas which do not allow variation.

Of the five parts of the lexical verb,[1] there is no variation at all in either the base form (and hence in the form of the present tense) or the -ing participle[2] (and hence in the form of the progressive), and very little variation in the S form.

This limited variation in present tense forms is particularly interesting in that it contrasts with studies of other varieties of English. Unlike Black English vernacular (BEV) (cf Labov et al. 1968: Wolfram and Fasold 1974), ISE shows little evidence of 's' deletion in third person singular present tense verbs. Such deletion is similarly observed by Cheshire (1982), notably with the verb do, in her study of Reading English, but examples of the positive form of do comparable with Cheshire's examples (1982: 35).

Well, how much do he want for it?
Your dad do play cricket, though, don't he?

did not occur in this sample of ISE, although the corresponding
negative form, (don't he?) is certainly present.

Cheshire (1982: 31) also notes a widespread use of the S-form
with non-third person subjects, for example:

I starts Monday, so shut your face
You knows my sister, the one who's small.
They calls me all the names under the sun, don't they?

Although there is some occurrence of a generalized 's' to non-
third person singular subjects in ISE, this usage appears to be a
stylistic device confined to a narrative context and the use of the
historic present tense. For example,

[1]   So I goes inside and she says, 'What've I gotta do?' I says
      'I don't know'. (7B/M/14–3)[3]
[2]   They were watching television so we gits on the floor and
      we crawls in my bedroom. (5A/F/14–7)

Moreover, the overwhelming majority of examples of this usage
– 95.5 per cent of instances – occur with verbs of saying/telling,
notably say and go, especially when used in speech tags. For
example,

[3]   Then 'e said 'e's gonna put me in a home. 'E says, 'Well,
      I'll throw you out on the street', and he said, 'I don't
      want to see you again'. N I goes, 'Well', I says, 'if that's
      the situation' [. . .] I says, 'just imagine if we're about
      eighteen or nineteen'. 'E goes 'Well, it's all right then.'
      (6A/F/13–11)
[4]   They were sitting there and we says, 'Stay there cause we
      gotta have tea'. (5A/F/14–7)

As these examples would suggest, this generalized S-form occurs
most frequently with first person subjects in both the singular and
plural, but it is also found with the third person plural, especially
in a narrative exchange in which the speaker is a participant.

[5]   We're on the bus [. . .] They says to us 'Stop that singing.
      stop that smoking.' (2A/F/13–11)

No occurrences with second person subjects were noted, but this
may be more a result of the low frequency of the pronoun you
as a subject, especially in narrative, than an indication of the unacceptability of this usage in the grammar of these speakers.

In addition, there is no evidence of variation in past tense forms of regular verbs in ISE although some instances of -*ed* deletion were noted, for example:

[6] An' he turn round, seen the shark, an' he goes up to the guy an' says, 'I think you need a bigger boat'. (3D/M/ 15–7)

Such variation will not be examined here, however: deletion of this type has been shown (Guy 1975: 2) to be inherently variable, being part of the process of consonant cluster simplification and evident among all speakers of English: 'This rule is very compelling, it affects virtually all speakers of English in all but the most self-conscious styles. It is intricately conditioned, but it is rarely categorical.'

The major area of variation which does occur in ISE is in the past tense and past participle forms of some irregular verbs, though even here the spread of this variation is not uniform. Some irregular verbs evidence much variation (for example, *come* as a past tense form occurs with a frequency of 67.1 per cent whereas many other commonly occurring verbs (for example, *say*, *tell*) evidence no variation at all. Indeed, for past tense forms, almost all variation (89.9 per cent) occurs with only five verbs *do*,[4] *see*, *come*, *give* and *run*.

The non-standard past tense and -*ed* participle forms evident in ISE may be classified according to their process of derivation as follows:

1. The form usually reserved for the -*ed* participle may be used for the simple past tense. For example, *seen*, *done* as in

    [7] I got a letter sent home an' me mum seen it. (2B/M/13–11)
    [8] The last time I done it real loud. (5A/F/14–7)

2. The form usually reserved for the simple past tense may be used with a perfective or a passive auxiliary. For example, *took*, *broke*, *went* as in

    [9] Someone might'a took 'em. (4A/F/14–0)

3. The uninflected base form of the verb may be used either to form the past tense or with a perfective or passive auxiliary. For example, *give*, *bring*, *stand* as in

    [10] His mate took a photo and give it to him. (8A/F/14–7)
    [11] If ya doin' that, ya coulda just stand still and ya woulda land on ya feet. (4A/F/14–0)

4. An ambiguous form – one which could be either the *-ed* participle or the base form where these two parts of the verb are identical – is used for the simple past tense. For example, *come, run* as in

[12] We were talking about when she run away from home. (7C/F/16–2)

5. A regularized *-ed* suffix is added to the base form of an irregular verb and this form is used to form either the simple past tense or with a perfective or passive auxiliary. For example, *fighted, breaked, catched* as in

[13] They went home an' got their friends an' that an' when they all come back they fighted. (4D/M/16–1)

[14] My two brothers, they have never fighted you know. Like they – my brother's been tempted to fight my Uncle, you know, but he's never fighted him. (9B/M/14–10)

6. A 'coined' form following the pattern of another irregular verb class is used to form either the simple past tense or with a perfective or passive auxiliary. For example, *brang, brung, writ* as in

[15] She never brang 'em no more. (6F/F/13–11)

[16] The receipt was writ in his name an' his address. (7B/M/14–3)

The frequencies of occurrence of verbs of the first four of these types are given in Table 10.1. Since frequencies are only calculated where there are at least five tokens of a particular form, no frequencies are given for types (5) and (6) and for some examples of other categories.

In Table 10.1, for each of types (1)–(4), the particular verbs involved are listed in column 1. Column 2 provided raw scores for the number of occurrences of the non-standard form compared with the number of potential occurrences in the data.

From these raw scores, a percentage frequency of the non-standard form is calculated and this is given in column 3. Columns 4 and 5 respectively give the number of speakers who use the form and the number using the form categorically.

All the processes listed above have their parallel in the formation of other past tense and *-ed* participle forms, so that in each case the resulting non-standard forms may be explained by analogy with an already existing pattern. The process of regularization by which irregular verbs follow the pattern of regular verbs provides an obvious example of this.

TABLE 10.1 Types of variation of past and -ed participle forms in ISE.

Verbs involved	Number of occurrences	% frequency[a]	Speakers using this form	No. of categorical speakers
Type 1: The -ed participle form may be used for the simple past tense				
Seen	113/181	62.4	28	14
Done	92/148	62.2	21	15
Rung	3/15	20	2	0
Sung	2/6	33.3	5	0
Sung	1/1	(100)	1	1
Swum	3/6	50	1	1
Type 2: The past tense form may be used as an -ed participle form				
Broke	5/16	31.3	4	3
Chose	1/1	(100)	1	1
Spoke	1/3	(33.3)	1	1
Tore	1/1	(100)	1	1
Bit	3/3	(100)	2	2
Hit	2/2	(100)	1	1
Forgot	1/1	(100)	1	1
Blew	1/4	(25)	1	0
Shook	1/1	(100)	1	1
Took	4/20	20	4	2
Gave	2/3	(66.6)	2	1
Fell	1/2	(50)	1	0
Rode	2/3	(66.6)	1	0
Beat	2/7	28.6	2	1
Rang	1/3	(33.3)	1	1
Ran	1/8	12.5	1	1
Went	13/40	32.5	9	6
Type 3: The uninflected form of the verb may be used for either the past or the -ed participle form				
Give	20/111	18	9	6
Bring	4/28	14.3	2	2
Break	2/49	4.1	2	1
Stand	1/4	(25)	1	1
Hang	2/9	22.2	2	2
Type 4: An ambiguous form – one which could be either the -ed participle form or the base form where these two parts of the verb are identical – is used for the simple past tense				
Come	288/429	67.1	38	15
Run	10/75	13.3	7	0
Become	1/1	(100)	1	1

Type 5: A regularized -ed suffix is added to the base form of an irregular verb and this form is used either as the past or the -ed participle form.

For example: *costed, hitted, spreaded, fighted, teared, breaked, lied, seed, feeled, catched, goed, winded.*

Type 6: A 'coined' form following the pattern of another irregular verb class is used either as the past or the -ed participle form.

For example: *brang, brung, git, writ, rid (ride).*

---

[a] % frequency = number of actual occurrences/number of potential occurrences.

But how, if at all, are these processes and the non-standard forms thereby derived related to one another? Is it possible to draw up an implicational scale relating these types of variation? And from this, what can be said about the direction of overall change?

Table 10.2 shows each informant's usage of non-standard past tense and -ed participle forms derived by each of the six processes mentioned.

Along the horizontal axis are the six processes of derivation of non-standard verb forms outlined above, ordered from left to right in terms of increasing frequency. That is, the ambiguous form used for the past tense occurs most frequently while the regularized form occurs least frequently.

The usage of each of these types of variation by each of the speakers listed along the vertical axis is recorded using three possibilities:

I   indicates that these forms were **invariably** used;
X   indicates that **variable** usage was apparent;
o   indicates that such non-standard forms were never used despite the potential for their occurrence.

Where no potential existed, that is, where verbs which might have occurred in such non-standard forms did not appear at all in the corpus, this was indicated by a dash.

If the data are displayed in this way, an implicational relationship may be assumed to exist if os occur only to the left of Xs, which occur to the left of is, that is,

    o X X X I I I

not

    o X X I X I o

TABLE 10.2   Individual speakers' usage of non-standard verb forms in ISE.

Speaker	Regularized form	'Coined' past tense form	Uninflected base form for past tense	Past tense for -ed participle	-ed participle tense	Ambiguous form for past tense
3A	o	X	—	|	—	—
4A	X	X	X	X	—	—
2C	X	X	X	X	—	—
3C	|	o	|	X	—	—
8A	o	o	o	o	—	—
6A	X	X	X	X	—	—
1D	o	X	X	|	X	—
9B	X	(o)	o	X	X	—
10B	o	o	o	X	(o)	—
1A	o	o	o	o	X	—
4C	o	o	(o)	o	X	X
8B	X	X	X	X	X	X
5C	X	X	o	X	X	X
1B	X	X	o	(1)	X	X
2B	X	X	o	X	X	X
4B	o	X	o	X	X	X
5D	o	X	(o)	|	X	X
10D	o	|	o	|	X	X
3D	o	o	o	X	X	X
2A	|	o	o	X	X	X
3B	o	o	o	X	X	X
7A	|	o	o	X	X	(o)
7C	|	o	o	X	X	X
9D	o	o	(o)	X	X	X
8D	o	o	o	X	X	X
7B	X	X	(o)	(o)	X	X

X X X X X X X X X X X X X   X

X X X X X X (o) X o o o o o |

o o o o o | o o X | o | | o | |

o o o o o o | o o o o o o o o

o o o (X) o | o o o o o o o o

o o o o o (X) o X X X o o o |

8C
6C
2D
7D
1C
10C
9C
6B
3A
4D
6D
9A
5B
10A

What such an implicational relationship means is that the occurrence of any form implies the concurrent occurrence of any form to its right in the table, but not vice versa.

In an 'ideal' table of this type, all the os should be congregated to the lower left-hand corner, all the 1s to the top right-hand corner, with Xs in a diagonal between.

In Table 10.2, those cells which do not fit this pattern are bracketed.[5] They show variation or lack of variation where it would not be predicted and thus deviate from the 'ideal'. The number of deviations may be used as an indication of how closely a given table approximates the model through the calculation of the table's 'scalability'. This is done by deriving a percentage from the number of non-deviant cells divided by the total number of filled cells. For Table 10.2, the scalability is 93.6 per cent indicating a high level of fit.

From Table 10.2 the following implicational scale may be suggested:

Coined form/ Regularized form for past		base form for past/ -ed participle		past form for -ed participle		-ed participle for past		ambiguous form for past
	>		>		>		>	

It is the regularized forms and the coined past tense forms which occur least frequently in ISE. Moreover, it is apparent from Table 10.2 that it is these processes which relate least systematically to the other processes considered. Indeed, when these two types of variation are removed, the scalability of Table 10.2 increases from 93.6 to 95.9 per cent. One possible explanation for this is that the regularized -ed form carries a separate meaning from the alternative past tense form so that the two forms function in much the same way as already existing pairs such as 'hanged'/'hung'. Or, alternatively, that these forms are carryovers of the developmental process of regularization common in child language (cf Brown 1973: 234) – hence, such non-standard forms are related differently to the process of change.[6]

On the other hand, it would appear from Table 10.2 that the process of levelling of different past tense/past participle forms to a common form is well under way in Inner-Sydney English. Either the form usually reserved for the -ed participle is extended so that it is used for the simple past tense as well (Table 10.1, type 1) or the reverse, the form usually reserved for the simple past tense occurs as the ed participle (Table 10.1, type 2). Together with historical evidence and similar patterns in other varieties of English, this would suggest that a general change in the language is in progress.

The verbs whose non-standard forms are derived by either of these two processes (types 1 and 2) are of two clear types:

1. Class[7] 6 verbs – *do* and *see* – which change their base vowel and take a nasal suffix in the *-ed* participle, for example: *see/saw/seen*; and

2. Class 7 verbs which change their base vowel but do not take a suffix in either the past or the *-ed* participle. For example: *ring/rang/rung*.

Note that two ambiguous forms (*come* and *run*) – type 4 variation in Table 10.1 above – in which the base form is identical to the *-ed* participle, are both in this class, suggesting that it is the tendency to use the *-ed* participle form with a simple past tense meaning which is occurring here. But while it is these same two groups which are involved in both processes, the only verbs which show variation in both forms are *ring* and *run*.

Verb	Past tense	-ed participle
Ring	Rang	Rung
	Ring	Rang
Run	Ran	Run
	Run	Ran

Hence, for most of these verbs the form for the simple past – whether the past or the -ed participle form – is identical to that used for the perfective/passive, for example,

He took/has took/was took.
He seen/has seen/was seen.

Given that ISE, like other varieties of English, evidences a merging of the two forms, past and *-ed* participle, does this mean that ISE does not have a distinct past participle form – indeed, that there is a weakening of the categories of past and perfect in this variety of English? As Wolfram and Fasold (1974: 153) express it:

'It is possible that some non-standard equivalents of the present and past perfect tenses do not consist of forms of *have* plus the past participle but rather involve a form of *have* plus a general past form.' Such a possibility has been suggested for other varieties of English, for example, Black English. Labov *et al.* (1968: 225) use the frequent occurrence of forms such as 'She has came over', and 'When any of the fellas has went [. . .]' to suggest that 'It is doubtful if there is a consistent differentiation between the preterite and the perfect forms of the verb in NNE'.

Dines, Henry and Allender (1979: 46) go further in extrapolating from the use of forms like *seen* for both the simple past and
the past participle in their Melbourne sample to suggest: '[. . .]
it appears that non-standard English may be collapsing aspectual
distinctions that are customary in the standard language.' For
such a possibility to be established, however, would require more
evidence than simply a common form shared for two functions.
After all, regular verbs and some irregular verbs (class 4, *eg met*)
similarly have only one common form yet maintain a meaning
distinction between the perfect and the simple past tense. In addition, we would expect to find some evidence of hypercorrection
in the speech of these informants. That is, if the distinction between past tense and past participle forms is indeed weakening
in ISE, we would expect to find distinct participial forms in which
the pattern of Standard English has been over-extended, thereby
suggesting the tenuousness of the distinction between past tense
and past participle forms. Wolfram and Fasold (1974: 153) suggest that such forms, for example 'They have cutten all them
trees', do occur in some varieties of English. Such forms, however, were never apparent in these data.

As well, if such a breakdown was occurring we would expect
to find much unsystematic wavering between past and *-ed* participle forms. That is, we would expect much two-way variation
with both possible forms occurring for both functions. Instead, as
pointed out above, we find only two of the twenty-five verbs involved showing such variation. For the other twenty-three verbs,
the variation is one-way only: the past or the *-ed* participle form
is extended to function as both past tense form and past participle. Moreover, with both past tense and *-ed* participle forms,
variation within individual speakers is not extensive. Indeed, for
many speakers in this sample, the form of the verbs involved is
shared for both these functions, producing a common past and
-ed participle form for that speaker. For example, 9B says:

[17] I stood there wondering what was goin' on an' I seen
     Mr Saunders comin' up.
[18] I've seen Tommy but I think you'd have to be an adult
     to understand it.

Interestingly, too, as Table 10.2 illustrates, in this sample of ISE
the incidence of non-standard past tense forms is greater than that
of *-ed* participles. More speakers use non-standard past tense
forms than past participles and many use at least some of these
forms invariably. Shnukal (1978: 167) draws similar conclusions
for her Cessnock, NSW, sample. Indeed, the degree of categori-

cal usage is obscured in Table 10.2 in that processes involving several forms are classified rather than individual verbs and verb classes. The relationship of such individual verb and class variation within the general processes could profitably be the object of further study.

10.4 What linguistic/non-linguistic factors affect this variation?

Studies in the past have suggested that the use of non-standard verb forms is independent of non-linguistic factors other than social status. Wolfram and Christian (1975) examining Appalachian English, Feagin (1979) investigating working-class Anniston English, and Shnukal (1978) writing on her Cessnock sample, all conclude that age and sex do not have a significant effect on the use of non-standard irregular forms.

My own study in ISE, however, would suggest that some variation in the use of non-standard irregular forms with respect to age, sex, style and context does occur. Female speakers decrease their use of non-standard forms with age and in more formal situations, whereas male speakers do not; if anything, their use of non-standard forms tends to increase with increased age and increased formality. This correlation has been reported elsewhere (Eisikovits 1982, 1987, 1989) so will not be described in detail here. Instead, attention will be focused on the linguistic factors which may affect the use of non-standard irregular verb forms. Surprisingly, this question has received little attention in the past[8] so that we have no detailed knowledge of the environments which favour the use of non-standard irregular forms.

Casual observation reveals that non-standard forms of the past in Inner-Sydney English may occur in both main and subordinate clauses. But does the type of clause affect the frequency of usage of such forms?

Anecdotal evidence would suggest that subordinate structures are less likely to favour the use of non-standard forms. Consider, for example:

[19] The last exam we did, no one passed [. . .] so we had to go through it again, an' we done that about four or five times [. . .] (6F/M/16–8)

[20] I seen a coupla gang fights. They fight real dirty, not very fair [. . .] I seen guys slashed up with bottles. I seen 'em get their eyes slashed; just poked with a broken bottle. When I saw that, no more. (9D/M/16–5)

To test this possibility, a comparison was made of the frequencies of occurrence of non-standard past tense forms in both main and subordinate clauses. For the purposes of this comparison, only the five most frequently occurring non-standard forms – *seen, done, come, run, give* – are considered. These include the majority of possibilities of variation of types 1, 3 and 4 (see Table 10.1 above) and constitute 88.9 per cent of variation in the data. For other non-standard forms where few occurrences were noted (for example, regularized forms of type 4 above), it was considered that too little data existed for a viable comparison. The results of this comparison are set out in Table 10.3.

TABLE 10.3 Use of non-standard forms of the past tense for clause types for five most frequently occurring verbs in ISE, in percentages:

	Younger girls (N) = 10)				Older girls (N) = 10)			
	Main		*Subordinate*		*Main*		*Subordinate*	
Seen	68.2	(15/22)	42.9	(3/7)	63.6	(14/22)	60	(3/5)
Done	100	(9/9)	88.9	(8/9)	50	(8/16)	40	(6/15)
Come	95.9	(47/49)	88.5	(23/26)	60.7	(34/56)	37.9	(11/29)
Give	52.2	(12/22)	25	(1/4)	17.7	(3/17)	0	(0/4)
Run	0	(0/9)	[50	(1/2)]ᵃ ᵇ	0	(0/10)	[50	(1/2)]

	Younger boys (N) = 10)				Older boys (N) = 10)			
	Main		*Subordinate*		*Main*		*Subordinate*	
Seen	60.5	(26/43)	53.9	(7/13)	73.2	(30/41)	50	(6/12)
Done	77.8	(14/81)	45.5	(5<11)	46.7	(13/23)	77	(6/8)ᵇ
Come	56.3	(45/80)	54.2	(13/24)	78.1	(50/64)	69.6	(16/23)
Give	48	(1/21)	0	(1/1)	16.7	(4/24)	0	(0/4)
Run	26.1	(6/23)	0	(0/3)	0	(0/11)	0	(0/5)

ᵃ The results for both female groups for this verb in subordinate clauses are bracketed because of the very few potential occurrences of non-standard run in these contexts; hence the limited conclusions which can be drawn here.
ᵇ Deviant pairs.

Of the twenty pairs of main/subordinate clauses compared in Table 10.3 seventeen show the non-standard form of the past occurring more frequently in the main rather than the subordinate clause. Even among the three deviant pairs, two may be explained by the particularly low frequencies of occurrence; that is, in both the female groups, only one instance of *run* was noted in subordinate clauses in only two potential occurrences for each group.

Looking now at non-standard past participles, it is clear that the past form for the past participle may occur in either a perfective or a passive structure. However, when the frequencies in these two structures are compared, it is found that the past form occurs more than four times as often in the perfective. See Table 10.4. In Table 10.4 39 of the 84 perfective structures – 46.4 per cent – have the past form, whereas it occurs in only 4 of the 36 passive structures, that is, 11.1 per cent.

TABLE 10.4: Use of V-*ed* form for past participle in ISE.

Perfective Occurrences	Passive occurrences
$\dfrac{39}{84}$ $\% = 46.4$	$\dfrac{4}{36}$ $\% = 11.1$

Indeed, for many verbs not only is the occurrence of this form of the past participle more likely to occur in the perfective, but it in fact occurs exclusively in this context. Where a passive structure occurs, the alternative -*ed* past participle is used.[9] This usage is tabulated in Table 10.5.

In Table 10.5, with the verb *take,* for example, the four occurrences of the *took* form of the past participle all occur in the perfective (4 in 15 or 26.7 per cent) and the alternative *taken* form occurs in all five of the passive occurrences of this verb. A more telling example is the verb *break* for which the five instances of this verb in the perfective all have the *broke* form. There are no occurrences of *broken* in the perfective. The eleven occurrences of *broken* which do occur are all in the passive. A similar pattern of usage occurs for all but one verb. Only with *bite* does the past tense form of the past participle occur in both the perfective and the passive:

[21] He might've come home drunk an' the dog mighta bit 'im (4A/F/14–0)
[22] I know a kid who got bit by a horse. (4B/M/14–11)

Furthermore, of the four passive examples with the past form of the past participle, only one occurs with a *be* passive, the remaining three occur with a *got* passive. And this one example was with the verb *shake:*

TABLE 10.5 Occurrence of -ed participle forms in the perfective and the passive in ISE.

Verb	Perfective			Passive		
	-ed participle	Occurrences	% freq.	-ed participle	Occurrences	% freq.
Break	Broke	5/5	100	Broke	0/11	0
	Broken	0/5	0	Broken	11/11	100
Speak	Spoke	1/2	50	Spoke	0/2	0
	Spoken	1/2	50	Spoken	2/2	100
Bite	Bit	1/1	100	Bit	2/2	100
	Bitten	0/1	0	Bitten	0/2	0
Blow	Blew	1/1	100	Blew	0/3	0
	Blown	0/1	0	Blown	3/3	100
Take	Took	4/15	26	Took	0/5	0
	Taken	11/15	73.3	Taken	5/5	100
Give	Gave	2/2	100	Gave	0/1	0
	Given	0/2	0	Given	1/1	100
Fall	Fell	1/2	50	Fell	–	–
	Fallen	1/2	50	Fallen	–	–
Beat	Beat	2/2	100	Beat	0/5	0
	Beaten	0/2	0	Beaten	5/5	100
Ring	Rang	1/3	33.3	Rang	–	–
	Rung	2/3	66.7	Run	–	–
Run	Ran	0/2	0	Ran	1/6	16.7
Go[a]	Run	2/2	100	Rung	5/6	83.3
	Went	13/40	32.5			
	Gone	27/40	67.5			

[a] Go, being an intransitive verb, does not allow a passive.

[23]   The woman was all shook up.

which may well be a special case in that through the influence of a popular song it may have acquired the status of a set phrase among younger speakers.

What appears to be taking place, then, is a separation of meanings of the past participle which is reflected in the choice of the form used. The more stative, adjectival sense of the past participle which emerges in the passive, especially the *be* passive, tends to favour the *-ed* participle form, while the more active/dynamic meaning is more likely to be expressed in the non-standard past form borrowed from the simple past tense.

Such a development is particularly interesting in the light of earlier developments in some past participle forms. Many older participial forms in -en (for example, *sodden, drunken, shrunken, molten, shaven*), which have been replaced by alternative forms, are nevertheless retained as adjectives in the -en form (compare Pyles 1964: 198–203).

Compare, too, the use of invariant *be* which occurs in ISE with an active, non-stative meaning, for example:

[24] If she ever wants anythink of mine, she always bees nice to me but I just be mean back to her when she bees nice. (2A/F/13–11)

[25] He just bees silly and takes his clothes off. (4B/M/14–11)

A second important factor affecting the use of the past form for the past participle is tense. While the overall frequency of use of this form in the perfective is 46.4 per cent, there is much difference in frequency with respect to tense. See Table 10.6. In Table 10.6 the past form of the past participle occurs in the past perfective with a frequency of 70.7 per cent, but in the present perfective with a frequency of 30.2 per cent – it is thus more than twice as likely to be used in the past perfective than in the present.

TABLE 10.6 The effect of tense on the use of the past form for the past participle in the perfective in ISE.

Past tense occurrences	Present tense occurrences
$\frac{29}{41}$	$\frac{13}{43}$
% = 70.7	% = 30.2

Again this trend is borne out with individual verbs. A particularly striking example of this is the verb *go* for which 11 of the 13 occurrences of the *went* form of the past participle occur in the past perfective. Only 5 of the 27 occurrences of *gone* as past participle occur in a similar environment, making the frequency of the *went* form in a past perfective structure 68.8 per cent (11/16). With the present perfective, however, only 2 in 24 present perfective structures, that is, 8.3 per cent, occur in this form.

Similarly with *take,* 37.5 per cent or 3 in 8 occurrences in the past perfective, have the *took* form, whereas only 14.3 per cent, 1 in 7 in the present perfective examples, occur in this form. Table 10.7 summarizes this difference.

TABLE 10.7 Occurrence of non-standard *-ed* participle forms in the perfective for two verbs in ISE.

Verb	Past perfective occurrences	Present perfective occurrences
go (went)	$\dfrac{11}{16}$	$\dfrac{2}{24}$
	% = 68.8	% = 8.3
take (took)	$\dfrac{3}{8}$	$\dfrac{1}{7}$
	% = 37.5	% = 14.3

A third factor which appears to have some influence on the form of the past participle used is the presence of a preceding modal. Twenty per cent (17 in 85) of the modal-perfective structures in the past occurred with the past form of the past participle, whereas only 12.2 per cent of all perfective structures without a modal auxiliary had this form.

These same trends may be observed in the practice of individual speakers. Most of the 21 speakers who use this form (14 in 21) use it categorically for each of the verbs they use, generally with the same form for the simple past tense. For those speakers who evidence variation in the forms of the past participles they use, this variation tends to be dependent upon either the type of structure in which the past participle occurs – whether perfective or passive – or its tense.

What all this would suggest, then, is that the environment which most favours the occurrence of the past tense form of the *-ed* participle in ISE is a perfective structure in the past tense with a modal preceding. The next step in research would be to test these results on other varieties of English to see if the patterns evident here are similarly evident elsewhere.

Notes

1. Quirk *et al.* (1972: 70) describe the five forms of the normal English verb as follows: the base, *eg call, drink,* the S-form, *eg calls, drinks,*

the past, *eg called, drank,* the *-ing* participle, *eg calling, drinking,* the
-ed participle, *eg called, drunk.* This terminology will be followed
throughout this chapter.
2. Of course the form of the *-ing* participle varies between *-ing* and *-in'*
forms.
3. The letters and numbers following quotations from transcripts
identify the speaker and provide information about his age and sex.
For example, 7B/M/14–3 indicates that 7B is a male and aged 14 years
3 months.
4. The *do* referred to here is, of course, the lexical verb *do* rather than
the auxiliary *do.* Sentences such as:
 *He *donen't* do nothing
 **Done* he do it?
 (Q: Did anyone go?) *I *done.*
did not occur in ISE. In such past tense negative questions and ellipses the *did* form was always used. In addition, emphatic do (*did*) as in
 He did so do it
was never found to occur in the *done* form. Occurrences of past tense
do in these environments were therefore not included in this analysis.
5. Table 10.2 shows implicational scaling for individual speakers rather
than for the overall community of speakers, although there is obviously a strong tendency in that direction. Hence, only those cells which
do not conform for a given speaker are bracketed.
6. For a discussion of the relationship of child morphology to historical
change, see for example Bybee and Slobin (1982).
7. The term 'class' is used following the classification of Quirk *et al.*
(1972: 110ff.) This classification will be referred to throughout this
discussion.
8. One notable exception is the work of Jenny Cheshire (1978).
9. The verb *go* is an exception to this in that, being an intransitive verb,
it does not form a passive. Hence, any possible variation must occur
in the perfective. This pattern is, however, evident with other verbs
which do allow a passive.

References

BAILEY, CHARLES-JAMES N. (1973) *Variation and Linguistic Theory.* Vir-
ginia: Center for Applied Linguistics.
BROWN, ROGER, (1973) *A First Language.* London: George Allen and
Unwin.
BYEE, JOAN and SLOBIN, DAN (1982) 'Rules and schemas in the develop-
ment and use of the English past', *Language,* **58** (2): 265–89.
CHESHIRE, JENNY (1978) 'Present tense verbs in Reading English' In
Peter Trudgill (ed.) *Sociolinguistic Patterns in British English,* London:
Edward Arnold.
CHESHIRE, JENNY (1982) *Variation in an English Dialect.* Cambridge:
Cambridge University Press.
DINES, ELIZABETH, HENRY, PATRICIA and ALLENDER, SUSAN (1979). *Formal
and Functional Variation in Urban Children's Language.* Report

prepared for Education Research and Development Committee, March.

EISIKOVITS, EDINA (1982) 'Cultural àttitudes and language variation', *Australian Review of Applied Linguistics*, **5**(1): 129–42

EISIKOVITS, EDINA (1987) 'Sex differences in inner- and intra-group interaction among adolescents'. In A. Pauwels (ed.) *Women, Language and Society in Australia and New Zealand*. Sydney: Australian Professional Publications.

EISIKOVITS, EDINA (1989) 'Girl-talk/boy-talk: Sex differences in adolescent speech'. In P. Collins and D. Blair (eds) *Australian English: The Language of a New Society*. Queensland: University of Queensland Press, *pp* 35–54.

FEAGIN, CRAWFORD (1979) *Variation and Change in Alabama English: A Sociolinguistic Study of the White Community*. Washington, DC: Georgetown University Press.

GUY, GREGORY (1975) 'Variation in the group and the individual: The case of final stop deletion', *Pennsylvania Working Papers on Linguistic Change and Variation* **1**(4).

LABOV, WILLIAM (1966) 'The linguistic variable as a structural unit', *Washington Linguistic Review*. **3**: 4–22.

LABOV, WILLIAM (1969) 'Contraction, deletion and inherent variability of the English copula', *Language*, **45**(4): 715–62.

LABOV, WILLIAM (1970) 'The study of language in its social context', *Studium Generale*, **23**(1): 30–87.

LABOV, WILLIAM (1972) *Language in the Inner City; Studies in the Black English Vernacular*. Philadelphia: University of Pennsylvania Press.

LABOV, WILLIAM, COHEN, PAUL, ROBINS, CLARENCE and LEWIS, JOHN (1968) *A Study of the Non-standard English of Negro and Puerto-Rican Speakers in New York city*. Office of Education, Cooperative Research Project No. 3288.

PYLES, THOMAS (1964) *The Origins and Development of the English Language*. New York: Harcourt, Brace & Wold.

QUIRK, RANDOLPH, GREENBAUM, SIDNEY, LEECH, GEOFFREY and SVARTVIK, JAN (1972) *A Grammar of Contemporary English*. London: Longman.

SHNUKAL, ANNA (1978) 'A Sociolinguistic study of Australian English: phonological and syntactic varation in Cessnock, N.S.W', unpublished Ph.D. dissertation. Washington, DC: Georgetown University.

WOLFRAM, WALTER and CHRISTIAN, DONNA (1975) *Sociolinguistic Variables in Appalachian Dialects. Final Report*. Washington, DC: National Institute of Education of the Department of Health, Education and Welfare.

WOLFRAM, WALTER and FASOLD, RALPH (1974) *The Study of Social Dialects in American English*. Englewood Cliffs, NJ: Prentice-Hall.

Part three

Aspect

Chapter 11

Aspect in English dialects

Peter Trudgill and J. K. Chambers

We have already noted that a considerable number of the chapters in this volume have to do with variation between dialects in modal and auxiliary verbs. The three chapters in this section are all concerned with the use of forms of the auxiliaries *do* and *have* in the expression of aspectual differences in the English verb, where aspect is taken to mean not location of an event in time, as with tense, but its distribution in and through time.

It emerges that a number of non-standard dialects have a rather richer range of aspectual distinctions available than does the standard dialect. As far as the expression of aspect through formal means is concerned, Standard English distinguishes between simple and progressive forms:

I go	I'm going
I went	I was going.

and between perfective and non-perfective forms:

she went   she has gone   she had gone.

Also available are the past habitual forms:

she used to go   she would go.

Ossi Ihalainen's chapter shows that many of the dialects of the south-west of England (and this is also true of South Wales dialects, although Ihalainen does not deal with them) have an additional distinction. In these dialects, unstressed auxiliary *do* can be used to express habitual or generic aspect:

I sees the doctor tomorrow	I do see him every day
I seen the doctor last month	I did see him every day.

This form, which is also mentioned by Gachelin in Chapter 16, is shown by Ihalainen formerly to have been much more widespread in English than it is today. It is possible, too, that unstressed *do,* pronounced /də/, is the antecedent of the progressive aspect *de* found in many English-based Atlantic creoles.

Ihalainen also discusses the fascinating south-western distinction between intransitive/objectless infinitives, with *-y* and transitive infinitives without, dealt with at greater length by Gachelin:

Can you zewy?   vs Can you zew up thease zeam?
'Can you sew?'   'Can you sew up this seam?'

It is not an accident that Ihalainen is the only scholar to have two chapters in this volume. He is a pioneer and leading authority in the study of the grammar of English dialects, and an expert on the dialects of Somerset. The English Department at the University of Helsinki, moreover, has become, under the guidance of Ihalainen and his colleagues, a very important centre for the study of English dialects. There are probably more students carrying out serious investigations of the grammar of English English dialects in Helsinki than there are at all English universities combined.

Feagin's chapter also looks at a form of *do* as an aspectual marker. Her chapter is based on extensive and sensitive research carried out in Anniston, Alabama, USA, and employs data obtained through both systematic and casual observations. She concludes that *done,* as in

You've done spent your money.

functions as a perfective and/or intensive marker which can be paraphrased as *completely* or *already*. Since *done* can co-occur with other auxiliaries and modals, as in

He may have done retired,

Feagin's data present us with the same problem as that faced by Brown. (Ch. 8): is *done* in this usage a true auxiliary, or is it an adverbial?

Harris's chapter is included in this section because it deals with perfect verb forms in Irish English, such as

She's nearly her course finished,

but it also deals with the interesting Irish English syntactic phenomenon of cleft sentences of a type that are not found in most other types of English:

It is looking for more land a lot of them are.

Feagin argues, very convincingly, for multiple causation in the historical development of *done*. She and Harris have to deal with the issue of contact with languages other than English as a causal mechanism in the development of richer aspect systems. Harris, however, warns us that we should not be too quick to look for substratum influence as the sole cause of linguistic change. He too favours multiple causation. Irish English, like Alabama English, may demonstrate certain characteristics because of language contact, but, as Gachelin also reminds us (Ch. 16), archaism and innovation must also play a role. The conclusion seems to be that there are so many things that can happen in linguistic change, that changes which have more than one causal factor in their favour are more likely to happen than those that do not.

Chapter 12

Periphrastic *do* in affirmative sentences in the dialect of East Somerset

Ossi Ihalainen

One of the interesting features of the dialect of East Somerset[1] is the use of periphrastic *do* in affirmative sentences. The following attempt to describe this phenomenon is based on interviews with speakers of East Somerset who were recorded in the summers of 1972 and 1974.[2]

By the term 'periphrastic *do* in affirmative sentences' I refer to sentences where *do* is simply used as an unstressed tense marker. This *do* should be kept apart from the so-called emphatic *do* which carries sentence stress and is used to indicate emphasis, specifically contrast. The phonological difference between these two can be seen from the following examples:

[1] He did 'burn it. (periphrastic *do*)
[2] He 'did burn it. (emphatic *do*)

The difference between the unemphatic and emphatic forms is also seen from their behaviour with respect to certain frequency adverbs. Contrast the following sentences:

[3] We did always have the wheat and take it in the barn wi a good, thick, heavy, wooden floor.
[4] We always *did* close the gate.

My discussion will deal only with the non-emphatic variation. Furthermore, to simplify the description, I shall deal only with the past tense form.

Although the periphrastic use of *do* is a provincialism today, it was common in Standard English until the end of the eighteenth century. The decline in the use of *do* in affirmative sentences can be seen from the treatment of tenses by various eighteenth-century grammarians. In his *Four Essays on the English Language*

(1758), John Ward gives the following verb paradigm: 'The action denoted as now doing: *I write, do write,* or *am writing a letter.* . . . The past imperfect tense: *I did write* or *was writing a letter.*[3] There is no indication in Ward's discussion that he regarded the periphrastic formation as non-standard.

James White (*The English Verb,* 1761), too, seems to regard the periphrastic formation as a standard feature:

> *Do* and *did* are very often used as the Signs of the Present and First Past Tenses in the Indicative Mood . . .: Present Tense *I love* or *I do love: thou lovest, thou dost love.* . . . *Do* therefore, is the Sign of the Present tense, though not always used. First Past Tense: *I loved,* or *did love, thou lovedst, thou didst love. Did* in such cases, therefore, is, and ought to be considered as the Sign of the First Past Tense of the Indicative Mood.

Samuel Johnson (1755: 8) also notes the periphrastic form but discourages its use: '*do* is sometimes used superfluously, as *I do love, I did love:* but this is considered a vitious mode of speech'.[4] The rapidity of the decline in the use of periphrastic *do* in affirmative sentences can be seen from the fact that Charles Coote, writing in 1788, already feels that it is archaic: 'The old English writers frequently used this verb [*ie do*] as an auxiliary in affirmative sentences, whether an emphasis was required or not . . . . At present we do not use this auxiliary in mere affirmations, unless we wish to lay some stress on what we affirm' (Coote 1788: 101).[4]

Although periphrastic *do* disappeared from Standard English during the New English period, dialectologists have attested its appearance in some local dialects. In his 1875 study of the dialect of West Somerset, Elworthy (1875: 21) notes the following:

> Generally, the present tense of all our verbs is formed with the auxiliaries *do* for active, and *be* with the present part. for neuter verbs; but by no means unfrequently for emphasis we use the usual inflexion. In that case, however, we have no notion of tacking on a simple consonant and saying 'he walks.' Our inflexion would be *ai wau·kus,* if we wished distinctly to assert that he does not ride; if merely that he is walking, we should say *ai du wau·kĕe.*

Elworthy makes it quite clear that periphrastic *do is* used unemphatically, but otherwise his description of the distribution of *do* is rather vague. For example, he does not discuss the past tense at all.

Elworthy takes up the question of periphrastic *do* again in his 1877 study of the dialect of West Somerset. He starts by giving a general account of the periphrastic form (1877: 191) 'In the dialect the use of the periphrastic form with *do*, and of the auxiliary verbs generally, is so much the rule that the infinitive of the principal verb is the part most used in ordinary sentences, while the tense, state, etc., are formed by the auxiliaries.'

His verb paradigm (1877: 192) makes the basic distinction between transitive and intransitive verbs or usages of a verb. Intransitives add an intransitive ending to their stems, showing the following word structure: stem +EE (+inflectional ending). Thus, in Elworthy's dialect a distinction is made between the two verbs *dig* in sentences like *I dig ditches* and *I dig*. According to Elworthy, the latter sentence would be realized as *I do digĕe* or *I digus*.[5]

I have attested no instances of the intransitive ending in my recordings of either West or East Somerset dialects. The usage seems to be obsolete today.

Besides the transitive/intransitive distinction, Elworthy's paradigm shows the following aspectual differences in the present: (a) habitual; (b) actual. In Standard English the distinction between the above categories is brought out by the use of the simple and progressive forms, respectively (*He plays the piano* vs *He is playing the piano*). In West Somerset the present habitual is expressed by the following forms: *I do dig* or *I digs* (Elworthy 1877: 192)[6]

Elworthy does not discuss the term 'habitual', but his examples suggest that he uses it in the usual sense of repeated or characteristic activity.

In the past, the situation is complicated by the fact that instead of the two distinctions that were postulated for the present (habitual/actual), there are now three categories: (a) past general; (b) imperfect; (c) past habitual. Under 'imperfect' Elworthy gives the progressive form. In other words, while the present tense form *I be diggin the ground* is called 'actual', the corresponding past tense form is called 'imperfect'. The difference seems to be terminological rather than real.

The past habitual form corresponding to the present habitual *I do dig/I digs the ground* is *I used to dig the ground*. However, in addition to the category 'past habitual' Elworthy postulates the category 'past general'. The verb forms denoting the past general are *I digged all the lot* and *I did digĕe*. In other words, *did* occurs only in intransitive sentences. His paradigm (1877: 218) makes this point quite clear.

The difference between the categories 'habitual' and 'general' is not explained. Accordingly, there is no way of knowing what difference Elworthy believes there to be between the forms *He used to dig* and *He did dig*.

In the light of my recordings, it is interesting to note that in present-day East Somerset periphrastic *do* is often interchangeable with *used to*, ie it is used to express the past habitual in transitive and intransitive sentences. On the other hand, I was unable to attest a single instance of periphrastic *do* denoting one specific completed action in the past.

Besides the environments discussed above, Elworthy points out that periphrastic *do* also occurs in *if*-clauses, where it has the force of the subjunctive auxiliary *should*. He gives the following examples: (a) *neef (=if) I do dig;* (b) *neef I did dig.*

He comments on (b) as follows: 'This is really equivalent to *if I should dig, ie* pure hypothesis' (Elworthy 1877: 192).

To summarize, Elworthy's description of the distribution of periphrastic *do* is the following:

[5] Present habitual, both transitive and intransitive ((a) and
     (b) respectively):
     (a) *I do dig the ground.*
     (b) *I do digěe.*
[6] Past general, intransitive only:

         I did digěe.[7]

Periphrastic *do* is used to denote the present habitual. Periphrastic *did* denotes what Elworthy calls the past general. The past habitual is expressed by *used to*. This is a curious kind of distribution. However, since Elworthy does not define the terms 'habitual' or 'general', it is impossible to say whether the difference between these categories is real or terminological.

In his *Dialect Grammar* Wright (1905: 297), too, attests the use of periphrastic *do* in certain dialects. In a note to his chapter on tense formation he writes: 'The periphrastic form *I do love,* & c. for *I love,* & c. is in gen. use in the south-western dialects.'

Wright does not mention the periphrastic form in his discussion of the past tense or of the subjunctive. Furthermore, no attempt is made to analyse the possible aspectual meaning of the periphrastic form.

After this survey of the previous descriptions of the use of periphrastic *do* in dialectal English, I would like to review the verbal categories in modern English that I feel are of particular relevance to my analysis of periphrastic *do* in present-day East Somerset. The non-progressive verb forms show the following aspectual categories in Standard English:

[7] He worked in the garden.
[8] He would work in the garden./He'd work in the garden.
[9] He used to work in the garden.

Sentence [7] is ambiguous between what I would like to call specific and generic time reference.[8] When [7] refers to a specific action in the past, it is said to have specific time reference, or the verb form is said to denote the specific aspect. In the following discourse the past tense form has specific reference:

X: What did Bill do between two and three o'clock Monday afternoon?
Y: He worked in the garden.

On the other hand, [7] can also denote repeated or habitual activity, *ie* activity that was carried out every now and then. In that case the reference is said to be generic. Generic time reference can be illustrated by the following example: *Bill worked in the garden every Monday afternoon.* On this interpretation, [7] means the same as [8] and [9].

However, *would/'d, used to* and the simple past tense form are not interchangeable. Specifically, it would seem that *would/'d* has a more limited distribution than the simple form or *used to*. For example, *would/'d* cannot be used if the verb indicates a state, as can be seen from the following examples:

[10] There was a pub here.
[11] There used to be a pub here.
[12] *There would be a pub here. (The asterisk indicates that the sentence is impossible.)
[13] He liked her.
[14] He used to like her.
[15] *He would like her.[9]

The basic distinction that I believe is relevant to the description of periphrastic *do* in present-day East Somerset is the aspectual generic/specific distinction. In the following section I shall give examples of non-progressive past tense forms in East Somerset and try to show that periphrastic *do* typically occurs in contexts where the speaker describes some habitual or characteristic activity.

12.1 Simple past tense form

In the eight interviews (varying between 47 and 73 minutes in length) on which this analysis is based, the following kinds of non-progressive past tense forms were attested:

[16] So they went on first, and they went on to three hundred and something, I don't remember the exact number, and the other and I went till we got to five hundred and sixty, and then we give up. (W.B.)

[17] Yes, I went to work early. I went out – me father died and we were left poor, mother and I. 'Course I had about nowt to keep meself then, because we were poor, but we got on. I am thankful to say that I worked and helped me mother and we made life between us and done very well. (W.B.)

[18] And there was a big firm and little – few miles away – village called Mark, and he went down there. (F.B.)

In [16] the speaker is talking about a specific bet that he made with his friends. The simple tense forms *went on* and *got* are used to mark specific reference.

In [17] the verb *went to* is used in the sense 'began'. Since one single incident in the speaker's life is involved, *went* has specific reference. The forms *worked* and *helped*, however, do not refer to any specific occasions. Their reference is generic. Passage [18] refers to a specific occasion.

As the above examples show, the simple past can denote both the specific and the generic aspect. However, with some verbs, say *come*, the simple past form is rare in generic contexts. On the other hand, verbs such as *want* and *have* (=*possess*) seem to have the simple form regardless of the aspect involved. Here are some examples of the simple form in generic contexts:

[19] The longer it went on the stronger the cider did get. (L.V.)

[20] Then he did cut up the various joints what you wanted. (L.V.)

[21] Oh, what they called the curry comb, the curry comb and brush. (L.V.)

[22] Well, you always had plenty of wood on the farm to burn, always. (L.V.)

[23] Before we went to the fair, used to wait for ponies from Bridgwater. Used to hunt the ponies. (J.S.)

There may be a semantic explanation for why certain verbs

favour the simple form over the periphrastic form in generic contexts. Interesting as the question is, I shall not pursue it here.

12.2 Periphrastic *do*

The following sentences will illustrate the use of periphrastic *do* in East Somerset. All the passages quoted show the generic aspect. In spite of the high frequency of periphrastic *do*, I did not find a single instance of periphrastic *do* in specific contexts.

[24] We did come back then and we did have a glass or two of cider, and then we did go and have a bit of breakfast, come out again and then we did have another drink before we did start off. (J.S.)

[25] That did go to a milk factory . . . . The surplus milk they did make into cheese and then the cheese did go to the different markets, that's how that did work. (L.V.)

[26] If you did, perhaps you did get the peg, get the ring on the peg. That did count twenty-five. If you get en in the next ring beside of the peg, he did count ten, and the outside ring did count five. You did chart that up and you did play for so many hundred. Come on later, we did have darts. (W.B.)

12.3 *Used to* and *would/'d*

The use of the verbs *used to* and *would/'d* in East Somerset does not differ from their use in Standard English. The following passages show some typical examples:

[27] I used to carry me little firkin, as they called it, little – like a little barrel. And I used to have he filled up, used to hold three pints. I used to have he filled up perhaps twice a day when we was workin'. (J.C.)

[28] Two or three of em would get hold of the pig, tip im on the stool, which he couldn't get off, and then he'd cut that pig's throat. (L.V.)

[29] A few shillings would keep us for a week. (W.B.)

[30] There was various fairs. There was fairs held at – there was one at Wedmore, Cheddar, Shipham and Banwell, which them fairs would come annually. (L.V.)

It was shown above that periphrastic *do*, *would/'d* and *used to* all mark the generic aspect in East Somerset. There is a noticeable tendency to adhere to one form in a discourse unit (answer to a question, story, etc.). However, it is in no way exceptional that one form alternates with the rest in a single discourse. Consider the following passages:

[31] A few shillings would keep us for a week. People used to – a – man that used to earn about thirty bob a week, he did keep his family an' smoke and have a drink out of that very well. (W.B.)

[32] Then after tea they used to go off milkin' and I used to go down the field again. They come back from milkin' and then we did go on [tɪ] ten o'clock at night – – overtime – – and then after that we did go and have a good – – another good supper – – lettuce and everything cut up – – and then we'd have a damn good sing-song. (J.S.) (The past tense form of *come* is pronounced in the same way as the present form *come*: [kʌm]. Therefore, it is impossible to say whether the word *come* in the above passage is the simple past tense form of *come* or whether it is the historic present.)

[33] You'd learn from that experience. You [dɪ] learn your own experience and that's how you did go on. I mean, if the boss did see that you was a bit pushing, you was a bit energetic, he – – he [ʔ] give you – – he wouldn't never stop in your way, you know. (H.T.)

[34] They used to keep em up on the hills, you see, and a man used to look out to em. Very often they'd run astray and come down over, you see, and the man did come and track them up over again. (J.C.)

[35] (Interviewer: Where did you take the milk? Oh, we did – – at that time, well, you used to take it to the factory. They did make cheese and butter. (W.B.)

[36] I did get me knees into his back [*ie* the pig's back] and hold his hind leg back, and he'd just have the knife and cut through it. (W.B.)

It should be noted, however, that although *used to* and *would* are interchangeable with periphrastic *do* most of the time, there is a specific context where only *do* seems to occur. Older varieties of English would show the subjunctive here. Consider the following temporal and conditional clauses:

[37] If the boss did see that you was a bit pushing, . . . he would . . . (H.T.)

[38] If you did buy up a load of peat in them days, it used to cost you ten shillings. (A.G.)

[39] And they'd chew this bit till they did get a nice mouth. (W.B.)

[40] After he [= the pig] did finish bleeding, he'd take en off the stool. (L.V.)

[41] If you did – – perhaps you did get the peg, get the ring on the peg, that did count twenty-five. (W.B.)

[42] Before you did put this ferret where the rabbits is, you put down nets at the holes and then put the ferret in. (L.V.)

The above examples show that Elworthy's observation about periphrastic *do* being equivalent to the subjunctive auxiliary *should* in some contexts still holds for East Somerset.

12.4 Simple and periphrastic forms contrasted

In the remaining part of my study I shall discuss in detail the evidence which suggests that periphrastic *do* occurs only in generic contexts. I shall then hypothesize that a sentence such as *Bill did come to see me yesterday* is unacceptable in Somerset English. Clearly, this is a claim that can be tested in the field.

On the basis of the interviews, however, it is possible to quote only indirect evidence to support the hypothesis that periphrastic *do* marks the generic aspect. Specifically, one can try to show that in passages that show specific time reference periphrastic *do* does not occur, whereas in generic contexts it does. Contrast the following passages:

[43] It was like this in them days, years ago, you see. A lot of the villagers did rent this land, this peat land, did rent a plot you see, half an acre, you see, for ten years, perhaps take a lease on this land for ten year, you see, for to excavate it, you see. Well, all as their fire stuff did cost them then, you see, in the home was their labour, you see. (F.B.)

[44] Well, he bought a business then at another village, a place called High Ham, an' he was there four year, I think he said he was there four year. Well, in the meantime this man what was here, you see, was giving up, and so he seen father and he told im what he were doing and he said, 'If you like to come and buy the business', he said, 'you could have it.' All the same, my father, he came and bought the business. Eighty pound the goodwill cost. (F.B.)

These extracts come from the same speaker. The first one shows generic reference. Periphrastic *do* is used consistently throughout. Notice that the form *take* is clearly an instance of the non-repetition or omission of the auxiliary, so that *take* can be traced back to *did take* exactly the way *done* can be traced back to *has done* in some contexts.

The critical verb is *cost*. In [43] showing the generic aspect the past form of *cost* is *did cost*. In [45] the speaker is referring to a specific occasion. He is telling a story about his father. The aspect is specific, and the simple form of the verb is used rather than the periphrastic form.

The following extracts illustrate the verb *go*. Three speakers are involved here. In [44] the speaker tells how he first started working. The reference is specific and the simple form occurs:

[45] Yes, I went to work early. I went out – me father died and we were left poor, mother and I. (W.B.)

That the reference is specific is clearly shown by the fact that the speaker is about to mention the place that he went to. However, something else occurs to him and he starts a new sentence without finishing the previous one.

Consider also the following sentence, where the speaker tells about a competition that he had with his friends:

[46] So they went on first, and they went on to three hundred and something. (W.B.)

The reference is to a specific occasion, and the simple form is used.

Contrast [45] and [46] with [47] below. The speaker is the same, but this time the reference is generic. The speaker uses the *do*-periphrasis:

[47] We were paid three and sixpence a week for milking ten cows at a time, fifteen times a week, and I did go to work on Saturdays – – on the farm, in the garden, and I had a shilling and me food. (W.B.)

Similar examples can be quoted from other speakers. Consider the following passages. In [48] an informant tells how he left school and how his brothers went to war. He is describing a specific occasion in his life. The simple form of the verb is used:

[48] I was about, I believe, eleven year old when I come out of school. All me brothers went to the war [*ie* the First World War] and Dad were home. (J.S.)

Passage [49] is a description of a typical day in the informant's life. The reference is generic. This time the periphrastic form occurs:

[49] We did come back then and we did have a glass or two of cider and then we did go and have a bit of breakfast. (J.S.)

In the following extracts the verb *take* occurs. In [50] the speaker tells about a specific occasion in his life: an old man had healed his warts. The informant describes the treatment. The aspect is specific. In [51] the informant talks about pig-killing. The aspect is generic. Notice again how the simple form and the periphrastic form alternate:

[50] And he just looked and he took me fingers in his hands like that and just smoothened me hands over like that and lo and behold, in 'bout three weeks I hadn't got a wart left. (W.B.)

[51] (We did) hang im up and cut en down the belly and take the inwards out and then we did take the – – in – – run the inward, run en out. (W.B.)

Finally, consider a longish passage from a speaker who uses periphrastic *do* quite frequently. However, this time he is telling a story about a specific incident in his life. The aspect is specific. The simple form runs throughout the story:

[52] Something rather funny happened here. Once there was a couple went to the church to get married, and the old vicar, he been using his right arm too – he been lifting his arm up a good bit. When they got im in the church, ee'd nearly read all the burial service before anybody knowed he was wrong. And then ashes to ashes and dust to dust he was going, an' – – somebody thought, 'Surely to goodness! He's going to bury em.' So they went and got the old verger and he was a blacksmith at the time, you know. So he come down to the church wi his old – – used to wear leathery aprons – – and I always remember he had one leg 'about six inches longer than the other, you know. Stump on, he come up and took the book away and looked at en and told the old vicar he was wrong, you see. 'You got the wrong service, sir.' 'Oh, no, no, no, I haven't.' Anyhow, they lock en in the church. Everybody went out and locked ee in and got out – – went to Il-minster for a – – I forget what they call im – – what was

– – eh – – another vicar, a little bit higher, you know. So
he come. Anyhow, the old chap lost his – – lost his – –
eh – – gown, you know, he lost his job. Yeah, they took
him to the Shire Hall in Taunton and he was tried in
there. (H.A.)

12.5 Summary

I have argued above that periphrastic *do* in East Somerset shows
a characteristic distributional pattern in that it only occurs in
generic contexts, whereas the simple past tense form can occur
in generic and specific contexts. *Used to* and *would/'d* are also
used in generic contexts. The distribution of periphrastic *do*, however, is not identical with the distribution of *used to* and *would/'d*
because *do* is also used in temporal and conditional clauses.

Notes

1. According to Elworthy (1875) and Wright (1957), the dialect
   boundary between East and West Somerset runs along the
   Quantocks.
2. Eight interviews, recorded between 1972 and 1974, were analysed for
   this study. The total length of the recordings is some 400 minutes.
   The interviews are free in form. The informants, all members of small
   agricultural communities and aged between 64 and 81, were asked to
   tell about their everyday activities, such as haymaking, harvesting,
   tending horses, selling and buying cattle, slaughtering, fishing, catching rabbits, digging peat, social activities, etc.
3. Quoted by Visser (1969: 1508).
4. Quoted by Visser (1969: 1508).
5. Quoted by Visser (1969: 1509). For an extensive discussion of the
   development of the auxiliary *do* see Ellegard (1953).
5. Judging from Elworthy's examples the *ee*-suffix has two forms: [i]
   when final and [ə] when not final.
6. Since Elworthy's principles of phonetic spelling are obsolete and since
   I am dealing with a syntactical problem, I have written out his examples in conventional spelling. When the pronunciation of a word
   is grammatically significant, I have given it by using the International
   Phonetic Association (IPA) alphabet. Elworthy spells *do* in (a) 'du',
   indicating a reduced central vowel (schwa). He also attests the emphatic form. His emphatic form is spelled 'dùe'. This corresponds to
   the IPA transcription [dY:].
7. Elworthy spells *did* 'dud', indicating a reduced central vowel. Emphatic *do* is spelled 'daed'. Elworthy's symbol 'ae' stands for a very
   open [ɛ] sound.

8. For a discussion of the term 'generic' see Joos (1968: 109–12). My term 'generic' in this chapter covers the cases that Joos would further specify as instances of the 'characterizing generic aspect' (1968: 110).
9. Sentences [12] and [15] would only occur as constituents of hypothetical sentences. For example, [15] might occur as a part of the sentence *If she weren't so stubborn, he would like her.*

References

ELLEGARD, A. (1953) *The Auxiliary do: The Establishment and Regulation of its Use in English.* Stockholm: Almquist & Wiksell.

ELWORTHY, F. T. (1875) *The Dialect of West Somerset.* The English Dialect Society, Series D, Miscellaneous. London: Trübner.

ELWORTHY, F. T. (1877) 'The Grammar of the Dialect of West Somerset', *Transactions of the Philological Society*, 1977–79, Part II, *pp* 143–257. London: Trübner, 1878. (First published in 1877).

JOOS, M. (1968) *The English Verb: Form and Meanings.* Madison: The University of Wisconsin Press.

MICHAEL, I. (1970) *English Grammatical Categories and the Tradition to 1800.* Cambridge: Cambridge University Press.

ORTON, H., and WAKELIN, M. (eds) (1967) *Survey of English Dialects,* vol. IV. Leeds: E. J. Arnold.

VISSER, F. T. (1968) *An Historical Syntax of the English Language,* vol. III, First Half. Leiden: E. J. Brill.

WRIGHT, J. T. (1957) 'Studies in the linguistic geography of Somerset', unpublished Leeds University MA thesis.

WRIGHT, J. (1905) *The English Dialect Grammar.* Oxford: Henry Frowde.

Chapter 13

Preverbal *done* in Southern States English

Crawford Feagin

Of all the grammatical forms in Southern White US English which are claimed to be derived from the mesolect creole spoken by Blacks during the era of American slavery, preverbal *done* (also called quasi-modal *done*) is the most likely candidate in the verb system. It occurs in sentences such as [1].

[1] You buy you a little milk and bread and you've done spent your five dollars! (Myrtice J R62).[1]

The creolist viewpoint on this issue is that Atlantic English creole has a *done* which is the same as, or similar to, the form in Southern Non-standard White. That form is the predecessor of current Southern non-standard White *done* because of the extensive language contact between Black creole-speaking slaves and Southern White small farmers over 100 years ago. English specialists point out that, on the contrary, this form is no new importation into the English language but that it existed in Middle English before any contact with creole. While the arguments of both the creolists and of the English historical and dialect specialists have merit, I am not convinced that its historical relationship with Southern White English must be exclusive. Rather, I prefer to see both possible sources of the form as complementary, the creole form reinforcing a tendency already in the language, what Traugott (1972b) has called the convergence of two systems in contact.

The treatment of *done* which follows opens with a discussion of data from Anniston (Alabama)[2] – the occurrence of *done* in positive declarative sentences, in questions, with tag questions, and in negative sentences – followed by a summary of the syntax of *done*. A second section consists of a discussion of the meaning of *done*. A third section deals with *done* outside Southern White English – creoles, Black English, Middle and Early Modern English and other varieties of English – and my explanation for the existence of *done* in Non-standard Alabama English (NAE).

13.1 Anniston data

The data for *done* which are discussed in this section are based on both recorded interviews and on (often) anonymous observations which provided more than half of the examples. The instances of *done* from the observations were more varied syntactically than those in the interviews because of the social and syntactic constraints of an interview.

Although nearly half of the observation data comes from one informant, a rural White woman, age 62, with an eighth-grade education, it must be emphasized that this imbalance is due to the amount of contact time and to intimate style, since she was a member of my household. The absence of particular forms of *done* in other working- and lower-class groups means very little since the total amounts of data aside from hers are so small. On the other hand, each working-class age and sex category shows some use of the form in both recorded interviews and in observations, if not in all its syntactic variations. The data are sufficiently distributed to suggest that with a comparable corpus, these rare forms would be found in every cell of the older working class, urban as well as rural.

Adverbial *done* is very much a class marker in Anniston and probably throughout the South. During all the time of my fieldwork, I never heard this form from the middle and upper classes, except in cases of downward quotation, joking or baby talk; it is a shibboleth in those classes. Moreover, until recording the data for *done,* I could not have either explained the meaning or given examples aside from perhaps the most frequent and obvious forms such as *He'(s) done gone,* despite the fact that I am a native of the town, since for all practical purposes it was foreign to me.

In order to substantiate this hypothesis that *done* is a class marker, the data taken from the tapes were quantified in two ways. First, the actual occurrences of *done* within each cell were enumerated with totals for age groups and sex. This is presented in Table 13.1. Second, since there seemed to be no practical way to decide when *done* could have been expected to appear, but did not, I counted the number of individuals who used *done* out of the number in the cell and computed the percentage of persons using the form in the interviews by cell, also shown in Table 13.1.

TABLE 13.1 *Done:* Occurrence in interviews. By age, sex and social class, with hours of tape per group.

	Absolute occurrence of done	*Informants using* done *by cell*	*Per cent informants using* done	*Hours of tape by cell*
Upper-class – teenagers				
Girls	0	0/11	0	11
Boys	0	0/8	0	7
Upper class – over 60				
Women	0	0/7	0	9
Men	0	0/6	0	6.9
Working-class – urban				
Teenage girls	5	4/7	57	75
(informal girls)	(4)	(3/21)	(14)	(2.7)
Boys	10	3/8	37	5.6
Working-class – over 60				
Women	36	6/9	66	14.6
Men	14	4/7	57	12.6
Rural – over 60				
Women	12	6/9	66	9.5
Men	6	2/7	28	6.1
Total all classes	83	25/79	31	

This is followed by the number of hours of taped interviews from which the data were taken, by cell, since the amount of time was not the same for each one. (The total hours of tape by age-group may not be the sum of that of the male and female cells, since in some cases there were male–female combinations on the tape, *eg* brother and sister.) As one would expect with such a rare form as *done*, there were times when the person being interviewed never used the form during the interview and then, after the machine was turned off, used it several times, although in no case did this happen with the upper class. To further demonstrate that the non-use of *done* in the upper class and its use in the working class was not a matter of chance, a chi-square test on the use of *done* in the interviews was carried out, showing that the difference between the two classes was significant at the 0.001 level (see Table 13.2).

The only instances recorded in the anonymous observations of *done* used by members of the upper class over a period of six years are the following, all occurring in the presence of intimate

TABLE 13.2 Chi-square test for *done*. Occurrence in interviews of the upper class and urban and rural working class, by individual

	Yes		No		Total
Upper class	0	10.53	32	21.47	32
Working class	26	15.47	21	31.53	47
Totals	26		53		79

$\chi^2 = 26.38$ d.f. $= 1$ $p < 0.001$

family members. The first two are instances of baby talk used with a dog, spoken in a high pitch.

[2] Pittipat says her mama's done chewed her bone up (Virginia L. 61).
[3] Pittipat! You've done et, you little wretch! (Virginia L. 61).

Two others were downward quotations, in the presence of a granddaughter in the first case, and a first cousin in the second.

[4] A lot of em [towels] have 'done give out' (Julia K. 89).
[5] I don't know if he 'done done it' (Barbara K. 16).

The signals for downward quotation vary from change in intonation and vowel length, to kinesics (rolling eyes, shrugging shoulders, tossing head), to no auditory or visual signal at all. In the latter case it is simply understood by all hearers that quotations are intended.

13.1.1 Positive declarative sentences
The working class and poor whites of Anniston and the surrounding rural area seem to have the same *done* as has been reported for Black English by Labov (Labov et al. 1968: 265-6, Labov 1972: 55-6) and Dillard (1972: 47, 94-5, 219-21). Dillard divides *done* into two forms, one with an auxiliary preceding *done* as in *he's done come,* the other in initial position in the verb phrase as in *he done come.* This rather artificial division is attributed to the source of the respective forms: AUX + *done* is supposed to be the White form, (Ø) + *done*, the Black form. Dillard attributes the fact that Black English has both forms to dialect mixing. Since both kinds of done occur in almost equal frequency in the Anniston data and from the same speakers, they will be separated here only for the purposes of exposition. There is no evidence calling for a distinction between them on the basis of either syntax or meaning.

The auxiliaries preceding *done* in the Anniston data are *have, be, should have,* and *may have* in their various tensed forms. In all cases of *be* + *done* + past participle, *be* seems to be a relexification of *have*. With certain rare exceptions, *done* is followed by a past participle. The exceptions, which will be discussed later, are cases of *done* followed by uninflected verb (presumably present tense), preterite, uninflected copula, present participle, adjective or adverb and preceded by ∅, inflected *be,* or modal. *Been* may precede the past participle, but it may not precede *done* as reported by Rickford for Gullah (1975: 169). The longest verb phrase with *done* had five verbs: *should have done been gone.*

Since *done* is such an unusual form to White non-Southerners, Tables 13.3 and 13.4 present an extensive display of the forms of *done* and its co-occurrence with auxiliaries found in both anonymous observations and interviews for positive declarative sentences. Examples for each of the subtypes follow.

TABLE 13.3 AUX + *done* + past participle: distribution by age, sex, rural/urban among working class. Interviews and anonymous observations

	Urban						Rural	
	Teen		Middle		Older		Older	
	M	F	M	F	M	F	M	F
BE + DONE + PP[a] (*N* = 13)								
'm done PP								1
is done PP	2				1			2
was done PP					1	2		4
HAD + DONE (BEEN) + PP (*N* = 39)								
've done PP								7
has done PP					1	1		2
have done PP	2	3		1	3	7		11
had done been PP								1
HAVE/BE + DONE + PP (*N* = 26)								
's done PP	1		2	2	2	4	2	13
MODAL + HAVE + DONE (BEEN) + PP (*N* = 3)								
shoulda done PP								1
shoulda done been PP								
may have done PP						1		
Totals	5	3	2	3	9	15	2	42

[a] PP = past participle.

TABLE 13.4 $\emptyset$ + *done* + past participle: Distribution by age, sex, rural/urban among working class. Interviews and anonymous observations

	Urban						Rural	
	Teen		Middle		Older		Older	
	M	F	M	F	M	F	M	F
DONE + BEEN + PARTICIPLE (N = 4)								
Done been ⎧ pres. part. ⎫			1					
⎪ past part. ⎪				1				
⎨ and got ⎬								1
⎩ in ⎭						1		
DONE + GOT + (+NP)								
+ ⎧ PP ⎫ (N = 16)	2							1
⎪ ADJ ⎪					1			2
⎨ ADV ⎬	2	1	1			1		4
⎩ NP ⎭		1						
DONE + DONE + NP (N = 3)								
Done done NP			1					2
DONE + PP (+ PRES. PART.) (N = 57)								
Done forgot	5	3			1	1		3
[All other]	4	2	1	9	4	8	5	11
Totals	13	6	5	9	6	12	5	24

AUXILIARY + DONE + PAST PARTICIPLE
AUX = BE

[6] Lord, I'm done died! (Myrtice J. R62).
[7] Some of the unions is done gone too far (Melvin H. W72).
[8] It was so quiet I thought everybody was done gone to bed (Myrtice J. R62).

AUX = HAVE

[9] I think that Mr Kershaw has done passed away (Myrtice J. R62).
[10] Well, he had done retired then. He useta work at Monsanto (Billy H. W18).
[11] Well, they had done that two or three times that night, and they uz already lookin' for em (Diane B. W15).
[12] She said the soap had done been dumped and they have to be done by hand in the morning (Myrtice J. R62).

AUX = 's

[13] When they went to bury him they said there was some little ole girl jus' screamin' and hollerin' and fallin' over the casket. I said, too late to fall after he's done dead (Milly B. W77).

[14] He's done got a hole wallered out in the carpet in there where he watches TV (Tom G. W17).

AUX = MODAL + HAVE

[15] They started it and then they stopped it. It shoulda done been gone (Myrtice J. R62).

[16] [Did you bring it?] Yes, but I may have done lost it (Ada P. W60s).

[17] He may have done retired (Myrtice J. R62).

Ø + DONE + PARTICIPLE
DONE + *been* + PAST, PRESENT PARTICIPLE

[16] An, you notice, he wouldn't go on TV. McGovern tried to get him in a debate, but he 'uz too smart. He done been whipped oncet and on that, and he wouldn't do it! (Sam C. W70).

[19] I done *been* playin'! (Jack W. 50s, dance-band leader).

DONE + *got* (+ NP) + PP, ADJ, ADV, NP

[20] We done got the other shell made (Clint L. W18).

[21] An' I said, No, you can't come in. You done got wet (Myrtice J. R62).

[22] He done got out (Ray M. W50s).

[23] You got Ruby on it and he done got somethin'! (Ed C. 20s).

Done done + NP

[24] This is the third bobbin that done done it (Dana G. W15).

[25] Oh, I done used all my thread (Diana B. 15).

[26] The buses done quit runnin' (Myra T. W74).

Table 13.5 summarizes the total occurrences of *done* with past participle by age, sex, locale (rural/urban) for the working class.

There are several examples of *done,* mostly from Myrtice Jordan, which do not fit with *done* as just described, that is, (AUX) + DONE + PP. In these unusual cases, *done* is followed, not by

TABLE 13.5 Total (aux) + *done* + past participle: Distribution by age, sex, rural/urban among working class. Interviews and anonymous observations

	Urban						Rural	
	Teen		Middle		Older		Older	
	M	F	M	F	M	F	M	F
Total *done*	18	10	6	12	15	27	7	66
	28		18		42		73	
Grand total: 161								

a past participle, but by some other verb form, an adverb or an adjective. (See examples [27] – [42].) In many of these cases, *done* is used as an adverb, usually to mean 'already', perhaps as a result of relexification. In four cases, *done* precedes the preterite. That these are preterites rather than Ø-HAVE is established by replacing *done* + VERB with HAVE + PP without *done,* as in the asterisked (not English) and crossbarred (not equivalent) examples in [27]–[30]. The adverbial in the sentence – *yesterday, years ago, four o'clock this morning, two, three year ago* – blocks such an interpretation. Nor can *already* or *completely* substitute for *done* in any of these cases of *done* + PRETERITE: *done* here appears to be an intensifier of some sort.

DONE + PRETERITE

[27] They done had the tables fixed yesterday [context: referring to tables which had been set for a banquet] (Myrtice Jordan R62).
'They had the tables set up yesterday, already.'
*They have had the tables set up yesterday.
They had had the tables set up yesterday.

[28] I done quit years ago, cause I know that the poor class of people have no right in the 'lection (Lamar N. R86).
'I quit [voting] years ago.'
*I have quit years ago . . .
#I had quit years ago . . .
*I already quit years ago . . .
?I absolutely quit years ago . . .
I quit years ago, absolutely, because . . .

[29] You done woke me up four o'clock this mornin pullin' dishes! (Milly B. W77).

'You woke me up at four o'clock this morning washing
dishes!
*You have waked me up at four o'clock this morning . . .
#You had waked me up at four o'clock . . .
*You already woke me up at four o'clock . . .
You woke me up at four o'clock this morning, damn it!

[30] You know, Parker Memorial, they spent another million
dollars on their church. Done built that new part on it
over there two, three year ago [context: decline in atten-
dance at church and Sunday school resulting in unused
buildings] (Melvin H. W72).
'[They] built that . . . two years ago.'
*They have built that . . . two years ago.
#They had built that . . . two years ago.
*They already built that . . . two years ago.
They just built that . . . two . . . years ago.
They built that . . . two . . . years ago, of all things.

Wolfram and Christian also found this (1975: 329-30); see
example [96]. In two more cases, [31] and [32], *done* is followed
by the uninflected form of the verb or the copula; in three others
[33]- [34], it is followed by the present participle. Of those forms
having a preceding auxiliary, one of the examples of a modal
[32]; the rest [33]-42] have inflected BE. In no case is the copula
before *done* a relexification of HAVE, as seen in the more usual
AUX + DONE+ PP.

DONE + UNINFLECTED FINITE VERB

[31] They done know what it's all about (Myrtice J. R62).
'They already know what [Christmas] is all about.'

The verb appears to be in the third person plural, present tense.
Wolfram and Christian (1975: 328) found a similar example in
West Virginia. (See example [98].)

MODAL + DONE + UNINFLECTED COPULA

[32] It should done be up [two times] [context: Because of
heavy spring rains, the farmers were just then planting the
cotton which should already have been growing.] (Myrtice
J. R62).
'[The cotton] should already be up [by now].'

(BE) + DONE + VERB + ING

[33] By the time he got up there it was done jus' lightnin' an'
      rainin' (Myrtice J. R62).
      'By the time he got up there it was already lightning and
      raining quite a lot.'
[34] I'm tellin you, I could jus' see that train done bearin'
      down on me! [context: story of car caught on railroad
      tracks] (Myrtice J. R62).
      '. . . at that exact moment, I could see that train already
      bearing down on me!'
[35] My hair was done standin' out! (Jewel M. 70 Gadsden).
      'My hair was standing straight out!'

Wolfram and Christian have an example of this in their West
Virginia data (1975: 328; example 78a); see [97].

BE + DONE + ADVERB

[36] I said, I'm like bad money. I'm done back again! (Myrtice
      J. R61).
[37] I'm done here (Myrtice J. R61).
      'I'm already here.'
[38] Mine's done out of fix [three times] (Myrtice J. R62).
      '[My figure] is completely out of shape'.
[39] You done ready to go to bed? (Myrtice J. R61).
      '[Are] you already ready to go to bed?'

There seems to be no common characterization, such as
'locative', for the adverbs following *done*.

BE + DONE + ADJECTIVE

[40] Some of em's done dead an' gone (Mattie D. R83).
      'Some of em are already dead and gone.'
[41] Of course, Floyd 'uz done dead then, y'know (Flora P.
      W74).
      '. . . Floyd was already dead then.'
[42] Well, she 'uz done dead (Ruby T. W78).
      '. . . she was already dead [by then].'

It should be noted that in all the cases of DONE + ADJECTIVE
in the Anniston data, the adjective is *dead*.

13.1.2 Other environments

In addition to occurring in positive declarative sentences, *done*
was found in questions, sentences with tag questions and in
negated sentences.

Question

The only full questions found with preverbal *done* are the following:

[43] Had you done seen this, Corky? [context: newspaper in hand] (Myrtice J. R62).
'Have you already seen this, Corky?'

[44] Had you done gone to bed? [context: to person in bed] (Myrtice J. R62).
'Have you already gone to bed?'

[45] Has he done come back? (Ruby T. W78).
'Has he already come back?'

[46] Hadn't y'all done gave Christmas gifts? (Sherry W. W16).
'Haven't you already given [each other] Christmas presents?'

All the other questions (six examples) are non-inverted:

[47] What's the matter? You done tuck up some cold? (Myrtice J. R61).

[48] You done paid yet? (Regina W. W20s).

[49] You done checked her oil? (teenage boy, service station attendant).

Tag question

The only tag questions noted occurred both with and without a preceding auxiliary:

[50] The son had done left, hadn't he! (Myrtice J. R61).

[51] He done back me off, ain't he! (Billy S. 50s, salesman).

Negation

On the basis of rather meagre evidence, it seems that the negative of adverbial *done* (*ie* meaning 'already') is HAVE + NEG which occurs as *hadn't done* or *ain't done,* based on both the two tag questions already cited and the following:

[52] I carry it if somebody hadn't done got it (Imogene D. 50s, news-stand clerk).
'I carry-it [*Time*] if somebody hasn't already bought it.'

13.2 Syntax of *done*: Summary

The following summarizes the environments of *done* as found in the Anniston data.

13.2.1 'Normal' *done*

(a)   BE
(MODAL) HAVE _____ (been) PAST PARTICIPLE
                    (+PAST)$_{(\alpha)}$ (α)
                              BE = HAVE

Read: A verb phrase with normal positive *done* can consist
of an optional copula or (an optional modal followed by)
have, done (optional *been*), and a past participle; it can also
consist of only *done* and a past participle. The initial copula
or *have* may occur in either the past or non-past form. If they
occur in the past, then *been* does not occur. The copula is a
relexification of *have*.

  I'm done died!

(b) Negation (conditional):
    if NP $\left\{ \begin{matrix} \text{hadn't} \\ \text{ain't} \end{matrix} \right\}$ _____ PAST PARTICIPLE

                        $\left\{ \begin{matrix} \text{hadn't} \\ \text{ain't} \end{matrix} \right\}$ = hasn't, hadn't, haven't
                                        = HAVE + NEG

Read: A conditional negative verb phrase with *done* consists
of *if*, a noun phrase, *hadn't* or *ain't, done,* and a past participle. *Hadn't* and *ain't* are forms of negative *have; hadn't* is
used for *hasn't, hadn't* and *haven't*.

  . . . if somebody hadn't done got it.

(c) Tag:
NP (HAVE) _____ PAST PARTICIPLE $\left\{ \begin{matrix} \text{hadn't} \\ \text{ain't} \end{matrix} \right\}$ NP
         (+PAST)

Read: A tag question with *done* in the verb phrase consists
of a noun phrase, optional *have* in the past or non-past, optional past, past participle, *hadn't* or *ain't,* and a noun phrase.

  The son had done left, hadn't he!

(d) Question:
(HAVE) NP _____ PAST PARTICIPLE
       (+PAST)

Read: A yes/no question with *done* consists of optional have in the past or non-past, a noun phrase, *done,* and a past participle.

Has he done come back?

13.2.3 'Extended' *done*
(a) MODAL be + ADVERB be # HAVE

> *Read:* A verb phrase with 'extended' *done* consists of a modal, *done, be* and an adverb. *Be* is not a relexification of *have.*

It should done be up.

(b) (BE ———
   (+PAST) $\left\{ \begin{array}{l} \text{VERB + ING} \\ \text{ADVERB} \\ \text{ADJECTIVE} \\ \qquad\qquad \text{dead} \end{array} \right\}$ BE ≠ HAVE

> *Read:* A verb phrase with 'extended' *done* can consist of a copula in the past or non-past and a present participle, an adverb or the adjective *dead.* The copula is not a relexification of *have.*

My hair was done standing out.

(c)   VERB   (i) ——— [+STATIVE]
   $\left\{ \begin{array}{l} \text{PRESENT TENSE} \\ \text{PRETERITE} \end{array} \right\}$ present
                                tense

                       (ii) ——— [−STATIVE]
                                preterite

> *Read:* A verb phrase with 'extended' *done* can consist of *done* and a stative verb in the present tense or a non-stative verb in the preterite.

They done know what it's all about.

(d) NP ——— VERB+ING

> *Read:* A verb phrase with 'extended' *done* can consist of a noun phrase, *done* and a present participle.

I could jus' see that train done bearin' down on me!

It is interesting to note that for every environment in which *done* appears, the adverb *already* also may appear:

'Normal' *done*
(a) = [6] – [26]   John is already finished.
                           John has already finished.
                           John had already finished.
                           John had already been finished.
                           John had already been seen.
                           John should have already finished.
                           John should have already been finished.
(b) = [52]   . . . if John hadn't already finished.
(c) = [30] – [51]   John's already finished, ain't he!
                           John has already finished, hadn't he?
(d) = [43 – [49]   Has John already finished?

'Extended' *done*
(a) = [32]   John should already be here.
(b) = [36] – [42]   John is already finishing it.
                           John is already up.
                           John was already dead.

(c) = [27] – [30]   (i) John already knows.
                           (ii) John already jumped. (?)
(d) = [33] – [35]   That was John already running.

On the other hand, *done* cannot occur in some positions where
already can, such as in clause-initial or clause-final position.

   Already many people had arrived.
   *Done many people had arrived.

   John has come already.
   *John has come done.

Nevertheless, since *done* shares a subset of the environments in
which *already* appears, it seems logical to claim that *done* has the
same functions as, and a meaning closely equivalent to, *already*.

13.3 Meaning of *done*

This study approaches the meaning of Southern White *done* from
four types of evidence: (a) spontaneous translations; (2) the fact
that its privileges of occurrence and meanings seem to match
those of *already;* (3) its co-occurrence with manner adverbs; and
(4) the linguistic context for some of the examples.
   In the Anniston data, there was an interesting series of repeti-
tions by a *done* speaker trying to talk to a partially deaf person,
a non-*done* speaker.

[53]   I done seen em.
(louder)   I done seen em!
(yet louder) I already seen em!! (Myrtice J. R61).

Apparently Myrtice Jordan considers *already* to be the equivalent of *done*. This is not an idiosyncrasy of Mrs Jordan. On two different occasions a Black speaker also used *already* in attempting to communicate with the same partially deaf speaker as shown in example [75] and [76] in the discussion of *done* in Black English.

Already as a marker of perfective in English has been studied in some detail by Traugott and Waterhouse (1969), who assume the existence of three forms of *already: already*$_1$ is the perfective marker; *already*$_2$ involves emphatic stress and an element of surprise and may occur with both future *will* and adverbs with a specific time reference. It does not supplete to *yet* in interrogatives and means 'so soon, as early as now/then, right now/then' (Traugott and Waterhouse 1969: 288). *Already*$_3$ apparently modifies the quantifier system in some way and alternates with *not yet* (Traugott and Waterhouse 1969: 288).

Already$_1$, the main subject of their paper, is not really an adverb of time in English but a perfective marker, 'the realization of a feature or set of features associated with PERFECT' (Traugott and Waterhouse 1969: 302). It suppletes with *yet* for negation except in embedded sentences, implies some state of change and occurs only in copula sentences allowing *become* or some other inchoative. It cannot occur with future *will,* in generic sentences, with adverbs having specific time reference in the present, with verbs or adjectives that block perfect, or in sentences that cannot have deep structure perfect.

The eight Traugott and Waterhouse constraints on *already* were tested against *done* using the Anniston data:

1 It suppletes with *yet* for negative except in embedded sentences. (Questions present a special case.)

The only negative with *done* occurred in an embedded sentence. The only co-occurrence of *yet* with *done* was in a question, which is a special case and will be discussed below.

[52] I carry it if somebody hadn't done got it.
[48] You done paid yet?

2. It implies some state of change.

This seems to be the case for *done* in all the Anniston data.

[7] Some of the unions is done gone too far.
    [it has come about [the unions go too far]]

[22] He done got out.
    [it has come about [he get out]]

3. It occurs only in sentences with a copula which allow *become* or some other inchoative.

In every case of true copula + *done* (as opposed to *have* relexified as *be*), *it has happened* or *it has come to pass* underlies the surface sentence as in

[36] I'm done back again.
    It has come to pass   that I am back again.
    It has happened

4. It cannot occur with future *will*.
    *You'll done be tall soon.
    *You'll done go with me.

5. It cannot occur with generics.
    *Birds done fly.

6. It cannot occur with adverbs with specific time reference in present tense.
    *I done see you at five o'clock.
    *Jack is done working tonight.

The time adverbials (adverbs, adverb phrases, and adverb clauses) occurring with *done* are listed in Table 13.6 arranged according to Crystal's taxonomy of time adverbials (Crystal

TABLE 13.6 Time adverbials occurring with perfective *done* in NAE. Arranged according to Crystal's (1966) taxonomy

A.	How often? Frequency of occurrence
	Single occurrence: once
	Fresh occurrence: again
	Frequent occurence: too many times
B.	How long? Restricted duration.
	Limits of duration explicit or known: over six months
C.	When? Time reference explicit.
	In past removed: yesterday, years ago, two, three years ago, a long time (ago), so long ago
	In daytime period: four o'clock this morning
D, F	When? Requires previously explicit time reference (from A, B or C)
D.	Time referred to precedes explicit time reference
	Non-specific overall: already
	End-point known: by the time
F.	Time referred to follows explicit time reference
	Overall period: after

1966: 11–14). The one specific-reference time adverbial, [at] *four o'clock this morning,* occurs in the past rather than in the present. The meaning of *done* in the sentence with that adverbial, however, is not perfective *already,* but intensive, as with the other cases of *done* + preterite, perhaps more like emphatic $already_2$ as described by Traugott and Waterhouse which can occur with [+ specific time] adverbs. *Done* in this sense, though, does not occur with *will* as can $already_2$.

7. It cannot occur with verbs or adjectives that block perfect.
   *He is done small.
   *John is done writing a book.

8. It cannot occur in sentences that cannot have deep
   structure perfect.
   *I done plan to go tomorrow.
   *I'm done working at Sears on Mondays.

Since these are the reasons for proposing *already* as a surface realization of perfect, then *done* would also qualify as a surface structure perfective marker.

One subject brought up in the Traugott and Waterhouse discussion, questions with the perfective, deserves more attention.

Traugott and Waterhouse (1969: 301) point out that 'Q[uestion] + NEG with PERFECT involves expectation (*ie* "imperfection")'. They distinguish *already* and *yet* in questions in the following manner.

Expectation that 'you' will pay:
   Have you paid yet?
   [Q it has already come about that you have paid]
No such expectation:
   Have you paid already?
   [Q it is the case that you have paid already]
Neutral as to expectation:
   Did you pay?
   [Q you pay]

Thus, in the only case of *yet* occurring with *done,* and that in a question,

   [48] You done paid yet? [to another girl at soda fountain]
        (Regina W. W20s)

the expectation is that she had not at that time paid.

On the other hand, a negative question without *yet* implies that *it is the case that X.* For example, if someone sees a friend who should have already gone somewhere, he will say, *Haven't you gone yet?* Obviously, the friend has not gone since he is standing

there. However, the questioner can ask a mutual friend *Has X
gone already?* in which case it is assumed that X has indeed gone.
Did you go?, on the other hand, does not imply one way or the
other whether or not X went anywhere. Thus, the question from
the Anniston data:

[46] Hadn't y'all done gave Christmas gifts?

assumes that 'y'all' had actually exchanged Christmas presents.
The situational context is that the crowd had given Christmas
presents early to a member because she was moving away. She,
therefore, thought that they had at the same time exchanged
Christmas presents as a group, which actually was not the case.
The rest of the Anniston questions with *done* are of this sort,
implying an expectation of the question action having been completed. For example, on several occasions, Myrtice Jordan asked
in regard to the newspaper, which had obviously been read by
the other members of the household, '(Had) [=HAVE] you done
seen this?' Obviously, the expected answer was 'Yes, I have'. If,
instead, she had asked, '(Had) [=HAVE] you done seen this
yet?' it would imply that she thought that the others had not seen
it.

   Co-occurrence with adverbials other than time adverbials and
clues from the linguistic context were examined in further analysis
of the meaning of *done*. The few adverbials co-occurring with
done which do not refer to time seem to be manner adverbials.
Most are intensives and generally mean 'completely'; for example, *plumb, long, all, just*:

[54] Jeff is done long gone, though [context: buddy recently
     married] (Tom G. W17).
     'Jeff is a complete loss [to the gang], unfortunately.'
[55] An' I lived on Walnut for years and years, and 'ey done
     took Walnut Street plumb over (Ruby T. W78).
     '. . . [the Negroes] have by now taken Walnut Street com-
     pletely over.'

[56] You didn't know about it until it was all done planned
     and fixed (Myrtice J. R61).
     '. . . until it was completely and totally planned and
     fixed.'

[57] By the time he got up there, it was done jus' lightnin' and
     rainin'! (Myrtice J. R61).
     '. . . it was already lightning and raining quite a lot.'

In these cases, *done* has the meaning 'intensive' in addition to its
perfective function. Friedrich (1974: S38), referring to Slavic or

Ancient Greek, mentions the possibility of aspect having 'certain emphatic or intensifying functions'.

One last adverbial, *'bout,* hedges on or qualifies the perfective meaning of *done,* as shown in [58]

[58] I done 'bout forgot. It's been a long time (Billy H. W17).
'I have almost completely forgotten.'

Aside from the intensive uses of *done* with the preterite and with intensive adverbs, it is clear from the linguistic context that it is used as a perfective marker:

[59] I heard her when she went in there, but I think I done gone to sleep when she come out (Myrtice J. R61).

[60] When 'ey get that age, gen'lly, their mind is done gone, but . . . (Myrtice J. R61).

[61] He died in Ohio. He 'uz done married again 'n I 'uz done married again, so hit didn't bother me (Ruby T. W78).

[41] . . . an' so me and him married. Of course, Floyd 'uz done dead then, y'know (Flora P. W74).

[62] We got a phone call . . . to come at once; Donna was in the hospital. Well, we had to rush over here, and they had done operated on her for appendicitis. An' she'uz up 'n runnin' around in the hall! (Ruby T. W78).

[63] . . . That's where she died . . . I run and told Mama . . . And they come out there and pick' Will up and carried her to the house. Well, she 'uz done dead (Ruby T. W78).

[64] I useta play a long time ago, but I done quit playin'.
I quite playin' when I quit singin' (Ruby T. W78).

[65] An' then he worked at the Fort in the canteen about three months, I reckon. An' went in one Sunday mornin' an' the lady manager of 'em told him to go to a beer store. He said, 'Well', says, 'Is that all you can put me on?' She said, 'Yeah, that's what they said do'. An' [he] said, 'Will you write me a showin' for my time?' 'Oh', [she] says, 'You not a-gonna quit!' [He] says, 'No, I ain't'. Says, 'I done quit'. Said, 'I'm not goin' to the beer store!' (James H. R81).

Done is mainly a surface marker of perfect aspect, functioning as an adverb closely equivalent to *already* and, as such, carries the meaning 'completed action'. (Other aspectual phenomena express a continuing [progressive] or not necessarily completed [imperfect] action.) *Done* also acts as an intensifier.

As a perfective marker, *done* is largely redundant in sentences with *have +en* or *already* as the surface realization of perfect.

Done with *have* +*en* or *already* adds emphasis to the perfect meaning of the sentence *He may have retired* as in [66a]–[66c].

[66a] He may have done retired (Myrtice J. R61).
[66b] He may have already retired
[66c] He may have already done retired.

Southern White speech is full of pleonasms of various sorts, so the redundancy in [66c] is in keeping with all varieties of Anniston English rather like the following:

[67] My partner and I, we were . . . (Newt B., state trooper in county court).
[68] She got off out of school at two-thirty (Jenelle B. 40s, beauty shop proprietor).
[69] I'm usually always at the Teen Center . . . (Allison B. U16).
[70] Where's your parents live at, up here in town? (Gene M. W18, glass repair shop).

Multiple negation in Alabama White English is another good example of the Southern tendency toward pleonasm.

Done is totally non-redundant only when perfect is realized overtly only by *done*, rather than by *done* with *have* +*en* or *already*:

[32] It should done be up. [37] I'm done here.

The perfective function of *done* is most clearly seen in such cases as there is nothing else in the sentence to indicate the perfect.

Altogether, out of the 161 examples of *done* displayed schematically in Tables 13.3 and 13.4, only 39 occur unequivocally with *have* + *en*. Another 26 occur with the ambiguous *'s*, 13 with some form of *be* and 3 with a modal. The remaining 80 have no auxiliary. Absence of an auxiliary gives no information as to what tense or aspect is intended, leaving the past participle to indicate tense and aspect. However, the past participle which partly signals the perfective does not function well in English. In Standard English, the preterite and past participle of regular verbs is the same -*ed* form. Only in irregular verbs is the distinction maintained. In non-standard Southern White English the preterite and past participle of irregular verbs is very unstable. Thus the participle cannot be relied on to disambiguate the verb phrase between preterite and perfect, and occasionally, the present tense.

Thus, if *done* is eliminated from *they done give you one*, the result in non-standard Southern White English could be interpreted three ways:

(a) They give [present] you one.
(b) They give [preterite] you one.
(c) They give [perfect] you one.

A study of the possible complementary distribution of *done* and *already,* either in the community or in the individual would be worth while. It seems likely that heavy users of *done* use *already* less than light users or non-users. However, one or another of the forms is needed for the non-standard speaker to make distinctive the meaning of perfect.

13.4 *Done* outside Southern White

Preverbal *done*, as mentioned in above, presents an interesting example of possible creole (and therefore Black English) influence on Southern White speech. However, this same form, or a similar one, can be found in English before any contact with creole. It seems likely that there are both creole and archaic influences at work here, reinforcing each other, unless this phenomenon is considered simply as a case of drift whereby four unrelated dialects of English – Southern White non-standard, Atlantic creole, Black English and Tristan da Cunha English – come up with the same form which had previously existed in much earlier stages of the growth of the language, Middle and Early Modern English.

13.4.1 Creoles

Various creoles have markers which function in much the same way as preverbal *done,* although they also have such markers in post-clausal position. Jamaican creole and Guyanese creole have such a post-clausal *done* in their basilects.

[71] wen mi kuk don, me a hosl fid op me pikni
'When I finish cooking, I hurry and feed my children.'
Guyana Creole (Bickerton 1975: 40)

[72] mi dis iit don
'I just finished eating.'
Jamaican Creole (Bailey 1966: 42)

The preverbal *done* also exists in these creoles.

[73] wen dem don plau dem tship
'When they've finished ploughing, they harrow.'
Guyana creole (Bickerton 1975: 40)

[74] me don nuo se im naa go
'I know full well that he won't go.'
Jamaican creole (Bailey 1966: 42)

In no case does creole *done* have an auxiliary preceding it (D. Bickerton 1973: personal communication). John Rickford, a native of Guyana, says that 'extended *done*' (*done up, done back*) does not exist in Guyana creole (1975), although William Stewart reports that *He done sick* does occur in Gullah (1975: personal communication).

Both Bickerton (1975: 40–59) and Dillard (1972: 47) point out the similarity of this *done* to completive markers in other Creoles: neo-Melanesian *pinis* (from English *finish*), French Creole *fek* (from *faire* 'do, make'), Sranan *kaba* (from Portuguese *acabar* 'finish'), as well as *done* in the creoles of Jamaica and Guyana, Krio (Sierra Leone) and Wescos (Cameroon). Some of these occur in clause final position as well as in the preverbal position, and are in the process of shifting to preverbal position as they get further away from pidgin. Bickerton sees the preverbal *done* of Black English as reported by Labov as a mesolectal form, the first step in decreolization being the shift of *done* to preverbal position. Next is the replacement of *done* by *finish* or other constructions, which may be what is happening if *done* is indeed dying out in Northern Black English.

13.4.2 Black English

Black English has a preverbal *done* which Labov refers to as 'another Southernism, widely used among whites' (Labov *et al.* 1968: 265). All but one of his eleven examples are of *done* without an auxiliary. The exception, *I'll be done put,* does not match any of the Alabama White data. He found that in the northern ghetto areas, preverbal *done* does not seem to be maintaining itself and may be disappearing.

Dillard explicitly states that Southern Whites have both AUX + *done* and Ø + *done,* while Black English basilect has only Ø + *done.* As mentioned above, he claims that any AUX + *done* in Black English is a result of borrowing from other dialects of English, *ie* Southern White (1972: 220).

That the *done* in Black English has the same meaning as the *done* in Southern White can be seen in the following natural expansion in which a Black woman from Autauga County, Alabama (in the Black Belt) is trying to communicate with a partially deaf White woman, a non-*done* speaker:

[75] We done turned it [the mattress].
      (louder) We already done turned it! (Mattie Lou McC. 45).

On another occasion the same two speakers went through a similar routine regarding the dog:

[76]   M: He just got through lickin' it [a plate].
            What?
       M: (louder) He done already licked it.
            What?
       M: (yet louder) He have done licked it!
            (Mattie Lou McC. 45).

13.4.3 Middle and Early Modern English

Preverbal *done* is not limited to Atlantic Anglo-creoles, Black
English or Southern White non-standard English. There was a
done in Middle English, Medieval Literary Scots and Early
Modern English which had the same meaning of 'already' or
'completely'. However, unlike Southern White, every example of
this *done* has a preceding auxiliary *have/has/had*.

Chaucer and Gower repeatedly used this form which Mustanoja (1960: 605–6) characterizes as 'perfect tense *Hath done*
followed by the past participle of the principal verb'.

[77]   an oratorie . . . Hath Theseus doon wroght in noble wyse
       (Chaucer, *Canterbury Tales,* 'The Knight's Tale', line)
       1913; in Mustanoja 1960: 605)
[78]   thise marchantz han doon fraught hir shippes newe
       (Chaucer, *Canterbury Tales*, 'The Man of Law's Tale', line
       171; in Mustanoja 1960: 605).

Ellegård (1953: 143) assumed it was characteristic of uneducated
usage since it was common in the fifteenth century *Paston Letters*
and in the sixteenth-century Machyn's *Diary*.

[79]   I have . . . doon dewely examyned the instrument (*The
       Paston Letters,* ed. J. Gardiner (1904): letter 12, p. 26,
       line 5; in Ellegård 1953: 143).

Visser points out that while the *Oxford English Dictionary*
mentions that Scottish poets of the sixteenth century extended the
periphrastic use to the infinitive and past participles, 'the com-
pilers appear to have overlooked the occurrence of the idiom in
Earlier English as well as in non-Scottish writings' (1969: 111,
1493). Some of his examples:

[80]   . . . told hym . . . how he *hadde don forrsake* God and
       his holy Religion (*c.* 1445–50, *Peter Idleys Instructions*
       (ed. D'Evelyn 1935), Bk. II, 249).
[81]   He *hes done* petuously devour The noble Chaucer
       (1508, Dunbar, *Lament for the Makaris,* line 49)

Traugott (1972a: 146, 193) reports that this form died out in
the south of England in the fifteenth century, though it remained
common in Northern English.

[82] And many another false abusion/The Paip *hes done invent*
(1578 *Scottish Poems of the Sixteenth Century,* ed. J. G.
Dalyell (1801), vol. II, line 189; in Traugott 1972a: 146)

In Craigie's *Dictionary of the Older Scottish Tongue* (n.d.: II,
178) there are ten examples of *done* used 'in the infinitive, past
and present participles' and three 'with past participles':

[83] As I afore haue done discus.
(1556 William Lauder *Office and Dewtie of Kyngis,*
340)

[84] Quhone I haue done considder This warldis vanite
(1570–86, Richard Maitland, Maitland Folio Ms cii. 1).

[85] Thay ar . . . volfis and toddis [foxes], wuha . . . haue
violentlie done brokin the dyk of the scheipfald (1581
Nicol Burne, *The Disputation,* 78b).

However, A. J. Aitken, who worked on that volume and is now
editor of the dictionary, insists that these forms were from Middle
English *do* and were literary in Medieval Scots (1973: personal
communication).

13.4.4 Other varieties of English

The only other references to *done* in the literature cite Literary
Scots or American uneducated speech, generally Black English.
Curme (1931: 23; 1935: 210) gives examples from older Scots
English and *Uncle Remus,* as well as from a story about West
Virginia lumbermen. Mustanoja (1960: 606), after discussing the
Middle English forms, notes that 'roughly parallel constructions
are common in the language of uneducated American English
speakers', giving citations from Norman Mailer's *The Naked and
the Dead.* Atwood (1953: 7, 44) has *done* as a form peculiar to
Black English.

There are references, however, to the existence of this form in
the speech of Whites in West Virginia, the Great Smoky Mountains, the Ozarks, Arkansas in general, and on the island of
Tristan da Cunha in the South Atlantic. Since the data are
generally so meagre, they will be presented in their entirety, except for the sixty-five examples recorded by Wolfram and
Christian (1975: 335) in West Virginia.

Hackenberg provides four examples of *done* in a collection of
miscellaneous interesting grammatical forms found in Nicholas
County, West Virginia (1973: 149):

[86] They done sent that (54, male, mine electrician).
[87] The other one's done eighteen (60, male, miner).

[88] He's done went home (18, female, miner's dependant).
[89] It had done started then (unidentified).

In the West Virginia counties of Mercer and Monroe. Wolfram and Christian (1975) found constructions such as the following with *done*:

[90] I done forgot when it opened.
[91] And the doctor done give him up, said he's got pneumonia.
[92] . . . because the one that was in there had done rotted.
[93] We thought he was done gone.
[94] If she had, she woulda done left me a long time ago.
[95] . . . the next thing you know she's done throwed herself plumb to the dogs.
[96] . . . and I come back by the house and done got my feet wet.
[97] . . . that little bush was done giving over and I didn't know what there to do.
[98] I mean, you done understand it and then, you know, he'd keep on explaining it, you know.

Most of their examples (twenty-six out of sixty-five) were from men over 40.

Three other sources provide the remainder of examples:

[99] I done done it (Smokies; Kephart 1913: 285).
[100] Lee Gifford's done dead (Ozarks; Randolph 1927: 3).
[101] Th' chores done been done (Ozarks; Randolph 1927: 3).
[102] She's done went t' Bentonville (Ozarks; Randolph 1927: 3).
[103] I done ploughed (Arkansas, uneducated; Thanet 1892: 121).

Except for Wolfram and Christian, Randolph and Hackenberg give the most lengthy discussion of this phenomenon, a paragraph each. Wolfram and Christian (1975: 321–35) explore the syntactic, semantic and pragmatic properties of *done* in their data and conclude with remarks on the historical development of *done*. Their comments on my work refer to an early draft, not the version presented here which was developed independently of their work, although our analyses have converged in many respects.

In his survey of the Upper Midwest, Allen (1975: 46) reports that 'only one bona fide instance appears, in the conversational "I done never heard it" of a Type I [old, with elementary education] South Dakota farmer of South Midland parentage, inf. 314'. This informant, 85 years old when interviewed in 1952, lived in Stanley County in central South Dakota. However, he was born (1867) in St Joseph, Missouri, and lived there until he was 16 (Allen1973: 82).

There are no references to *done* used in this manner in Wright's *English Dialect Dictionary* (1898: II, 95–9, 120) nor in the *Scottish National Dictionary* (Grant and Murison 1952: III, 6–8, 104). Since the literature yielded no other information, I began asking native speakers. A. J. Aitken, a native speaker of Scots and editor of the *Dictionary of the Older Scottish Tongue*, maintains that *done* as found in Alabama (see my examples [6]–[52]) is unheard of in today's working-class Scots (1973: personal communication). Other linguists, native speakers or those familiar with the regional dialects of Yorkshire and Devon (M. A. K. Halliday) and of Cheshire (D. Bickerton), had the same reaction as Aitken (1973: personal communications). Neither had ever heard the form before except in the context of Black English, Atlantic Anglo-creole or White Southern vernacular.

One other kind of English which has *done* is that of Tristan da Cunha (Zettersten 1969: 85–6). (Perhaps this is not a dialect of English but a creole, although Hancock (1971) does not include it in his list of creoles.) Zettersten records the following perfective *done* forms:

[104] When you done went down Gough . . .
[105] I done went to the doctor and he gave me a
        hinjection and I's better now.
[106] Edwin's done drawn his stone.
[107] I's done tell her she must be married before Lent.

Zettersten (1969: 136) singles out the following as components of the dialect of Tristan da Cunha:

(1) The various dialects spoken by the early settlers. Mainly Southern [England] dialects or Cockney; (2) Features of the nautical jargon of the time. Mainly vocabulary; (3) The influence, mainly on morphology and syntax, due to the settlers from St Helena, and possibly Peggy White from Bombay; (4) Certain loan-words due to the influences from South Africa; (5) A certain influence from American whalers who settled down on Tristan.

Absence of information can be misleading, since it is always possible that the form exists, but has not been noted. However, I must tentatively conclude that *done* as discussed in this section indeed does not exist today outside of White Southern vernacular, Appalachian English, Tristan da Cunha English, Black vernacular and Atlantic Anglo-creoles.

13.5 Origin of Southern White *done.*

The question still remains of how *done* could have originated in Southern White English. If one should be so rash as to disregard Aitken's statement that *done* was limited to being used as a literary device in Late Medieval Scots, it is possible to explain its occurrence in Southern White as an inheritance from the Scotch-Irish. The argument would go as follows. The lowland Scots who settled in Ulster after 1600 were poor, often uneducated. For those who were educated, their education had been in Latin rather than English (Leyburn 1962: 44) so that their English would have been less affected than one would expect. The mass immigration of the Scotch-Irish to America began in 1717 and continued until 1775. Arriving at Philadelphia, they settled along the frontier, first in western Pennsylvania, then western Maryland, then on south – the Shenandoah Valley of Virginia, the Piedmont of the Carolinas and, lastly, central Georgia (Leyburn 1962: 184–255). These people were often uneducated and isolated.

Georgia was the last southern colony to be settled because of the hostile Spanish presence to the south. Early settlement (1733–38) went slowly because of various restrictions on the settlers, including a ban on slaves. In 1738, however, the policies changed. Slavery was allowed, and more extensive settlement began. The Indians were pushed back successively in some fourteen divisions and treaties between 1783 and 1835 until they were removed in 1836, opening up North Georgia to White settlement. Georgia seems to have been settled largely by people from the Piedmont of the Carolinas and Virginia who were mainly Scotch-Irish in origin. It seems possible that these people brought *done* with them. Evidence in support of this suggestion is the occurrence of *done* in Nicholas, Mercer and Monroe counties in West Virginia, which, in 1930, had a Black population of 2.2 per cent, 11.4 and 4.2 per cent respectively, and in the Great Smoky Mountains, also a white area, except for the Cherokees who lived in a single small region. See also Ščur (1978) who argues along these lines for the origin of *done* in the southern United States.

On the other hand, it is a matter of record that many slave-owners were small farmers who worked in the fields with their slaves and who owned as few as a single family of slaves.

Flanders, 1933: 127 for example, reports that in Georgia in 1860, 'of the total number of slaveholders, 66 per cent owned less than 10 [slaves] each, while only 5 per cent held more than 100. The great majority of owners, therefore, possessed less than 20 slaves.' He goes on to say, 'It was by no means unusual for the average slaveholder to labor with his Negroes in the field. . . .' (1933: 128). Here was an obvious point of close contact where *done* in creole could have reinforced and been reinforced by the *done* which may have existed in the English of these farmers.

I suggest that *done* was brought to Alabama by both the poorer settlers from Georgia and the Carolinas (Wood 1971: 5) and the slaves who came with – or were later sold to – the planters.

The maintenance and/or borrowing of *done* may be attributable to the fact that the primary marker of perfect in English (*have* + *en*) has lost its distinctiveness in Southern White, especially non-standard Southern White; *have* has become severely reduced, is often dropped and is no longer clearly distinguished from *had*. Furthermore, the past participle and preterite generally share the same form, even in the frequently used irregular forms which are distinguished in Standard English. In terms of a system, *done* fills a weakness in the patterning important to the system of tense and aspect markers.

13.6 Conclusion

Southern White Non-standard English has a form, *done,* which is distinct from preterite and past participle *done*. This adverbial *done* occurs in the verb phrase after the auxiliary (if any) and before the past participle. It can also, though rarely, occur as a true adverb before prepositions and adjectives. It carries two meanings, 'perfective' and 'intensive', which can generally be paraphrased, respectively, as *already* and *completely*.

Perfective *done* occurs in Appalachian and Ozark English, in Black English, in Atlantic Anglo-creoles, in the English of Tristan da Cunha and in Non-standard Anniston English. Historically, it was last recorded in Standard English in sixteenth-century Scots poetry. In modern varieties of English it is an archaic feature which was reinforced by the creole English of the Black slaves in the American South.

Notes

1. Informants are identified by their age and by R = rural, U = upper class or W = working class.
2. Anniston is an industrial town with a population of 60,000 located between Birmingham, Alabama and Atlanta, Georgia.

References

ALLEN, HAROLD B. (1973–76) *The Linguistic Atlas of the Upper Midwest:* In three vols: 1 (1973), 2 (1975). Minneapolis: University of Minnesota Press.

ATWOOD, E. BAGBY (1953) *A Survey of Verb Forms in the Eastern United States.* Ann Arbor: University of Michigan Press.

BAILEY, BERYL (1966) *Jamaican Creole Syntax.* Cambridge: Cambridge University Press.

BICKERTON, DEREK (1975) *The Verb System of Guyana Creole.* Cambridge: Cambridge University Press.

CRAIGIE, WILLIAM A. (1937) *Dictionary of the Older Scottish Tongue from the Twelfth Century to the end of the Seventeenth.* Vols 1–5. Chicago: University of Chicago Press.

CRYSTAL, DAVID (1966) 'Specification and English tenses', *Journal of Linguistics* 2: 1–34.

CURME, GEORGE O. (1931) *A Grammar of the English Language, vol. 3 Syntax.* Boston: D. C. Heath.

CURME, GEORGE O. (1935) *A Grammar of the English Language, vol. 2. Parts of Speech and Accidence.* Boston: D. C. Heath.

DILLARD, J. L. (1972) *Black English: Its History and Usage in the United States.* New York: Random House.

ELLEGARD, ALVAR (1953) *The Auxiliary do: the Establishment and Regulation of its Use in English.* Gothenburg Studies in English, vol. 2 Stockholm: Almqvist and Wiksell.

FANDERS, RALPH BETTS (1933) *Plantation Slavery in Georgia.* Chapel Hill: University of North Carolina Press.

FRIEDRICH, PAUL (1974) 'On aspect theory and Homeric aspect', *International Journal of American Linguistics* 40 (4): 2 (Memoir 28), S1–44.

GRANT, WILLIAM, and DAVID D. MURISON (eds) (1929–76) *The Scottish National Dictionary.* Edinburgh: The Scottish National Dictionary Association.

HACKENBURG, ROBERT G. (1973) 'Appalachian English: a sociolinguistic study.' Washington, DC: dissertation. Georgetown University

HANCOCK, IAN F. (1971) 'A map and list of pidgin and creole languages.' In Dell Hymes (ed.) *Pidginization and Creolization of Languages.* Cambridge: Cambridge University Press, ff. 509–23.

KEPTHART, HORACE (1913) *Our Southern Highlanders.* New York: Outing.

LABOV, WILLIAM (1972) *Language in the Inner City: Studies in the Black English Vernacular.* Philadelphia: University of Pennsylvania Press.

LABOV, WILLIAM, COHEN, PAUL, ROBINS, CLARENCE and LEWIS, JOHN (1968) *A Study of the Non-Standard English of Negro and Puerto Rican Speakers in New York City*, vol. 1. US Office of Education Cooperative Research Project No. 3288.

LEYBURN, JAMES G. (1962) *The Scotch-Irish: A Social History.* Chapel Hill: University of North Caroline Press.

MUSTANOJA, TAUNO F. (1960) *A Middle English Syntax*. I. *Parts of Speech*. (*Memoires de la Sociéte Néophilologique de Helsinki*, 23). Helsinki: Société Néophilologique.

RANDOLPH, VANCE (1927) 'The grammar of the Ozark dialect', *American Speech* 3: 1–11.

RICKFORD, JOHN R. (1975) 'Carrying the new wave into syntax: the case of Black English BIN.' In Ralph W. Fasold and Roger W. Shuy (eds) *Analyzing Variation in Language*. Washington, DC: Georgetown University Press, *pp* 162–83.

SCUR, G. S. (1978) 'Concerning some peculiarities of the perfect in English'. In D. Hartmann, H. Linke and O. Ludwig (eds) *Sprache in Gegenwart und Geschichte: Festschrift für Heinrich Matthias Heinrichs zum 65. Geburtstag*. Köln: Böhlau, *pp* 174–87.

THANET, OCTAVE [ALICE FRENCH] (1892) 'Folklore in Arkansas', *Journal of American Folklore* 5: 121–5.

TRAUGOTT, ELIZABETH CLOSS (1972a) *A History of English Syntax: A Transformational Approach to the History of English Sentence Structure*. New York: Holt, Rinehart & Winston.

TRAUGOTT, ELIZABETH CLOSS (1972b) 'Principles in the history of American English – a reply', *The Florida FL Reporter* (Spring–Fall), 5–6, 56.

TRAUGOTT, ELIZABETH CLOSS, and JOHN WATERHOUSE (1969) ' "Already" and "yet": a suppletive set of aspect markers,' *Journal of Linguistics* 5: 287–304.

VISSER, F. TH. (1963–73). *An Historical Syntax of the English Language*, 3 vols. + 1 part. Leiden: Brill.

WOLFRAM, WALTER A., and DONNA CHRISTIAN (1975) *Sociolinguistic Variables in Appalachian Dialects*. Final report. Washington, DC: National Institute of Education of the Department of Health, Education and Welfare.

WOOD, GORDON R. (1971) *Vocabulary Change: A Study of Variation in Regional Words in Eight of the Southern States*. Carbondale, Ill.: Southern Illinois University Press.

WRIGHT, JOSEPH (ed.) (1898–1905) *The English Dialect Dictionary: Being the Complete Vocabulary of all Dialect Words Still in Use, or Known to Have Been in Use During the Last Two Hundred Years*. London: Henry Frowde.

ZETTERSTEN, ARNE (1969) *The English of Tristan da Cunha*. Lund Studies in English, vol. 37. Lund: Gleerup.

Chapter 14

Conservatism versus substratal transfer in Irish English

John Harris

14.1 Introduction

Tracing the origins of vernacular language varieties which have emerged in colonial conditions of language shift continues to be the subject of lively debate. The two positions that are particularly well represented in the more recent literature concern the role of language universals versus substratal transfer in creole genesis (see, for example, the papers in Muysken and Smith 1986). One of the main difficulties facing those arguing the substratum case relates to the multitude of base languages implicated in the emergence of creoles spoken in the the areas most frequently studied, such as the Caribbean. On the face of it, the task of isolating specific areas of substratal influence would appear to be much easier in the case of contact vernaculars for which a single substrate language can be unambiguously identified.[1] Varieties of this type would thus seem to constitute one of the most fruitful research sites for those interested in testing substratum hypotheses. One such vernacular is Irish English.

It has long been the practice in studies of Irish English to start from the premiss that any markedly non-standard linguistic feature can be attributed to influence from Irish Gaelic (*eg* van Hamel 1912; Hughes 1966; Bliss 1972; Sullivan 1980). Typically, this assumption is based on no more than anecdotal evidence. In this chapter, however, I discuss the results of more recent systematic research which provide qualified support for this position. The focus will be on two areas of Irish English syntax: *it*-clefting and a number of forms and constructions used to express the range of tense–aspect relations associated in Standard English with the present perfect. At the same time, however, I wish to sound a note of caution by drawing attention to the danger of neglecting a third component in the internal history of contact vernaculars – the retention of superstrate features which have either disappeared from standard usage or have always been restricted to non-standard dialects. In some cases, the relevant evidence is not easy to come by – frequently because the relevant features in Old World English are restricted to poorly documented dialects. Acknowledging the significance of this element is hardly anything new, but it would be fair to say that it has not been at all fashionable to pursue this line of enquiry in the context of the recent universals-vs-substrata debate. The adverse effects of this neglect can be exemplified in a number of cases where substratists and universalists have been disputing the origins of some linguistic feature which turns out on closer inspection to have less to do with claims made by either side and more to do with the conservative nature of many contact vernaculars (see, for instance, Harris 1986).

The most obvious place to seek parallels between the history of Irish English and that of other contact vernaculars would seem to be the various other varieties that have a Celtic substratum background, *eg* English as spoken in Wales, Cornwall and the Highlands and Western Isles of Scotland, or French as spoken in Brittany. However, there are several reasons why it is justifiable to discuss Irish English in the same context as Anglophone Caribbean creoles and other New World Black Englishes. First, their formative periods (roughly speaking, the seventeenth century) coincide to a great extent. Second, there was a significant Irish presence in both the Caribbean and the American colonies at that time. And third, many of the features traditionally attributed to substratal transfer in Irish English are similar and in some cases identical to those found in the New World Black varieties which have been focused on in the substrata-vs-universals debate. These include: palatal reflexes of historical velars in the environment of historical *a,* as in *kyat* 'cat', *gyap* 'gap'; a mid back round pronunciation of the vowel corresponding to standard Λ; and the existence of distinctive habitual aspect markers constructed with invariant *be* or derivatives of *do.* The potential significance of these parallels (including the possibility of a borrowing connection) has been discussed recently in a number of suggestive notes (*eg* Bailey 1982) and in more detail by Harris (1986, 1987) and Rickford (1986).

An additional aim of this chapter is to explore the possibility of developing the parallelism between contact Englishes spoken on both sides of the Atlantic even further. In particular, I will address the issue of whether it is justifiable to speak of a lectal continuum in Irish English which might correspond to the classic post-creole continua encountered in the Carribean. If so, it would be worth checking the extent to which the more 'basilectal' features of Irish English could be equated with an early contact jargon, showing the greatest degree of substratal input from Irish, as well as the extent to which 'mesolectal' varieties might reflect a historical process of convergence towards the superstrate. I begin the comparison by briefly outlining the main similarities and differences between the external histories of Irish English and New World Black Englishes.

14.2 External history of Atlantic contact Englishes

Among the points of comparison that any account of the external histories of Irish English and west Atlantic contact Englishes must take into consideration, the following would seem to be particularly important: the number of substrate languages represented in the initial contact situation; the rate of shift to the superstrate; the degree of motivation to acquire the superstrate; the continuity (or otherwise) of the functional link between an emergent contact vernacular and the superstrate; the length and intensity of contact with native speakers of the superstrate; and the range of varieties spoken by superstrate models.

One of the historical factors that clearly distinguishes Irish English from New World Black Englishes concerns the number of substrate languages that were represented in the initial contact situation. Whereas the African base in the latter case consisted of numerous languages with varying degrees of genetic relationship, only one substrate language has been involved in the development of the former, namely Irish Gaelic. Moreover, the rates at which the subjugated populations have shifted towards the superstrate differ markedly. In the New World, the shift was more or less abrupt and complete. In Ireland, on the other hand, the process has been ongoing for almost three centuries and has not gone to completion throughout the whole island. Irish survives as a first language in the *Gaeltacht* enclaves on the west coast and enjoys institutional status in the Republic of Ireland.

These two factors (a single substrate and the incompleteness of the shift to English) make the task of identifying points of substratal transfer potentially easier in Irish English than in New World Black Englishes. One of the most obvious research sites for those concerned with elucidating the substratal contribution in Irish English would seem to be the speech of present-day Irish–English bilinguals. Surprisingly, however, relatively little work with this specific goal has been carried out. (An exception is Ní Ghallchóir 1981.)

No account of the establishment of vernaculars which evolve in colonial conditions of language contact can be complete without giving due consideration to the social–psychological factors constraining the acquisition of the superstrate language by a subjugated population. This aspect of the sociolinguistic matrix contains a number of internal contradictions – most notably, a tension between the economic reasons favouring the adoption of the colonizers' language and factors of ethnic identity and solidarity which are likely to have inhibited it. For Blacks in the New World, the rewards for acquiring some kind of English were evidently high and were born out of the necessity not just to communicate with Whites but also, given the diverse linguistic backgrounds of the slave population, with one another. In Ireland, there has long been a dual perception of English. On the one hand, it is viewed by many as a symbol of Saxon oppression, while Irish retains strong associations of national identity. On the other hand, English represents a key to better employment opportunities in urban areas of Ireland as well as overseas. The continuing shift in the direction of English testifies to the ascendancy of the latter consideration over the former (see de Fréine 1977). Nevertheless, the conflict between economic necessity and nationalist sentiment continues to be reflected in contradictory language attitudes among the nationalist population. A majority speaks English as a first language, but a majority also sees Irish as the national language and supports its official status (see Edwards 1984).

An important factor in the subsequent development of varieties which initially evolve under conditions of language shift concerns the question of whether contact with the lexical donor language is maintained. The structural impact of the functional link being broken is illustrated by a number of New World Anglophone creoles spoken in communities where English has been replaced as the institutional language. The most widely held view is that varieties which develop in isolation from their lexical source language (eg Sranan and Saramaccan in Suriname) tend to exhibit a greater degree of structural divergence from the latter than those which remain in contact with the superstrate (see, for instance, Alleyne 1980). (However, for reservations about this account, see now Holm 1986a.) What we typically find in communities where the functional link with the lexical donor language has been retained is a continuum of varieties reflecting varying degrees of convergence towards the superstrate (eg Bickerton 1975). In

Ireland, the functional connection with English has remained un-broken for almost 300 years. Whether this has produced a 'classic' lectal continuum of the type usually associated with post-creole communities is an issue that I address in subsequent sections of this chapter.

It is probably wrong to think of the post-creole continuum as reflecting a unidimensional historical progression from an 'earlier' creole towards a 'later' acrolectal variety via various intermediate mesolectal stages. A number of researchers have argued strongly that such continua are likely to have been in place more or less right from the outset, reflecting the social diversity of plantation society (eg Alleyne 1980). A particularly significant factor here is likely to have been the extent to which those acquiring the target language were exposed to superstrate models in the initial contact situation.

In Ireland, variation in the intensity of contact with English is most clearly manifested along the geographical dimension.[2] During the formative period of Irish English, the highest pro-portion of native English or Scots speakers was to be found in coastal towns and in those mostly eastern and northern rural areas which were the target of a concerted colonization effort. Elsewhere, at least in the early stages, contact with English was minimal. Later on, as English gained ground in rural areas which had remained relatively unaffected by colonial settlement, it is likely to have been transmitted to a great extent by speakers whose mother tongue was Irish. This development presumably contributed to the evolution of heavily substrate-influenced varieties of Irish English which in their turn became models for the further transmission of English. The original pattern of varia-tion in the degree of exposure to natively spoken English has been overlaid somewhat by the effects of later internal migration, particularly from rural to urban areas. Nevertheless, as the evidence to be presented in the following sections shows, the pat-tern still manifests itself in the differing extents to which substratal features are discernible in different regional varieties of Irish English.

Another significant factor contributing to the heterogeneity of language behaviour in early colonial societies relates to the diver-sity of superstrate varieties represented in the initial contact situation. The range of varieties represented in both Ireland and the New World is likely to have been quite wide, reflecting the diverse social and geographical backgrounds of native English speakers. It is reasonable to assume that relatively standard speech was restricted to the highest social classes, including senior officers in administration and the military, while the majority of colonists, such as soldiers, small farmers, indentured workers and the like, spoke a range of regional non-standard dialects. Moreover, it is the latter groups who had the closest contact with the subjugated populations. (For a summary of the New World evidence, see Rickford 1986.) We can take it therefore that, during the earliest stages of language shift, the superstrate targets were defined in predominantly non-standard terms. Unfortunately, the paucity of documentary material on Early Modern English vernaculars greatly complicates the task of trying to establish a clear picture of what these targets were like. This in turn renders it that much more difficult to gauge accurately the extent to which particular non-standard features in modern contact vernaculars represent retentions of older dialectal English. This is an issue that I take up in section 14.4.

14.3 Clefting

14.3.1 Introduction
One feature of Irish English which has been widely commented on concerns the *it*-cleft construction. Impressionistic accounts of its use in vernacular Irish English generally draw attention to two peculiarities: a wider syntactic distribution and a markedly higher overall frequency of occurrence than is usual in other varieties of English. Both characteristics are widely attributed to substratal influence from Irish (*eg* van Hamel 1912; Clark 1917: Henry 1957; Hughes 1966; Sullivan 1980.)

By far the most convincing presentation of the substratum case is provided by Markku Filppula (1982: Ch. 4, 1986: Ch. 4), and I will be drawing heavily on his work in the following discussion. His is the only study of *it*-clefts in Irish English that is based on the quantitative analysis of real speech data. Although his corpus cannot by any means be considered fully representative of the communities he investigated (only twenty-three speakers from three areas were recorded), it is sufficiently large (153, 906 words) for us to identify with some degree of confidence a number of systematic interdialectal differences. The three English-speaking areas were selected on the basis of the assumed strength of Irish influence: C. Kerry and C. Clare in the rural west of Ireland, where the impact of Irish is most recent and direct; a rural area of C. Wicklow just south of Dublin, where Irish as a first language has been extinct for at least 150 years; and Dublin city where the link with Irish is most tenuous. Filppula's study also included a control group of six speakers of educated southern British English (ESE) (40, 247 words).

14.3.2 Syntax and pragmatics of cleft sentences in Irish and English

Irish and English have parallel cleft constructions in which the initial clause contains a focal constituent introduced by a copula and the second clause is introduced by a relativizer. In the following examples, [1a] and [1b] are clefted versions of the thematically unmarked sentences [2a] and [2b]:

[1] (a) Is é Seán a chuaigh go Doire
    cop HIM JOHN rel GO+past TO DERRY
    inné
    YESTERDAY
    (Christian Brothers 1962).
    (b) It's John who went to Derry yesterday.

[2] (a) Chuaigh Seán go Doire inné
    GO+past JOHN TO DERRY YESTERDAY
    (Christian Brothers 1962).
    (b) John went to Derry yesterday.

In Standard English, the following elements can be extracted as focal constituents in *it*-cleft sentences: subject NP (as in [1*b*]), object NP, complement of preposition, PP complement and various types of adjunct. In contrast, VP and subject complement constituents cannot undergo the same operation. Moreover, there are restrictions on the type of adjunct that can be extracted. For instance, it is not usual for manner adverbials to appear in focal position (*eg* *It is slowly that he walked in*).

In Irish, the range of syntactic elements that can undergo fronting in the equivalent cleft construction is less restricted than in English. Only a tensed verb or the predicate of a copula cannot appear in focal position. In addition to the constituents that are capable of being fronted as in English, the copular clause in Irish clefts can contain the following: VP (as in [3]), subject complement (predicate adjective of the substantive verb *bí,* as in [4]) and adjunct of manner (as in [5]). (The examples marked with ? are ungrammatical in Standard English, although, as we will see, they are grammatical Irish English.)

[3] Is ag déanamh a chuid ceachtannaí atá
    cop AT DOING HIS PORTION LESSONS rel-BE
    Tadhg
    TIM
    (Stenson 1981).
? 'It's doing his lessons that Tim is'.

[4] Is   caochta   atá   sé
     cop DRUNK *rel*-BE   HE
     (Stenson 1981).
     ? 'It's drunk he is'.

[5] Ní   go maith   a   chonaic   sé   iad
     cop+neg WELL   *rel*   SEE+*past* HE THEM
     (Christian Brothers 1962).
     ? 'It's not well he saw them'.

The usual function of clefting in English is to highlight the fronted element. The construction tends to occur more frequently in formal planned discourse than in spontaneous speech where highlighting is more typically achieved by intonational means. Some researchers find it convenient to distinguish two types of thematic meaning associated with the use of cleft sentences (see Filppula 1986: 92ff). The most common use of the construction in Standard English involves what has been termed *stressed-focus clefts* in which the relative clause contains given information while the fronted constituent is highlighted as new information. Much less frequent is the so-called *informative-presupposition* type of cleft. Here the content of the relative clause constitutes information which is new but which is presented as something that is not at issue. That is, the truth value of the information is presupposed, even though it is new to the listener or reader. The focal constituent in clefts of this sort typically has anaphoric reference or in some other way represents given information.

In Irish, thematic markedness in speech is typically not achieved by intonational means, and clefting is virtually the only device available for achieving thematic fronting. It is not surprising, then, that the use of the construction in speech is much more common in Irish than in English. The Irish construction occurs with both of the thematic meanings just outlined, but the informative-presupposition function is very much more frequent than in English and is certainly not restricted to formal planned discourse. It is also not uncommon to find an extended type of informative-presupposition cleft in which the focal constituent represents new information but with no special thematic marking. In such cases the whole sentence can be said to carry new information, as in the following example (with deleted copula) cited by Filppula (1982: 118):

[6] 'Faoi Dhia, goidé tháinig ort?' ars an t-athair.
     ' "In God's name, what happened to you?" asked the father.'

'Mícheál   Rua   a   bhuail
[cop → ø] MICHEAL RUA   rel   BEAT
mé', ars an mac.
ME
' "It was Mícheál Rua who gave me a beating," said
the son.'

14.3.3 Clefting in Irish English

The range of elements that can be extracted as the focal constituent of clefts in basic Irish English is more or less identical to
that of Irish. Thus we find clefts involving subject complements
[7], VP [8] or various adjuncts [9] which would be unacceptable
in other varieties of English:

[7]   It's flat it was (Henry 1957).
      It was a great race was that (Filppula 1982).
[8]   It is looking for more land a lot of them are (Filppula
      1982).
      It must be working for her he was (Henry 1957).
[9]   It's badly she'd do it now (Henry 1957).
      My God it's often we said it (Filppula 1982).

TABLE 14.1 Frequencies of functional types of cleft sentence in three
Irish English (IrE) communities and ESE (based on figures in
Filppula 1986: 114–16).

Speaker group and corpus size (no. words)	Stressed-focus		Informative-presupposition		Overall total	
	N per 1000 words		N per 1000 words		N per 1000 words	
Kerry/Clare 69,747	124	1.77	68	0.98	192	2.75
Wicklow 41,986	55	1.31	22	0.52	77	1.83
Dublin 42,173	37	0.87	17	0.40	54	1.28
Total IrE 152,906	216	1.40	107	0.70	323	2.10
ESE 40,247	20	0.50	8	0.20	28	0.70

The figures given in Table 14.1 provide quantitative confirmation of the impression that the overall frequency of clefts in Irish English is greater than in spoken Standard English. All three Irish English areas in Filppula's study show a higher incidence of clefts than the ESE group. Moreover, the ranking of the different Irish English areas according to their *it*-cleft scores correlates with their ranking on the scale of presumed extent of Irish influence. A substratist could argue (as Filppula himself does) that both of these results reflect the differential effects of interference from Irish which, as noted in section 14.3.2, is characterized by a higher incidence of cleft constructions than is usual in most types of English. That is, the overall discrepancy in *it*-cleft scores between the Irish English areas on the one hand and ESE on the other could be attributed to the fact that the former all bear the marks of a historical connection with the Irish substrate. And the differences among the Irish English areas themselves could be interpreted as a synchronic recapitulation of a diachronic process of convergence towards the English superstrate.

The breakdown of the cleft scores in Table 14.1 according to functional type could plausibly be taken as further evidence in favour of the substratum case. The figures indicate a greater propensity of use informative-presupposition clefts in the more directly Irish-influenced area of Clare/Kerry than in the other Irish English areas, which are quantitatively more like the ESE group in this respect. Filppula cites the following example of a cleft sentence, produced by one of his Clare informants, which the supplied context identifies as being of the informative-presupposition type (1986: 120):

[10] We always worked in the shore you know burning kelp . . . Making iodine out of it. Well we was one year – my father and myself and my sister we used to – we – *It is the windlass we had taken with – you know windlass – with the rope folded up like.*

In this example (which was judged as unacceptable by all of Filppula's ESE informants), both the focal constituent and the relative clause contain new information. It thus has the same extended informative-presupposition status as the Irish example given in [6].

To summarize: the case for saying that the non-standard aspects of *it*-cleft usage in Irish English stem from an Irish substrate source can be made at two levels. First, there are clear structural parallels between Irish English and Irish with regard to the range of syntactic constituents that can be fronted into the focal position. Secondly, there are clear functional parallels between Irish and Irish English not only in terms of the relative frequency with which the construction is employed as a highlighting device but also in terms of the type of thematic meanings that it can be used to express. Furthermore, it is possible to argue that quantitative differences among Irish English dialects confirm the existence of a post-contact continuum with the most markedly non-standard varieties displaying a greater degree of substratal input than intermediate varieties which have undergone varying degrees of convergence towards the superstrate.

14.4 Tense–aspect

14.4.1 Introduction
Another area of Irish English grammar where many writers have claimed to be able to detect the effects of substratal transfer is the tense–aspect system. Particular attention has been focused on the way in which basic Irish English expresses aspectual distinctions that are associated with the present perfect in Standard English (eg van Hamel 1912; Bliss 1972; Todd 1975; Sullivan 1976). As we will see below, the parallels between Irish English and Irish in this area of the grammar are indeed striking. However, in this section I wish to discuss the results of research, reported in more detail in Harris (1984), which indicate that, in this instance at least, the substratum case is much weaker than has generally been supposed. There are good grounds for concluding that most of the non-standard characteristics of Irish English in this particular aspectual subsystem represent retentions of patterns that were present in Early Modern English.[3]

14.4.2 The Irish English 'perfects'
The 1984 study focused on four tense–aspect distinctions which are generally expressed by the present perfect form in Standard British English but which tend to be made grammatically transparent in basic Irish English:

[11] (a) **Resultative:** past event with relevance at the moment of speaking, eg *Peggy has swallowed an orange.*

    (b) **Indefinite present anterior:** events occurring at unspecified points in a period leading up to the moment of speaking, eg *I've been to Canada twice.*

    (c) **Hot-news:** event located at a point that is separated from but temporally close to the moment of speaking, eg *Al has just arrived.*

    (d) **Extended-now:** situation initiated in the past and persisting into the moment of speaking, eg *I've known Sam for some time.*

There are two resultative constructions which are characteristic of Irish English. The first, which following Greene (1979) we may refer to neutrally as PII, is a 'split' transitive construction in which an *en*-participle occurs to the right of the object NP, as in

[12] (a) I've it pronounced wrong
            (Susan X., Tyrone).
      (b) She's nearly her course finished
            (Sammy S., Belfast).

The second is an intransitive construction which is formed with a *be* auxiliary and an *en*-participle and is restricted to mutative verbs such as *leave, change, go, die*, as in

[13] I went back to school and all but I'm not too long left
      (Gerry M., Belfast).

A widely commented-on feature of Irish English is the use of a hot-news perfect (PI in Greene's terminology) of the form *be after doing* (= 'have just done'), *eg*:

[14] A young man's only after getting shot out there ('A young man has just got shot out there') (Tilly S., Belfast).

Standard English marks the contrast between indefinite present anterior and past anterior (then-time) by means of the perfect vs preterite distinction (*eg I've been to Canada twice* vs *I was in Canada last year*). Speakers of basic Irish English tend to use the preterite form in both cases, relying instead on adverbial means to signal the aspectual distinction. The following example contains a preterite form being employed in an indefinite present anterior context where a Standard English speaker would be much more likely to use the perfect:

[15] I never saw a gun in my life nor never saw a gun fired
      (Maggie H., Belfast).

As in many languages, extended-now time is signalled in Irish English by a simple or progressive non-past form:

[16] (a) I know his family all me life
            (Bernadette O'H., Lurgan, Armagh).
      (b) Field-worker: Have you always lived here?
            Answer: We're living here seventeen years
                            (Mick C., Belfast).

In summary, vernacular Irish English speech is characterized by the use of five verbal forms or constructions which, in a range of contexts, correspond to the Standard English perfect: hot-news PI, a 'split' perfect PII, an intransitive *be* resultative, a simple or progressive non-past form and the preterite (see Figure 14.1).

Standard form	Tense–aspect meaning	Irish English form
Preterite	Then time	Preterite
	Indefinite anterior	
	Hot-news	PI
Perfect	Resultative	PII (dynamic Vb) *be* Vb-*en* (mutative Vb)
	Extended-now time	Present
Present	Now time	

FIGURE 14.1   Coding of six tense–aspect distinctions in Standard British English and vernacular Irish English.

Table 14.2 presents the results of a preliminary attempt to quantify variability in the use of these forms in northern Irish English. The research is based on fifteen hours of tape-recorded conversation collected from nine urban (Belfast) and fifteen rural (South-west Ulster) speakers (a subset of the populations included in three much larger studies).[4] The figures were arrived at by counting tokens of forms which occurred as exponents of the four aspectual distinctions outlined in [11].

The figures in Table 14.2 reveal a good deal of variability among individual speakers. Some show a clear predominance of non-standard forms (*eg* 59A/3, 49A/2), some a predominance of standard perfect forms (*eg* Davy B., Gordon K., 58A/3), while others show both in more or less equal proportions (*eg* 59A/2 and 48A/2). But the main generalization to emerge from Table 14.2 is that, overall, there is a higher ratio of vernacular to standard forms among rural than among urban speakers. This of course parallels the findings relating to *it*-cleft usage discussed in section 14.3. So it is naturally tempting to seek a similar explanation of the distributional facts in this case. That is, does the higher incidence of non-standard perfect forms in the rural areas reflect a closer historical connection with the Irish substrate? In order to assess the plausibility of this suggestion, it is obviously

TABLE 14.2 Use of the Standard English present perfect and five corresponding non-standard forms in northern Irish English (from Harris 1984).

	PI	PII	be V + en	Preterite	Present	Total non-standard	Standard perfect
Urban speakers							
Maura D.	2	—	2	—	—	5	2
Maggie H.	—	1	—	7	—	7	3
Patsy	—	—	—	—	—	4	4
Mary X.	—	1	—	—	1	3	6
Eddy C.	1	—	—	—	—	1	2
Davy B.	—	—	1	4	—	5	14
Gordon K.	—	—	—	—	1	2	10
Tom M.	—	—	—	—	—	0	5
Maisie B.	—	—	—	—	—	0	4
Total % non-standard forms: 35							
Rural speakers							
59A/3	—	1	—	6	5	12	0
49A/3	—	—	—	—	2	6	0
48A/1	—	2	—	—	1	3	0
58A/1	—	1	—	5	—	7	0
68A/1	—	1	—	—	—	3	0
50A/1	—	1	—	6	—	7	1
49A/2	—	—	3	12	—	17	3
59A/1	—	1	2	9	—	9	2
48A/3	—	—	2	—	—	4	1
68A/3	—	—	4	—	—	4	1
59A/2	—	—	7	3	2	11	12
48A/2	—	2	—	—	—	5	8
68A/2	—	—	1	—	—	2	5
58A/2	—	1	—	—	—	2	8
58A/3	—	—	—	—	—	0	7
Total % non-standard forms: 66							

necessary to look closely at how the four aspectual distinctions mentioned in [11] are coded in Irish.

14.4.3 The Irish 'perfects'

The first thing to note about Irish in this connection is that it lacks a fully grammaticalized perfect form. Like basic Irish English, it does not signal the distinction between then-time and indefinite present anterior time by verbal means. The simple past form is used for both meanings:

[17] Chuaigh   sé   amach
GO+*past* HE   OUT
'He went/has gone out.'

In Irish English PI and PII (illustrated in [14] and [12] respectively) are often claimed to be calques on similar constructions in Irish (*eg* van Hamel 1912; Bliss 1972; Todd 1975; Sullivan 1976). In fact, Greene (1979) employs the same terms to describe them. The parallels between the hot-news PI constructions in the two languages are indeed difficult to ignore:

[18] Tá   sí   tréis   an   bád   a dhíol
BE+*non-past* SHE AFTER THE   BOAT SELLING
Irish English: She's after selling the boat.
'She has just sold the boat.'

(In fact, as Boretzky (1986) points out, the similarity between Irish and Irish English is only partial here. The parallel use of AFTER with some kind of gerund or verbal noun to code hot-news is indeed striking, but the position of the object NP is not the same in each case.) There are also undoubted similarities between Irish English PII and an Irish possessive construction which incorporates a verbal adjective as object complement. (Possession in Irish is expressed prepositionally as 'object-of-possession is at possessor'.)

[19] Tá   an   bád   díolta aici
BE+*non-past* THE BOAT   SOLD AT-HER
Irish English: She has the boat sold.
'She has sold the boat.'

The Irish constituent order NP plus verbal adjective is often assumed to be reflected in the NP plus *en*-participle order of the corresponding Irish English construction. (In fact, I have argued elsewhere (Harris 1985) that the structural parallels extend to their both being analysable as complex statal constructions consisting of a matrix clause indicating possession and an embedded clause containing the object NP, *ie* along the lines of [She has [the boat sold]].)

Irish is also similar to Irish English in employing a simple or periphrastic non-past form to express extended-now time, as in

[20] (a) Tá   sé   marbh le   fada   riamh
         BE+*non-past* HE DEAD WITH LONG-TIME EVER
         'He has been dead for a long time.'

    (b) Tá   sí   ag obair   ó   mhaidin
         BE+*non-past* SHE AT WORKING FROM MORNING
         'She has been working since morning.'

On the face of it, the clear parallels between Irish English and Irish in this area of the tense–aspect system support the substratum case. The evidence is perhaps most convincing in the case of the hot-news PI construction which, to the best of my knowledge, does not occur in any variety of English other than Irish English or Irish-English-derived dialects spoken in the New World. However, a number of considerations point to the conclusion that the evidence relating to the other forms is rather less clear-cut than might appear at first sight.

14.4.4 Earlier English

Virtually all of those who have claimed that the peculiarities of Irish English aspectual usage can be traced to a substratal source have based their conclusions on a straightforward comparison with present-day Standard British English. They make no reference to the fact that, in some cases, very similar patterns of usage are to be found in other regional varieties of English as well as in earlier forms of the standard language. Crucially, there is plenty of evidence to indicate that such patterns were widespread in the seventeenth century, the formative period of Irish English.

The use of the preterite to express indefinite present anterior time, for example, is a widely reported feature of Standard and non-standard American English and is occasionally even encountered in idiomatic Standard British English (see Leech and Svartvik 1975: 67). This was the usual pattern in Old English (*eg* 'Ne seah ic elθeodige' (*Beowulf*, line 336) 'I have never seen foreigners') and was still widespread in the seventeenth century. Among the many examples cited by Visser (1973: 754ff), we find 'You spoke not with her since?' (*Lear*, IV iii 35).

The 'split' PII construction of Irish English is of course structurally identical to the Germanic *Satzklammer*, *eg* Old English *Ic hæfde hine gebundenne* (see Traugott 1972: 93–4). The surface reflex of this construction in modern Standard English generally has a causative, 'indirect passive', or benefactive reading (as in *I had my car stolen* = 'I got someone to steal my car' or 'My car was stolen'). However, statal resultative readings were still common in the seventeenth century, as in 'Have you the lion's part written?' (*Midsummer Night's Dream*, I. ii. 68) and survive to some extent in Scottish and American usage (Kirchner 1952: 402ff). Impressionistically at least, we may say that, with regard to statal resultative readings of the older 'split' perfect, Irish English is distinguished from the latter varieties not so much qualitatively as quantitatively – both in terms of overall frequency of use and in terms of occurrence with a wider range of lexical verbs.

The intransitive *be* resultative of Irish English also has precedents in earlier forms of English. It is well attested in Old English (Visser 1973: 2042ff) and was still in widespread use during the seventeenth century, as in 'The Duke of Buckingham and I are come from visiting his majesty' (*Richard III*, I. iii 32).

Finally, we may note that the use of non-past forms to express extended-now time was apparently once a well-established feature of English. Seventeenth-century examples are not difficult to come by, as in 'Since the youth of the Count's was to-day with my Lady, she is much out of quiet' (*Twelfth Night*, I. i 23). Visser in fact supplies some even later examples, including 'We are here seven months' from James Barrie's *A Rolling Stone* (*c.* 1893). The construction still occurs sporadically in some present-day varieties of American and British English, particularly with the verb *go* (for examples, see Visser 1973: 2042ff).

It is widely accepted, on the basis of documentary evidence, that the present-day present perfect form is a relative newcomer to the English tense–aspect system (Traugott 1972, Visser 1973). As it has become increasingly established over time, it has gradually taken over functions that were previously fulfilled by other verbal forms and constructions, namely the older 'split' perfect, the *be* resultative, the preterite and non-past forms. This change has naturally not affected all varieties of English simultaneously. Some varieties (whether regional dialects or stylistically restricted registers of the standard language) are relatively conservative in that the incoming perfect has not fully established itself over the wide range of aspectual functions associated with the form in most types of Standard English. From this perspective, it is possible to argue that Irish English dialects are simply the most conservative of all in this respect.

In the light of this historical documentary and comparative dialect evidence, the case for substratal transfer in the area of the

Irish English 'perfects' is considerably weakened. It seems reasonable to conclude that, with the notable exception of the hot-news PI construction, the non-standard characteristics of Irish English usage in this particular aspectual subsystem represent retentions of archaic patterns that were once much more widespread in English. This interpretation fits well with quantitative findings, such as those summarized in Table 14.2, which confirm the existence of regional differences within Irish English in this area of aspectual usage. In this case, regional variation can be considered a reflection of the different rates at which individual dialects have participated in changes that have affected the standard. The higher incidence of vernacular forms among rural speakers can thus be taken as an indication that the newer perfect form has had less success in penetrating into more remote regions than in urban areas where normative pressures from the standard language presumably have more impact.

14.5 Conclusion

A few writers have pin-pointed specific features of Irish English which, they allege, show the effects of linguistic universals operating in conditions of language shift (see, for instance, Todd 1975 and Guilfoyle 1983 on the Irish English habitual aspect markers). However, as I have already indicated, the main research effort in Irish English studies has been directed towards proving the substratum case. As far as the research reported in this chapter is concerned, the evidence on clefting does indeed appear to support the latter position. Here the structural and functional characteristics which distinguish basic Irish English from other varieties of English are the very ones it shares with Irish Gaelic.

However, it would be wrong to suppose that the existence of any markedly non-standard Irish English form that has a direct parallel in Irish can immediately be attributed to substratal transfer. That at least is the conclusion forced on us by the evidence relating to the Irish English 'perfects' discussed in section 14.4. The finding that certain 'basilectal' features of Irish English can be traced not to an exclusive substratal source, as has hitherto been assumed, but to an earlier English base is by no means restricted to this particular area of the grammar. The same conclusion has been reached independently for a number of other Irish English features, including the distinctive *do* and *be* habitual aspect markers (Harris 1986) and palatalized reflexes of original velars before historical *a* (Harris 1987). This and other similar evidence relating to the history of contact vernaculars underlines the need to give due consideration to the sociolinguistic diversity which characterizes a superstrate language such as English in conditions of language contact and shift. The exact nature of that diversity cannot be extrapolated from our knowledge of the standard language. Its discovery depends primarily on the application of traditional historical and dialectological research methods. It is surely worth taking the trouble to pursue this line of enquiry before jumping to hasty conclusions about the contribution of substrata or linguistic universals to the evolution of particular features in contact vernaculars.

Of course, evidence relating to the retention of archaisms in contact vernaculars does not necessarily have to be interpreted as directly contradicting the substratist or universalist positions. Already some kind of reasoned synthesis of views appears to be emerging in the substrata-vs-universals debate (see, for instance, the comments in Holm 1986b). And there is no reason why this new consensus should not accommodate the line of research pursued in section 14.4. In fact, the outlines of a compromise between the latter position and the substratum case have already been sketched by a number of authors. Rather than seeking a unique substratal or superstratal source for a particular linguistic feature, it is often more illuminating to regard the two as mutually reinforcing. Several researchers working on Afro-American Englishes have traced particular forms to a convergence of sub- and superstratal inputs (eg Cassidy 1966; Dalby 1972; Rickford and Rickford 1976). The claim is that the integration of certain functions into the grammar of an emergent contact variety may be motivated by the presence of equivalent functions in the substrate language(s); and this process will be reinforced if forms with parallel functions already exist in at least some varieties of the superstrate, standard or non-standard. Applying this account to the Irish English 'perfects' case, we might say that the contribution made by the Irish substratum has been reinforcing or, to use Weinreich's (1953) term, 'preservative' rather than direct and exclusive.

Notes

This is a slightly revised version of a paper that was delivered at the *III Essener Kolloquium über Sprachwandel und seine bestimmenden Faktoren* and published in N. Boretzky, W. Enninger and T. Stolz (eds), 1987, *Bochum-Essener Beiträge zur Sprachwandelforschung* 3, Bochum: Brockmeyer, pp 143–62. My thanks to John Holm for his helpful comments on an earlier draft.

1. In this chapter, I will find it convenient to use the term *contact vernacular* to describe any non-standard language variety that evolves in conditions of large-scale language shift. Applied to English, the term thus includes Anglophone creoles as well as a number of dialects such as Irish English which, although not usually referred to as creoles, nevertheless share with the latter the property of having developed in communities where a subjugated population gives up its native language in favour of that of the colonial power.
2. Within particular regions, this pattern is probably also manifested to a certain extent along the social dimension, with relatively lower-status varieties exhibiting a greater degree of Irish influence. As far as I know, however, this impression has never been checked by empirical research.
3. All of the examples cited in section 14.4.2 are culled from the tape archives of the projects Language Variety and Speech Community in Belfast, and Sociolinguistic Variation and Linguistic Change in Belfast, both funded by the UK Social Science Research Council (grant nos. HR 3771 and HR 5777).
4. The larger studies are the two Belfast sociolinguistic projects mentioned in note 3 and the Tape-Recorded Survey of Hiberno-English Speech (UK Social Science Research Council).

References

ALLEYNE, M. (1980) *Comparative Afro-American*. Ann Arbor: Karoma.
BAILEY, C–J. N. (1982) 'Irish English and Caribbean Black English: another joinder', *American Speech* **57**: 237–9.
BICKERTON, D. (1975) *Dynamics of a Creole System*. Cambridge: Cambridge University Press.
BLISS, A. J. (1972) 'Languages in contact: some problems of Hiberno-English', *Proceedings of the Royal Irish Academy* **72**: 63–82.
BORETZKY, N. (1986) 'Regelentlehnung und Substrateinfluß in Kreolsprachen'. In N. Boretzky, W. Enninger and T. Stolz (eds) *Beiträge zum 2. Essener Kolloquium über Kreolsprachen und Sprachkontakte*. Bochum: Brockmeyer, *pp* 9–39.
CASSIDY, F. G. (1966) Multiple etymologies in Jamaican Creole. *American Speech* **41**: 211–15.
CHRISTIAN BROTHERS (1962) *New Irish Grammar*. Dublin: Fallons.
CLARK, J. M. (1917) *The Vocabulary of Anglo-Irish*. St Gallen: Zollikoler.
DALBY, D. (1972) 'The African element in American English'. In T. Kochman (ed.) *Rappin and Stylin Out*. Urbana: University of Illinois Press, *pp* 170–86.
DE FRÉINE, S. (1977) 'The dominance of the English language in the nineteenth century'. In D. Ó Muirithe (ed.) *The English language in Ireland*. Dublin: Mercier, *pp* 71–87.
EDWARDS, J. (1984) 'Irish and English in Ireland'. In P. Trudgill (ed.) *Language in the British Isles*. Cambridge: Cambridge University Press, *pp* 480–98.

FILPPULA, M. (1982) 'On some thematic and syntactic special features of spoken Hiberno-English', unpublished L.Phil. thesis. Joensuu: University of Joensuu.

FILPPULA, M. (1986) *Some Aspects of Hiberno-English in a Functional Sentence Perspective*. University of Joensuu Publications in the Humanities, 7. Joensuu: University of Joensuu.

GREENE, D. (1979) 'Perfects and perfectives in modern Irish'. *Ériu* **30**: 122–41.

GUILFOYLE, E. (1983) 'Habitual aspect in Hiberno-English', *McGill Working Papers in Linguistics* **1**: 22–32.

HARRIS, J. (1984) 'Syntactic variation and dialect divergence', *Journal of Linguistics* **20**: 303–27.

HARRIS, J. (1985) 'The Hiberno-English *I've it eaten* construction: what is it and where does it come from?' In D. Ó Baoill (ed.) *Papers on Irish English*. Dublin: Cumann na Teangeolaíochta Feidhmí, *pp* 36–52.

HARRIS, J. (1986) 'Expanding the susperstrate: habitual aspect markers in Atlantic Englishes', *English World-Wide* **7**: 171–99.

HARRIS, J. (1987) 'On doing comparative reconstruction with genetically unrelated languages'. In A. G. Ramat, O. Carruba and G. Bernini (eds) *Papers from the VIIth International Conference on Historical Linguistics, Pavia, September 1985*, Amsterdam: Benjamins, *pp* 267–82.

HENRY, P. L. (1957) *An Anglo-Irish Dialect of North Roscommon*. Dublin: University College Dublin.

HOLM, J. A. (1986A) 'The spread of English in the Caribbean area'. In M. Görlach and J. A. Holm (eds) *Varieties of English Around the World: Focus on the Caribbean*. Amsterdam: Benjamins, *pp* 1–22.

HOLM, J. A. (1986B) 'Substrate diffusion'. In Muysken and Smith (1986) *pp* 259–78.

HUGHES, J. P. (1966) 'The Irish language and the 'brogue': a study in substratum', *Word* **22**: 257–75.

KIRCHNER, G. (1952) *Die zehn Hauptverben des Englischen im Britischen und Amerikanischen*. Halle: Niemeyer.

LEECH, G. and SVARTVIK, J. (1975) *A Communicative Grammar of English*. London: Longman.

MUYSKEN, P. and SMITH, N. (eds) (1986) *Substrata Versus Universals in Creole Genesis: Papers from the Amsterdam Creole Workshop, April 1985*. Amsterdam: Benjamins.

NÍ GHALLCHÓIR, C. (1981) 'Aspects of bilingualism in northwest Donegal'. In M. V. Barry (ed.) *Aspects of English Dialects in Ireland*. Belfast: Institute of Irish Studies, Queen's University, *pp* 142–70.

RICKFORD, J. R. (1974) 'The insights of the mesolect.' In D. De Camp and I. F. Hancock (eds) *Pidgins and Creoles: Current Trends and Prospects*. Washington, DC: Georgetown University Press, *pp* 92–117.

RICKFORD, J. R. (1986) 'Social contact and linguistic diffusion: Hiberno-English and New World Black English', *Language* **62**: 245–90.

RICKFORD, J. R. and RICKFORD, A. E. (1976) 'Cut-eye and suck-teeth: African words and gestures in new world guise', *Journal of American Folklore* **89**: 294–309.

STENSON, N. (1981) *Studies in Irish Syntax*. Tübingen: Gunther Narr.

SULLIVAN, J. P. (1976) 'The genesis of Hiberno-English: a socio-historical account', unpublished Ph.D. dissertation. New York: Yeshiva University.

SULLIVAN, J. P. (1980) 'The validity of literary dialect: evidence from the theatrical portrayal of Hiberno-English forms', *Language in Society* 9: 195–219.

TODD, L. (1975) 'Base-form and substratum: two case studies of English in contact', unpublished Ph.D. thesis. Leeds: University of Leeds.

TRAUGOTT, E. C. (1972) *A History of English Syntax*. New York: Holt, Rinehart & Winston.

VAN HAMEL, A. G. (1912) 'On Anglo-Irish syntax', *Englische Studien* 45: 272–92.

VISSER, F. TH. (1973) *An Historical Syntax of the English Language*, 4 vols. Leiden: Brill.

WEINREICH, U. (1953) *Languages in Contact*. The Hague: Mouton.

Part four

Non-finite verb forms

Chapter 15

Non-finite verb forms in English dialects

J. K. Chambers and Peter Trudgill

When we turn our attention to English non-finite verbs, the forms which cannot be marked for tense or mood, we notice that the standard dialects reveal relatively little variation. The infinitive occurs invariably as the base form of the verb with the marker 'to', and the present participle occurs invariably as the base form with the suffix '-ing'. The present participle suffix is heard in a couple of well-known variants, as [ɪŋ] or [ɪn] (sometimes [ən], and, increasingly in North America, [in]). Although these variants have usually been considered purely phonological, Houston shows (in Ch. 18 below) that they have grammatical correlates as well.

Only the past participle shows much variation in Standard English. In the great majority of forms, the past participle is identical to the past tense form:

Infinitive	Present participle	Past participle	Past tense
(to) walk	(be) walking	(have) walked	walked
save	saving	saved	saved
end	ending	ended	ended

Even when the past tense form is 'irregular', the past participle is usually identical to it, as, for example, 'hit' takes no ending at all and 'find' and 'sit' replace the stem vowel, in both forms:

(to) hit	(be) hitting	(have) hit	hit
find	finding	found	found
sit	sitting	sat	sat

For about sixty verbs in Standard English, however, this identity of form between the past tense and past participle does not hold. Some of these are among the most frequently used verbs, such as:

Infinitive	Present participle	Past participle	Past tense
(to) sing	(be) singing	(have) sung	sang
see	seeing	seen	saw
eat	eating	eaten	ate
drink	drinking	drunk	drank
blow	blowing	blown	blew

Nevertheless, the tendency towards identical past tense and past participle forms is exerting a powerful influence on language change in English, as it has for many centuries. In standard dialects, several verbs now have past participle variants (perhaps more common in North America than in Britain) which are the same as the past tense forms alongside the traditionally different forms:

mow	mowing	mown/mowed	mowed
prove	proving	proven/proved	proved
saw	sawing	sawn/sawed	sawed

Other things being equal, we expect that this variability will be resolved in the next few generations as the traditional forms (*mown*, *proven*, *sawn*) become less frequent and ultimately disappear.

In non-standard mainstream dialects, the change towards identical forms has gone further. As discussed in Chapter 6 above and by Ihalainen in Chapter 9, some of these dialects have made changes not yet reflected in the standard dialects, replacing *taken* by *took*, for example, as in *They've took the net to the river*. A very interesting tendency is indicated in sentences such as *We seen the papers* and *John done it*. Here, the past participle form replaces the past tense form, whereas the overwhelming tendency in the history of the language has been just the opposite.

The present-day variability in past participle forms is, in one sense, the residue of the Old English distinction between weak and strong conjugations. Although the infinitive and present participle forms appear to be virtually invariable today, they too have undergone changes since the Old English period. As Gachelin points out in Chapter 16, the Wessex suffix -y can be traced to the Middle English infinitive ending -ie(n), from the Old English second conjugation infinitive marker -ian. The line of descent, however, is far from direct. In Wessex, as Gachelin carefully shows, the -y suffix occurs optionally not only on infinitives but on any uninflectable verb form (ie following a modal or *do*) whenever a direct object does not follow it. It has become a marker of surface intransitivity. He also shows that o'/ov occurs in Wessex as a marker of surface transitivity between present participles (and, 'marginally', some other verbal forms) and direct objects.

Gachelin's data includes, incidentally, several occurrences of present participles with *a*-prefixes, as in the line from a Wessex-folk poem, 'To work all day *a-meäken* haÿ'. These constructions are subjected to close study by Wolfram, in Chapter 17, using a corpus from the speech of Appalachia, an ocean away from Wessex. Much of the commentary on the *a*-prefixing constructions has been impressionistic. Wolfram's large sample from the south-western region of West Virginia, gathered in collaboration with Christian, who uses the same database for her work on personal datives in Chapter 3, allows him to test the claims of his precursors and propose an interlocking set of syntactic and phonological constraints.

Wolfram's syntactic analysis leads him to distinguish -*ing* forms that are verbal or adverbial, which allow *a*-prefixing, from those which are nominal or adjectival, which do not. Houston's Chapter 18 on the pronunciation variants [ɪŋ] and [ɪn] for -*ing* requires her to make a similar distinction in the categories of -*ing* words, based on the frequency with which the velar nasal occurs with each category. For Houston, however, the nominal and verbal categories cannot be treated as discrete but must be considered as poles on a continuum. Her data, mainly from British working-class speakers, reveal a tendency for the more 'noun-like' forms to occur with the velar nasal and the more 'verb-like' forms to occur with the alveolar nasal. That is, the velar nasal occurs less frequently as one moves down the continuum from proper names (*Corning*) to derived nominals (*the shooting*) and monomorphemic nouns (*morning*), to gerunds (*joggin' 4 miles can be harmful*) and progressives (*he was runnin'*).

Houston's discovery that the pronunciation of -*ing* correlates with the grammatical subcategory to which it is attached adds a new dimension to studies made on the assumption that the pronunciation variants are purely phonetic. The grammatical correlates, as she outlines in the second half of her chapter, apparently perpetuate a historical distinction in the verbal and nominal endings. In standard dialects today, at least in more formal styles, both of these have fallen together as [ɪŋ]. In non-standard dialects, the distinction between them is more or less retained as [ɪn] in the verbal forms and [ɪŋ] in the nominal forms.

Chapter 16

Transitivity and intransitivity in the dialects of South-west England

Jean-Marc Gachelin

Wakelin (1977: 125) has pointed out that 'syntax is an unwieldy subject which dialectologists have fought shy of'. This brushing aside of dialect syntax is regrettable because the study of grammatical variation can shed light on the workings of any language, and thereby enrich general linguistics. The present chapter deals with an area of dialect syntax – transitivity in south-west of England dialects – and attempts to characterize and explain, synchronically and diachronically, its salient features.

Gross (1969: 72) has written that 'Les notions "transitif" et "object direct" sont complètement inutiles pour les descriptions grammaticales.' We prefer the moderation of Kilby (1984: 40), who simply admits that the notion of direct object (DO) 'is not at all transparent in its usage'. The problem, therefore, should be not so much to discard but rather to improve our notions of transitivity and intransitivity. In this regard, the dialects of South-west England are important and interesting.

16.1 A description of transitivity and intransitivity in the dialects of South-west England

When compared with the corresponding standard language, any geographical variety may be characterized by three possibilities: (a) identity; (b) archaism (due to slower evolution); and (c) innovation. Interestingly enough, it is not uncommon in syntax for (b) and (c) to combine if a given dialect draws extensively on a secondary aspect of an older usage. This is true of two features which are highly characteristic of the South-west and completely absent in contemporary Standard English.

16.1.1 Infinitive+y

One of these characteristics is mentioned by Wakelin (1977: 120, 1984: 82), the optional addition of the -y ending to the infinitive of any real intransitive verb or any transitive verb not followed by a DO, namely object-deleting verbs (ODVs) and ergatives. The use of this ending is not highlighted in the *Survey of English Dialects* (*SED*, Orton and Wakelin 1967–68). It is only indirectly, when reading about relative pronouns, that we come upon *There iddn (=isn't) many (who) can* sheary *now*, recorded in Devon (Orton and Wakelin 1967–68: 1155). However, Widen (1949: 72f) gives the following examples heard in Dorset: *farmy, flickery, hoopy* ('to call'), *hidy, milky, panky* ('to pant'), *rooty* (talking of a pig), *whiny*. Three of these verbs are strictly intransitive (*flickery, panky, whiny*), the others being ODVs. Wright (1905: §439) also mentions this characteristic, chiefly in connection with Devon, Somerset and Dorset.

In the last century, Barnes made use of the -y ending in his Dorset poems (see Jones 1962), both when the infinitive appears after *to*:

reäky = 'rake' (*p* 116, *v* 26);
skimmy (*p* 119, *v* 66);
drashy = 'thresh' (*p* 162, *v* 48);
reely (*p* 168, *v* 32);

and after a modal (as in the example from the *SED*):

Mid (=may) happy housen *smoky* round/The church (*p* 193, *v* 35–6).
The cat vell zick an' woulden *mousy* (*p* 225, *v* 38).

But infin.+y can also be found after *do* (auxiliary), which in South-west dialects is more than a mere 'signal of verbality' (Samuels 1972: 174), serving as a tense-marker as well as a person-marker (*do* everywhere except for *dost*, 2nd pers. sing.). Instead of being emphatic, this *do* can express the progressive aspect or more often the durative-habitual (=imperfective) aspect, exactly like the imperfect of Romance languages (see Ihalainen, Ch. 12, on this topic). Here are a few examples culled from Barnes's poems:

Our merry sheäpes *did jumpy* (*p* 85, *v* 23).
 When I *do pitchy*, 'tis my pride (*p* 116, *v* 27 – for the meaning of the verb, *cf pitch-fork*).
How gaÿ the paths be where we *do strolly* (*p* 123, *v* 17).

Besides ODVs and intransitive verbs, there is also an ergative:

  doors *did slammy* (*p* 185, *v* 18).

In the imperative, infin. *-y* only appears with a negative:

  don't sobby! (*p* 187, *v* 1).

The optional use of the *-y* ending is an advantage in dialect poetry for metre or rhyme:

  Vor thine wull *peck*, an' mine wull *grubby* (rhyming with *snubby*, *p* 231, *v* 180).

And this ending probably accounts for a phonetic peculiarity of South-west dialects, namely the apocope of *to arguy* (the former dialect pronunciation of *to argue*), *to carry* and *to empty*, reduced to *to arg*, *to car* and *to empt* (Rogers 1979: 38, 72).

In the grammatical part of his *Glossary of the Dorset Dialect*, Barnes (1970: 25) insists on the aspectual connection between *do* and infin.+*y*:

> Belonging to this use of the free infinitive *y*-ended verbs, is another kindred one, the showing of a repetition or habit of doing as 'How the dog *do* jumpy', i-e keep jumping. 'The child *do* like to whippy', amuse himself with whipping. 'Idle chap, he'll *do* nothèn but vishy, (spend his time in fishing), if you do leâve en alwone'. 'He *do* markety', he usually attends market.

Barnes (1970: 25) also quotes a work by Jennings (1825) in which this South-west feature was also described:

> Another peculiarity is that of attaching to many of the common verbs in the infinitive mode as well as to some other parts of different conjugations, the letter *-y*. Thus it is very common to say 'I can't sewy', I can't nursy', 'he can't reapy', 'he can't sawy', as well as 'to sewy, to nursy, to reapy, to sawy', etc; but never, I think, without an auxiliary verb, or the sign of the infinitive *to*.

Barnes (1970: 25) claimed, too, that the collocation of infin.+*y* and the DO was unthinkable: 'We may say, "Can ye *zewy*?" but never "Wull ye *zewy* up theäse zêam?" "Wull ye *zew* up theäse zêam" would be good Dorset.'

Elworthy (1877) also mentions the opposition heard in Somerset between *I do* dig *the garden* and *Every day, I do* diggy *for three hours* (quoted by Jespersen 1971: 215, n. 4; and by Rogers, 1979: 37). Concerning the so-called 'free infinitive', Wiltshire-born Rogers (1979: 37) comments that 'it is little heard now, but was common in the last century', which tallies with the lack of examples in the *SED*. (This point is also confirmed by Ihalainen, Ch. 9.) Rogers (1979: 38) is quite surprised to read of a science-fiction play (BBC, 15 March 1978) entitled 'Stargazy in Zummerland', describing a future world in which the population was divided between industrial and agricultural workers, the latter probably using some form of south-western speech, following a time-honoured stage tradition already perceptible in *King Lear* (disguised as a rustic, Edgar speaks broad Somerset).

To sum up, after *to*, *do* (auxiliary), or a modal, the formula of the 'free infinitive' is

intr. V → infin. + $-y/\emptyset$

where 'intr.' implies genuine intransitives, ODVs and even ergatives. As a dialect-marker, -*y* is now on the wane, being gradually replaced by $\emptyset$ due to contact with Standard English.

16.1.2 *Of* + DO

The other typical feature of south-western dialects (and also of Sussex) is not mentioned by Wakelin, although it stands out much more clearly in the *SED* data. This is the optional use of *o'/ov* (occasionally *on*) between a transitive verb and its DO. Here are some of the many examples. Stripping the feathers off a dead chicken (Orton and Wakelin 1967–68: 458–9) is called:

pickin/pluckin *ov* it (Brk-loc. 3);
trippin *o'* en (= it) (D-loc. 6);
pickin *o'* en (Do-loc. 3);
pluckin(g) *on en* – (W-loc. 9; Sx-loc. 2).

Catching fish, especially trout, with one's hand (Orton and Wakelin 1967–68: 483–4) is called:

ticklin *o'/ov* em (=them) (So-loc. 13; W-loc. 2, 8; D-loc. 2, 7, 8; Do-loc. 2–5; Ha-loc. 4);
gropin *o'/ov* em (D-loc. 4, 6);
ticklin *on* em (W-loc. 3, 4; Ha-loc. 6; Sx-loc. 3);
tickle *o'* em (Do-loc. 1) (note the absence of -*in(g)*).

The confusion between *of* and *on* is frequent in dialects, but although *on* may occur where *of* is expected, the reverse is impossible. The occasional use of *on* instead of *of* of is therefore unimportant. What really matters is the occurrence of *of*, *o'* or *ov* between a transitive verb and the DO. The presence of the -*in(g)* ending should also attract our attention: it occurs in all the examples except *tickle o' em*, which is exceptional since, when the *SED* informants used an infinitive in their answers, their syntax was usually identical with that of Standard English, *ie* without *of* occurring before the DO: *glad to see you, (he wants to) hide it* (Orton and Wakelin 1967–68: 962–3, 1010).

Following Jespersen, Lyons (1968/71: 350–1) makes a distinction between real transitives (*I hit you*: action → goal) and verbs which are only syntactically transitives (*I hear you*: goal ← action). It is a pity that the way informants were asked questions for the *SED* ('What do we do with them? – Our eyes/ears') does not enable us to treat the transitive verbs *see* Orton and Wakelin 1967–68: 652 3 and *hear* (Orton and Wakelin 1967–68: 66) other than as ODVs.

The use of *of* as an operator between a transitive verb and its DO was strangely enough never described by Barnes, and is casually dismissed as an 'otiose *of*' by the authors of the *SED*, even though nothing can really be 'otiose' in any language system. Rogers (1979: 41) points out that 'Much more widely found formerly, it is now confined to sentences where the pronouns *en*, *it* and *em* are the objects.' This is obvious in the *SED* materials, as, incidentally, it is in these lines by Barnes (Jones 1962: 236, *vv* 8–9):

> To work all day *a-meäken haÿ*/Or *pitchen o't.*

Nevertheless, even if his usage is in conformity with present syntax, it is important to add that, when Barnes was alive, *o/ov* could precede *any* DO (*a-meäken* ov *haÿ* would equally have been possible). What should also be noted in his poetry is the extremely rare occurrence of *o'/ov* after a transitive verb with no *-en* (=*-ing*) ending, which, as we just saw, is still very rare in modern speech (Jones 1962: 484, *v* 62; 486, *v* 48):

> Zoo I don't *mind o'* leäven it to-morrow.
> Zoo I don't *mind o'* leäven o't to-morrow.

The second line shows a twofold occurrence of *o'* after two transitive verbs, one with and one without *-en*.

This *-en* ending can be a marker of a verbal noun, a gerund or a present participle (as part of a progressive aspect form or on its own), and *o'* may follow in each case. (From Jones 1962 unless otherwise stated).

VERBAL NOUN

> *My own a-decken ov my own* ('my own way of dressing my darling', *p* 517, *v* 16).

This is the same usage as in Standard English *he doesn't like my driving of his car.*

GERUND
That wer vor hetten o'n ('that was for hitting him', *p* 186, *v* 75)
. . . *little chance/O' catchen o'n* (*p* 365, *vv* 33–4).
I be never the better vor zee-en o' you (*p* 471, *v* 4).
The addition of *o'* to a gerund is optional: *Vor grinden any corn vor bread* (*p* 467, *v* 14) is similar to Standard English.

PROGRESSIVE ASPECT
As I wer readen ov a stwone (about a headstone, *p* 132, *v* 1).

Rogers (1979: 41) gives two examples of the progressive aspect:

I be stackin' on 'em up
I were a-peeling of the potatoes (with a different spelling).

PRESENT PARTICIPLE ON ITS OWN
To vind me stannen in the cwold,/A-keepen up o' Chris'mas (*p* 177, *vv* 19–20)
After any present participle, the use of *o'* is also optional:
Where vo'k be out a-meäken haÿ (Jones 1962: 114, *v* 2).

The general formula is thus:

trans. V → V + *o'*/∅

which can also be read as

MV (main verb) → trans. V + *o'*/∅ + DO.

Here, *o'* stands for *o'* (the most common form), *ov* and even *on*. In modern usage, the DO, which could be a noun or noun phrase in Barnes's day and age, appears from the *SED* materials to be restricted to personal pronouns. For modern dialects, the formula thus reads:

MV → trans. V + *o'*/∅ + pers. pron.

The *o'* is here a transitivity operator which, exactly like an accusative ending in a language with case declensions, disappears in the passive. Consequently, the phenomenon under discussion here has to be distinguished from that of prepositional verbs, which require the retention of the preposition in the passive:

We have thought *of* all the possible snags. →
All the possible snags have been thought *of*.

The use of *o'* as a transitivity operator in active declaratives is also optional, which represents another basic difference from prepositional verbs.

A similar problem can be found in French syntax, though prepositional verbs as such do not exist in this language. Gross (1969: 65) points out in this connection that 'le critère de présence ou d'absence de préposition est très insuffisant', preferring the criterion of an interrogative transformation:

[1] Il mange *des gâteaux* → *Que* mange-t-il?
[2] Il rêve *de gâteaux* → *De quoi* rêve-t-il?

Exactly the same opposition, interestingly enough, applies in south-western dialects also:

[3] He is (a-) eäten *o' ceäkes* → *What* is he (a-) eäten?
[4] He is (a-) dreämen *o'ceäkes* → *What* is he (a-) dreämen *ov*?

What remains a preposition in [2] and [4] works as a syntactic operator in [1] and [3], in French (the partitive article) as well as in south-western dialects (the link between a transitive verb and its DO). The compulsory deletion of the operator *o'* in questions relating to the DO demonstrates the importance here of the word order (V + *o'* + DO), as does also the similar triggering of deletion by passives.

Though now used in a more restricted way, *ie* before personal pronouns only, this syntactic feature is better preserved in the modern dialects than the -*y* ending of intransitive verbs, but, in so far as it is only optional, it is easy to detect the growing influence of Standard English.

16.2 Diachrony as an explanation of these features

Although the above description has not been purely synchronic, since it cites differences in usage between the nineteenth and twentieth centuries, it is actually only by looking back at even earlier stages of the language that we can gain any clear insights into why the dialects have developed in this way.

Both Widen (1949: 72–3) and Wakelin (1977: 120; 1984 : 82) remind us that the originally strictly morphological -*y* ending has since developed into a syntactic feature. It is a survival of the Middle English infinitive ending -*ie(n)*, traceable to the -*ian* suffix of the second class of Old English weak verbs (OE *milcian* → ME *milkie(n)* → south-west dial. *milky*). Subsequently, -*y* has been analogically extended to other types of verbs in south-west dialects under certain syntactic conditions: in the absence of any DO, through sheer impossibility (intransitive verb) or due to the speaker's choice (ODV or ergative). The only survival of medieval usage is the impossibility of a verb form like *milky* being anything other than an infinitive. Note that this cannot be labelled an archaism, since the standard language has never demonstrated this particular syntactic specialization.

So far no explanation seems to have been advanced for the origin of 'otiose *of*', and yet it is fairly easy to resort to diachrony in order to explain this syntactic feature. Let us start, however, with contemporary Standard English:

[5] They sat, sing*ing* a shanty. (present participle on its own)
[6] They *are* sing*ing* a shanty. (progressive aspect)
[7] I like them/their sing*ing* a shanty. (gerund)
[8] I like their sing*ing of* a shanty. (verbal noun)

Here [7] and [8] are considered nominalizations from a synchronic point of view. As far as [6] is concerned, Barnes (1970: 23) reminds his readers that the OE nominalization *ic waes on huntunge* ('I was in the process of hunting', cf Aelfric's *Colloquim*: *fui in venatione*) is the source of modern *I was hunting*, via an older structure *I was (a-) hunting* which is preserved in many dialects, the optional verbal prefix *a-* being what remains of the preposition *on* (see Wolfram, Ch. 17).

The nominal nature of V-*ing* is still well established in the verbal noun (with the use of *of* in particular), and it is here that the starting-point of a chain reaction lies. Hybrid structures (verbal nouns/gerunds) appeared as early as Middle English, as in

bi putt*yng* forth *of* whom so it were (1386 Petition of Mercers)

and similar gerunds followed by *of* were still a possibility in Elizabethan English:

Rend not my heart for nam*ing of* my Christ (Marlowe, *Doctor Faustus)*

together with verbal nouns not followed by any *of*:

. . . as *the* putt*ing* him clean out of his humour (B. Jonson, *Every Man out of his Humour).*

Having been extended from the verbal noun to the gerund, *of* also eventually spread to the progressive aspect in the sixteenth and seventeenth centuries, at a time when the V-*ing* + *of* sequence became very widespread in Standard English:

Are you cross*ing of* yourself? (Marlowe, *Doctor Faustus*).
He is hear*ing of* a cause (Shakespeare, *Measure for Measure*).

She is tak*ing of* her last farewell (Bunyan, *The Pilgim's Progress*).

However, what is definitely an archaism in Standard English has been preserved in south-western dialects, which have gone even further and also added an optional *o'* to the present participle used on its own (*ie* other than in the progressive aspect). Moreover, there is even a tendency, as we have seen, to use *o'* after a transitive verb without the *-en* (=-*ing*) ending. This tendency, which remains slight, represents the ultimate point of a chain reaction that can be portrayed as follows:

Use of o' in the environment following:

(A)	(B)	(C)	(D)
verbal noun →gerund	→ *be* + V-*ing*	→ pres. part.	→ V

V-*ing*

(A) evolution from Middle English to the Renaissance;
(B) evolution typical of English in the sixteenth and seventeenth centuries;
(C) evolution typical of south-western dialects;
(D) marginal tendency in south-western dialects.

The dialect usage is more than a mere syntactic archaism: not only have the south-western dialects preserved stages (A) and (B); they are also highly innovative in stages (C) and (D).

16.3 More about *of* + DO

Though this study deals primarily with dialect usage, it is tempting to compare this feature with another use of *of* (before a DO) in the history of English.

Stressing the tendency of the French prepositions *à* and *de* to become morpho-syntactic operators, Lafont (1978: 283) considers the former as 'le soutien (=support) du mouvement syntaxique', and the latter as its 'inverseur', hence *je pense à ton père* versus *je me souviens de ton père*. As far as the English verbal noun is concerned, (a) *the typing of your secretary* is subject-orientated (your *secretary* types), whereas (b) *the typing of your manuscript* is object-orientated (X types your *manuscript*). *Of* is indeed a syntactic inverter in (a) but certainly not in (b), and it is the latter that accounts for the dialect structure V-*en* + *o'* + DO in all its varieties.

The French partitive article *de* is not an inverter either: *je mange du pain/je ne mange pas de pain* only adds a nuance to *je (ne) mange (pas) le pain*, but the word order remains unchanged. Oddly enough, this brings us, finally, to a feature of biblical English, namely the tentative use of a partitive *of* after a transitive verb, exactly like Italian and especially French, following Vulgar Latin which resorted to the preposition *de* (+ablative). Thus the Vulgate offers *catelli edunt de micis*, a perfect calque of the Greek original (*apò* + genitive), hence *the dogs eat of the crumbs* (Mat. 15: 27) in the Authorized Version. Elsewhere, *sede et comede de venatione mea* (Gen. 27: 19) reads as *sit and eat of my venison*, and *Date nobis de oleo vestro* (Mat. 25: 8– Greek text: *ek* + genitive) accounts for *Give us of your oil*. Though the Revised Standard Version has here *Give us some of your oil*, it has none the less preserved the second of those three occurrences of *of* (*eat of my game*), a syntactic archaism due to the importance of calques in religious translations. An older use of a similar *of* can also be found in Middle English, where it is no doubt ascribable to French grammar: talking of the Prioress, Chaucer wrote *Of smale houndes had she*, . . . (Prologue to the *Canterbury Tales*. *v* 146), meaning 'she had *a number of/some* little dogs'.

Within the framework of transitivity, the only point in common between dialect *o'* (+DO) and the marginal oddity of Middle and Renaissance English, the partitive *of* as in Vulgar Latin and French, is their role as syntactic supports. This notion implies that both partitive *of* and dialect *o'* are not prepositions but syntactic operators. In fact, dialect *o'* represents a good example of both an interesting diachronic development, as described above, and a synchronic cline or squish (see Houston, Ch. 18): following a verbal noun, *o' can* be analysed as a preposition; in the rare cases where it occurs after an infinitive it is a very clear syntactic operator; as we move through the intervening categories along the cline, however – gerunds, progressives, present participles on their own – *o'* becomes less and less a preposition and more and more a syntactic operator. Forms such as *tickle on 'em* represent the end point of a diachronic development, and the ultimate in absence of prepositional characteristics.

References

BARNES, W. (1970) *A Glossary of the Dorset Dialect (with a Grammar)*. Dorchester, London, 1886. Guernsey: The Toucan Press.

ELWORTHY, F. T. (1877) *An Outline of the Grammar of the Dialect of West Somerset*. London.

GROSS, M. (1969) 'Remarques sur la notion d'objet direct en français', *Langue Francaise*, no. 1, Feb., 63–73.

JENNINGS, J. (1825) *Observations on Some of the Dialects of the West of England, Particularly Sommersetshire*. London.

JESPERSEN, O. (1971) *La philosophie de la grammaire*, Paris: Editions de Minuit.

JONES, B. (1962) *The Poems of W. Barnes*. London: Centaur Press, 2 vols.

KILBY, D. (1984) *Descriptive Syntax and the English Verb*. London: Croom Helm.

LAFONT, R. (1978) *Le travail et la langue*. Paris: Flammarion. 1978.

LYONS, J. (1968/71) *Theoretical Linguistics*. Cambridge: Cambridge University Press.

ORTON, H. and WAKELIN, M. F. (1967–68) *Survey of English Dialects*, vol. 4: *The Southern Counties*. Leeds: E. J. Arnold.

ROGERS, N. (1979) *Wessex dialect*. Bradford on Avon: Moonraker Press.

SAMUELS, M. L. (1972) *Linguistic evolution*. Cambridge: Cambridge University Press.

WAKELIN, M. F. (1977) *English Dialects. An introduction*. London: Athlone Press, 1972, rev. edn 1977.

WAKELIN, M. F. (1984) 'Rural dialects in England' In P. Trudgill (ed.) *Language in the British Isles*. Cambridge: Cambridge University Press, pp 70–93.

WIDEN, B. (1949) *Studies on the Dorset Dialect*. Lund: Lund Studies in English 16.

WRIGHT, J. (1905) *The English Dialect Grammar*. Oxford: Oxford University Press.

Chapter 17

Towards a description of *a*-prefixing in Appalachian English

Walt Wolfram

Of the variety of linguistic forms found in the Appalachian mountain range, perhaps the one that holds the most linguistic interest is the *a*-prefix that occurs with *-ing* participial forms.[1] Speakers in the area use sentences like the following:

> And John Boy, he come *a-runnin'* out there and got shot. [44: 6][2]
> It was a dreadful sight; fire was *a-flamin'* everything. [16: (434)]
> He just kept *a-beggin'* and *a-cryin'* and *a-wantin'* to go out. [83: 18]

Although forms such as these have been found in a number of varieties of American English, they are, according to Atwood (1953: 35), most frequently found in the rural varieties of the Appalachian mountain range.

What is referred to here as '*a*-prefixing' (since the *a*- is considered structurally to be a prefix attached to the following participial form) is a linguistic phenomenon with solid historical roots in the history of the English language. Krapp (1925: vol. 1; 268) is just one of many writers who note this form in the development of English:

> A very frequent syntactical form of contemporary popular speech is that which puts an *a* before every present participle, especially after *go*, as in *to go a-fishing, bye baby bunting, daddy's gone a-hunting,* etc. In phrases like these, the construction is historical, the *a*- being a weakened form of the Old English preposition *on* in unstressed position, and *fishing, hunting,* etc., being originally verbal nouns which have been assimilated in form and, to a considerable extent, in feeling, to present participles. Starting with these phrases, however, the *a*- has been prefixed to genuine present participles, after forms of *to be* and other verbs, with the result that in popular speech almost every word ending in *-ing* has a sort of prefix, *a*-.

Although the status of *a*-prefixing as an archaism is relatively secure and its historical source seems to be fairly well documented, its current use has not been analysed in detail. In most cases, *a*-prefixing is considered to be merely an insignificant alternant of its non-prefixed counterpart, an older form that has now become socially stigmatized in some settings. The form is simply added to an inventory of socially or regionally diagnostic linguistic variables without any attention to its structural details. As we shall see, however, some aspects of *a*-prefixing can be explained only by appealing to several levels of language organization, but these emerge only after a rigorous, detailed analysis.

17.1 The sample

To provide an adequate database for the analysis of *a*-prefixing, many tape-recorded samples have been obtained from Mercer and Monroe counties, located in the south-western part of West Virginia (Wolfram and Christian 1975). This area is in the heartland of Appalachia and therefore should be representative of a considerably broader area. The two counties also represent the two life-styles most typical of rural Appalachia. Monroe County is largely agricultural, whereas the economy of Mercer County centres on the mining industry.

In these two counties, over 100 tape-recorded, spontaneous-conversation interviews were conducted with informants representing five age levels: 7–11, 12–14, 15–18, 20–40, and over 40. Most of the informants were lower socio-economic class according to current sociological indices used to assess status. They were all interviewed by field-workers from the area, non-linguists who were trained to do sociolinguistic interviews. Conversations were flexible but typically related to local interests; themes included childhood games, hunting, fishing, ghost stories, the mining industry and local farming customs. These spontaneous conversations, of approximately one hour each, serve as the primary corpus for the analysis that follows.

In addition to the more than 300 examples of *a*-prefixing extracted from the primary corpus, the corpora of Hackenberg (1972) and Feagin (1976) have been checked as secondary data sources. Most of the examples cited here are quite similar to those found in these studies, which were conducted in different regions of Appalachia. If there is diversity in the use of *a*-prefixing, it should have been revealed by such a comparison, particularly with Feagin's study of the southernmost part of Appalachia extending into Alabama. It would appear, then, that the observations about *a*-prefixing in the present study have much wider applicability than the counties where the data were collected.

In the account that follows, I discuss *a*-prefixing in terms of its syntactic privileges, its phonological constraints and its semantic content. An adequate description of the structure and function of the form must deal with these levels of organization.

17.2 Syntactic properties of *a*-prefixing

Unfortunately, the common view of the syntactic properties of *a*-prefixed participles seems to have been represented by Krapp (1925: Vol. 2, 268) when he noted that 'in popular speech almost every word ending in *-ing* has a sort of prefix, *a*-'. Such a broad claim is clearly unwarranted, as will become obvious from the evidence presented below, and there is probably good reason to believe that it has never been the case in English. There are clear-cut syntactic contexts where it is permissible to attach *a*- to forms ending in *-ing;* but there are also syntactic contexts where it is clearly not permissible to do so.

To begin with, *a*-prefixing occurs most commonly with progressives, whether past tense, non-past tense or *be + ing* forms whose tense is realized elsewhere in the main verb phrase. Its occurrence with progressives is illustrated by sentences such as these:

I know he was *a-tellin'* the truth, but still I was *a-comin'* home.
[83: 1]
My cousin had a little brown pony, and we was *a-ridin'* it one day.
[124: 19]
Well, she's *a-gettin'* the black lung now, ain't she? [83: 25]
And he says, 'Who's *a-stompin'* on my bridge?' [16: (610)]
This man'd catch 'em behind the neck, and they'd just be *a-rattlin'*.
[28: 25]
He'll forget to spit, and he'll cut, and it'll just be *a-runnin'*,
    a-drippin' off his chin when he gets to catch them. [146: 25]

Another syntactic context in which *a*-prefixed forms can be found is with movement verbs such as *come, go,* and *take off*. In these cases, the participial *-ing* form functions as a type of adverbial complement to the verb:

All of a sudden a bear come *a-runnin'*, and it come *a-runnin'*
    towards him, and he shot it between the eyes. [44: 18]
And then I took off *a-ridin'* on the minibike. [4: 21]
They wasn't in there no more, and I went down there *a-huntin'* for
    'em [44: 20]

There are also cases in which *a*-prefixing occurs with verbs of continuing or starting, especially *keep*, but also sometimes *start, stay, get to* and so forth:

> He just kep' *a-beggin'* and *a-cryin'* and *a-wantin'* to go out. [83: 18]
> Then send the rope back down; just keep *a pullin'* it up 'til we got it built. [124: 2]
> You just look at him and he starts *a-bustin'* out laughing at you. [80: (683)]
> And we'd get plowed, and we'd get to *laughin'* and *a-gigglin'*. [85: 15]

Again, it appears that the *a*-prefixed form functions as a type of adverbial complement to the verb. (For a formal justification of the classification of these *-ing* forms as adverbial complements, see Wolfram and Christian (1975: 244–7.)

Finally, the prefix occurs in other types of adverbial constructions than complements to verbs of movement, starting or continuing:

> You was pretty weak by the tenth day, *a-lyin'* in there in bed. [37: 13]
> One night my sister, she woke up *a-screaming', cryin', hollerin',* and so we jumped up. [156: 25]
> Say Chuck would come by and want to spend a hour *a-talkin',* I always figure I'm not too busy to stop. [30: 4]
> Course a lotta times you can't, and grow up *a-huntin'* with them instead of huntin' for 'em. [31: 22]

All of the examples given above represent *a*-prefixing on the form to which the *-ing* is directly attached, but the prefix can be extended to compound forms as well, thus giving examples like these:

> I went *a-deer-huntin'* twice last year. [31: 31]
> I told her I was goin' *a-pheasant-huntin'*. [31: 30]
> We was goin' up there *a-squirrel-huntin'*. [159: 30]

The preceding paragraphs present the main types of syntactic structures in which *a*-prefixing is found with *-ing* forms. The types of structures in which it is NOT found also help to reveal the systematic nature of its syntactic properties. Most of the ungrammatical structures with *a*-prefixing listed below are those which are never found in our primary corpus, with confirming evidence from Hackenberg's (1972) and Feagin's (1976) corpora.

There is also some informal intuitional evidence by speakers from the area to support the ungrammaticality of the constructions cited here.

First, a-prefixing is not found with nominals. Although this is most obvious in nominals preceded by determiners or possessives (the first two sentences below), it is also true of other nominalized -ing forms (the last two sentences):

*He saw the a-shootin'.
*He watched their a-shootin'.
*A-sailin' is fun.
*He likes a-sailin'.

The -ing forms in such sentences appear to fit the classical definition of a gerund construction.[3]

Just as there is no a-prefixing with the nominalized constructions given above, there is none with adjectival -ing, whether the form occurs as a predicate adjective or has undergone modifier preposing. We therefore do not find sentences like these:

*The movie was a-shockin'.
*The a-shootin' hunters didn't hit the bear.
*The hunters shot the a-runnin' bear.

One additional restriction on the syntactic privileges of a-prefixing involves the overt realization of a preposition, so that we do not find sentences like these:

*He got sick from a-workin' so hard.
*He makes money by a-buildin' houses.
*He nearly died from a-laughin' so hard.

It is interesting to note that such sentences with a-forms in the same adverbial function, but without the overt preposition, are acceptable:

He got sick a-workin' so hard.
He makes money a-buildin' houses.
He nearly died a-laughin' so hard.

Such sentences clearly indicate that it is the overt appearance of the preposition that prohibits a-prefixing. The prepositional restriction is apparently due to the derivation of a-prefixing from the prepositions *on* or *at,* which would conflict with others such as *for, from* and *by.* In fact, Wolfram and Christian (1975: 247–

50) contend that the *a*-prefix is to be synchronically derived from an underlying preposition.

The examination of the syntactic privileges of *a*-prefixing in the preceding paragraphs demonstrates that the affix is restricted to -*ing* forms that function as verbs or adverbs. It occurs with progressives, after continuing verbs (like *keep*) or movement verbs, and with other types of adverbial complements. It is prohibited from occurring with -*ing* forms that function nominally or adjectivally.

The fact that, in the corpus, most *a*-prefixes occur with progressives seems to be a function of the greater frequency of progressives, compared with other constructions in which the prefix might occur. A tabulation of the incidence of *a*-prefixing in relation to the number of potential cases for some speakers in the corpus (Wolfram and Christian 1975: 252) indicates a different order of relative frequency – greatest with the continuing verb *keep* (41 per cent of all the cases where it might be realized), followed by movement verbs (28 per cent), progressives (20 per cent), and other adverbial complements (16 per cent).

17.3 Phonological constraints on *a*-prefixing

The delimitation of the syntactic privileges of *a*-prefixing given above does not account for all restrictions on it. There is rather an intersection of syntactic and phonological phenomena. The occurrence of an *a*-prefixed form is sometimes permissible in terms of its syntactic structure, but is blocked because of a phonological restriction.

One type of phonological restriction is the stress pattern of the verb. If the initial syllable of a verb base is stressed, then *a*-prefixing may occur:

> She was just standin' quietly *a-hollerin'*. [28: 26]
> So he kep' *a-follerin'* me around for a week. [77: 10]

There are, however, no instances of *a*-prefixing when the initial syllable is not stressed. That is, we do not get examples such as these:

> *He was *a-discoverin'* a bear in the woods.
> *He kep' *a-manipulatin'* things.
> *He was *a-retirin'* to his cage.

The absence of such items (confirmed in an examination of data from Hackenberg and Feagin) does not appear to be accidental;

it seems that in this environment a-prefixing is prohibited for phonological reasons. The prohibition may be related to a more general word-stress pattern in English which avoids two unstressed syllables at the beginning of a word. In terms of the syntactic privileges of a-prefixing, forms like those above should be permissible, yet they are blocked by the phonological restriction.

Another apparent restriction on a-prefixing relates to the canonical form of the verb. If the verb begins with a vowel, then a-prefixing typically does not occur. In the corpus, there are no examples of this kind:

*John was *a-eatin'* his food.
*He kep' *a-askin'* him the question.

Again, such forms are syntactically permissible. There is no reason why they should not occur unless we consider the canonical shape of the verb. Although there are certainly more English verbs beginning in consonants than in vowels, there are still sufficient numbers of vowel-initial verbs for some a-prefixing to have been realized if it were not constrained by the shape of the verb.[4]

Another constraint on a-prefixing affects its incidence variably rather than categorically. It is more likely to occur when the preceding word ends in a consonant than in a vowel. That is, we are more likely to get a form like *He was just standin' at the post a-hollerin'* than *He was just standin' quietly a-hollerin'*, even though both may occur. A-prefixing is almost twice as frequent after consonants as it is after vowels (Wolfram and Christian 1975: 257). The relative effect of the preceding phonological environment appears to be natural because of the general objection to contiguous vowels in English.

In addition to the phonological constraints mentioned above, there is a most interesting constraint on a-prefixing in co-ordinate constructions. Participles joined by a co-ordinating conjunction show a strong tendency to have a-prefixing on both -ing forms if it occurs on either:

They'll be all bushed up *a-struttin'* and *a-draggin'*. [146: 17]
He just kep' *a-beggin'* and *a-cryin'* and *a-wantin'* to go out. [83: 18]
Just keep *a-rockin'* and *a-rollin'*; rock the car and you finally can rock you a way to get out. [24: (218)]

Although there are only sixteen potential instances of coordination with an a-prefixed form in the corpus, twelve of them have a-prefixing on both -ing forms in the co-ordination. One ex-

planation for the high proportion is that *a*-prefixing has some
degree of code-specificity and that code-switching would not be
typical in close co-ordinate constructions of this type. It may also
be, however, that alliteration plays a role. Certain literary writers
have been known to use *a*-prefixing as an alliterative device in
their dialect representations (McKay 1974: 210). Additional
evidence may come from the fact that *a*-prefixes, if they are going
to occur on one of the forms of a co-ordinate, will tend to occur
on the second (and successive *-ing* forms in the series) rather than
simply on the first. That is, we are more likely to get expressions
like the first than the second:

> I heard her *barking* and *a-barkin'* and *a-barkin'*. [22: 26]
> ?I heared her *a-barkin'* and *barking* and *barking*.

Informal reactions of speakers from *a*-prefixing areas tend to
support the claim that co-ordinate constructions with *a*-prefixes on
all *-ing* forms are clearly preferred and that those with *a*-prefixes
on later forms rather than on earlier ones are preferred over the
reverse. The existence of the 'co-ordinate constraint' on *a*-prefix-
ing seems to be fairly straightforward, although the explanation
of this constraint by alliteration still needs to be investigated.

The discussion thus far clearly points to the intersection of syntactic and phonological constraints in accounting for the
occurrence of *a*-prefixing. Certain structures pass through the syntactic filter of permissible *a*-prefixing only to be constrained by
the phonological environment. Neither phonological nor syntactic
explanations are adequate by themselves, but together they account for the systematic occurrence of the form.

17.4 Semantic aspects of *a*-prefixing

The few recent attempts to describe *a*-prefixing have virtually ignored its syntactic and phonological aspects; instead, they have
focused on its semantic properties. Descriptions of *a*-prefixing by
Stewart (1967), Hackenberg (1972) and Feagin 1976) have all
focused on the potential semantic distinctiveness of *a*-prefixing as
a part of the verbal system of English. My consideration of the
semantic properties of this form will therefore be interwoven with
a discussion of these recent proposals.

Stewart (1967: 10) initially proposed that *a*-prefixing involves
an aspectual relationship of indefiniteness or remoteness. He
observes:

The prefix shows that the action of the verb is indefinite in space and time while its absence implies that the action is immediate in space or time. Thus, he's *a-workin'* in Mountain Speech means either that the subject has a steady job, or he is away (out of sight, for example) working somewhere. On the other hand, *he's workin'* in Mountain Speech means that the subject is doing a specific task, close by. A similar (though not identical) grammatical distinction is indicated in Negro Dialect by the verbal auxiliary *be*.

There are clear-cut counter-examples suggesting that Stewart's proposal cannot be justified even approximately. The following examples, which are typical, contradict any interpretation that restricts *a*-prefixing to indefiniteness or remoteness:

I's *a-washin'* one day, and to go under the door I had to go under
  that spider. [28: 21]
I's *a-cannin'* chicken one time. . . . [156: (229)]
All of a sudden, a bear come *a-runnin'* towards him and he shot it
  between the eyes. [44: 18]
Count to about 10 or 15 so we can see if this machine's
  a-working'. [13: 1]

In the first three examples, the adverbial modifiers *one day, one time* and *all of a sudden* imply a particular activity. Each sentence relates an incident located at a specific time and place. Even more specific is the fourth sentence, used by one of our field-workers, an authentic *a*-prefixing speaker. The sentence refers to the tape-recorder located at the place and time of the interview. Given such counter-examples, Stewart's proposal of the semantic distinctiveness of *a*-prefixing cannot be justified.

The breadth of semantic contexts in which *a*-prefixes can be found is indicated by their co-occurrence with various types of time adverbs. Feagin (1976), utilizing Crystal's (1966) taxonomy of time adverbs, shows the wide range of temporal and aspectual contexts in which *a*-prefixing can occur; and a similar pattern is revealed in the corpus examined here. Perhaps more important is the fact that there appears to be no systematic formal restriction in terms of the time categories identified by Crystal. This is quite unlike the pattern found in vernacular Black English for a form such as distributive *be,* whose meaning is indicated by its co-occurrence restrictions with certain time adverbs (Fasold 1969).

Hackenberg (1972), like Stewart, thinks *a*-prefixing represents a semantic aspect different from that of non-*a*-prefixed forms: he observes that 'the addition of the prefix seems to be a syntactic manifestation of semantic conditioning' (Hackenberg 1972: 116). Hackenberg's interpretation of *a*-prefixing is tied to an analysis of English progressives in which three main types of aspect are delimited: CONTINUOUS aspect, in which an activity is currently viewed in progress (*They're playing bridge right now*); INTERMITTENT aspect, in which an activity is viewed as recurring or habitual (They're playing bridge this year); and planned aspect, in which an activity is to take place in the future (*Tomorrow they're playing cards*). Hackenberg observes that *a*-prefixing is most frequent with intermittent aspect and least frequent with planned aspect.

The relevant question to ask about the observed preference for the intermittent aspect is whether the preference is a unique function of *a*-prefixing. That is, does intermittency correlate with *a*-prefixing or with the progressive? From all available evidence, it appears that the preference for intermittency is a function of the category of progressive and is not at all unique to *a*-prefixing. Sag (1973), for example, shows that the intermittent aspect (which he calls HABITUAL) is most common for the category of progressive, and the planned aspect (Sag's category FUTURATE) is the least. I conclude, then, that Hackenberg's observations concerning a unique semantic function for *a*-prefixing cannot be substantiated.

Finally, Feagin (1976: 184–85) is considerably more cautious than Stewart or Hackenberg in her semantic interpretation of *a*-prefixing:

> I want to propose that the *a* + verb + *ing* form has the meaning 'intensified action' or 'immediacy or dramatic vividness' which Leech suggested was an offshoot of the progressive in general. . . . [T]he prefixed participle tends to occur in emotional contexts such as narration of stories about ghosts, accidents, murders, tornadoes, fires, gossip, hunting, or childhood games and escapades. This could lead to opposite interpretations. First, that it occurs as a stylistic device to add colour and immediacy to the story. Second, that it occurs here because the speaker is caught up in his own thoughts and has let slip older, more rural forms which he normally edits out, especially in front of strangers like me.
> I believe the first interpretation to be the correct one, since 24 of the examples occur with the intensifier *just,* 16 with *keep* (which has an intensifying meaning of 'persevere'). Of these 16, 7 of the examples occurred with *just* as well, as in *kept on a-churning.* Thus the action described was triply intensified: *just kept on a-churning.*

It is unclear whether Feagin is proposing a formal semantic distinction of INTENSIFICATION of VIVIDNESS for *a*-prefixing, but if so, such a proposal is difficult to support. Although it is true that *just* is the most frequently co-occurring adverb with *a*-prefixes, intensifying *just* also occurs with non-*a*-prefixed forms. Furthermore, there does not appear to be a formal restriction of *a*-prefixing to intensifying adverbs such as *just* or *keep* as compared with a 'minimizing' adverb such as *hardly* (that is, we can find both *He's really a-talkin'* and *He's hardly a-talkin'*). *A*-prefixing can occur with both intensifying and minimizing adverbs, although there does appear to be a stylistic preference for the former. A stylistic preference, however, is not to be confused with a formal semantic distinction.

Feagin also observes that *a*-prefixing tends to occur in emotional contexts in narratives. Although it is very difficult to specify precisely the degree of emotion that would qualify as 'emotional', there is evidence that *a*-prefixing occurs more in narratives than in other discourse styles. (Approximately two-thirds of all *a*-prefixed forms occur in narratives.) Again, however, we are talking about a stylistic preference rather than a qualitative, formal distinction.

Feagin ultimately chooses between two interpretations for the meaning of *a*-prefixing, namely, that it is a stylistic device to add colour or that it is a narrative shift into an older, more rural form; but these interpretations are not mutually exclusive. The emotional narration of stories with dramatic vividness may certainly give rise to older, more rural forms, especially in cases where the forms carry no apparent formal semantic distinction.

My study has discovered no formal evidence for a distinct semantic category of *a*-prefixing, contrary to some current proposals. This, of course, is not to say that no formal distinction can be found, since we are always limited by the finiteness of our investigation. Some of the possible speculations have been eliminated, at least, and further examination of the phenomenon can start at this point.

Notes

1. There are occasional instances of *a*-prefixed forms other than -*ing* participles, for example, *I went through a house that's supposed to be a-haunted* [17: (1194)]. These forms include -*ed* participles and even non-participial adjectives and adverbs. They will not be considered here.
2. Sentences taken from the corpus described in section 17.1 are referenced by the informant number preceding the colon and the page on the typescript where the example is found following the colon. In the case of informants for whom there is no typescript, the counter num-

ber on the tape-recorder is included within parentheses. Due to the regular realization of -ing as [ɪn] or [ɪn] phonetically, I have adopted the popular convention by which it is indicated as in orthographically.

3. Some of the sentences cited previously as permitting a-prefixing (those called 'adverbial complements' above) have also been treated traditionally as gerunds. In the analysis followed here (justified formally in Wolfram and Christian 1975), only sentences like the starred ones above are considered to be true gerunds.

4. Although there are no examples of a-prefixing for vowel-initial verbs in this corpus. Feagin (personal communication) has brought one such item to my attention from her corpus. Hackenberg (1972) has no examples in his corpus. Given Feagin's example, it is possible that this constraint is variable rather than categorical for some speakers.

References

ATWOOD, E. BAGBY (1953) *A Survey of Verb Forms in the Eastern United States*. Ann Arbor: University of Michigan Press.

CRYSTAL, DAVID (1966) 'Specification and English tenses', *Journal of Linguistics* 2: 1–33.

FASOLD, RALPH W. (1969) 'Tense and the form *be* in Black English', *Language* 45: 763–76.

FEAGIN, CRAWFORD (1976) 'A sociolinguistic study of Alabama White English: the verb phrase in Anniston', dissertation Georgetown University.

HACKENBERG, ROBERT (1972) 'A sociolinguistic description of Appalachian English', Georgetown University dissertation.

KRAPP, GEORGE PHILIP (1925) *The English Language in America*, 2 vols. reprint. New York: Ungar, 1960.

MCKAY, JANET (1974) 'A linguistic study of Samuel Clemens' style,' dissertation, Princeton University.

SAG, IVAN (1973) 'On the state of progress on progressives and statives.' In Charles-James Bailey and Roger W. Shuy (eds) Washington, DC: Georgetown University Press, pp 83–95.

STEWART, WILLIAM A. (1967) *Language and Communication Problems in Southern Appalachia*. Washington, DC: Center for Applied Linguistics.

WOLFRAM, WALT, and CHRISTIAN, DONNA (1975) *Sociolinguistic Variables in Appalachian Dialects*. Final report, NIE grant no. 74–0026.

WOLFRAM, WALT, and FASOLD, RALPH W. (1974) *The study of Social Dialects in American English*. Englewood Cliffs, NJ: Prentice-Hall.

Chapter 18

A grammatical continuum for (ING)

Ann Houston

18.1 Introduction

The sociolinguistic variable (ING) has shown a remarkable consistency across English speech communities around the world with respect to its regularly observed patterns of social and stylistic variation. Converging results of these external factors have been reported for American (Labov 1966, Shuy, Wolfram and Riley 1967; Anshen 1969), Canadian (Woods 1979; Gregg 1984), British (Trudgill 1974), and Australian speech communities (Wald and Shopen 1981).

This chapter will explore evidence for a different type of effect observed for (ING). This effect exhibits sensitivity to the grammatical status of (ING), associating the apical nasal variant /n/ with verbal categories, and the velar nasal variant /ŋ/ with nominal ones.

The earliest report of a grammatical effect is found in a dialect survey of Central Texas English, which was conducted by Stolz and Bills during the 1960s. Although quantitative results are not provided, it is stated in a footnote that 'the reduction of *ing* and *in* was different for gerunds than for progressive verbs. Several speakers regularly pronounced *hunting* with the *ing* when using it in a noun phrase, but reduced the suffix to *in* when using it as a verb' (Stolz and Garland n.d.: 19). The first quantitative study of this phenomenon was carried out in the Philadelphia speech community by William Labov's field methods classes. Table 18.1 illustrates the grammatical effect with results from one Philadelphia study (Fishtown). It shows the highest occurrence of /ŋ/ with nouns, and the lowest occurrence of /ŋ/ with the present participle. Gerunds fall in between.[1]

TABLE 18.1 Percentage of velar variant /ŋ/ in Fishtown (Philadelphia) according to grammatical category (Abdel-Jawad 1979)

	%	N
Nominals/adjectives	59	215
Gerunds	28	86
Participles	20	221
Total		522

18.2 Grammatical effect observed for British (ING)

The presence of grammatical conditioning on (ING) is also observed for British speech. The British data are taken from tape-recorded interviews conducted by William Labov in the 1970s. The data represent British working-class speech. Map 18.1 indicates the location of the urban centres represented by these data (Houston 1985).

Based on the evidence to be presented in this chapter, I will argue that the basic categories in English where (ING) may occur do not constitute a set of discrete elements, but are linearly related along a continuum. Furthermore, this continuum shows geographical differences which exhibit a continuity with the past history of (ING).

The concept of a *grammatical continuum* appears in earlier work on English syntax. Ross (1972, 1973) argues for the existence of grammatical continua in English on the basis of a number of syntactic diagnoses applied to a range of sentence types. The continuum of relevance here is shown in Table 18.2

TABLE 18.2 Ross's continuum (Ross 1973b)

THAT < FOR TO < Q < ACC ING < POSS ING < ACTION NOM < DERIVED NOM < NOUN

Ross considers the possibility that the categories shown in Table 18.2 might correspond to cardinal points along a continuum, ranging from the least nominal at the left to the most nominal at the right, with intermediate values in between.

A detailed discussion of Ross's diagnoses which provide evidence for this continuum is beyond the scope of the present chapter. However, Ross's general conclusion is that the application of various tests to the syntactic types in Table 18.2 does not result in discrete grammaticality judgements. The gradient ac-

Map 18.1   Cities representing British synchronic corpus for (ING); relation of probabilities of velar variant /ŋ/ in modern urban areas in relation to isogloss, c. 1450

ceptability of a rule application (or co-occurrence relation), forms the basis for the continuum. What is important is that acceptability judgements align in a ranked progression of increasing or decreasing acceptability along the continuum.

One example which illustrates the gradience of acceptability is the presence of *not* in various types of subjects. Examples [1]–[7] below give Ross's judgements for a range of subject types. The subject in [1] is sentential, whereas the subject in [7] is a derived nominal. The more sentential the subject is, the more acceptable it is to have the sentential negator *not*.

[1] *That he does not prepare dinner* is good for her health.
THAT

[2] *For him not to prepare dinner* is good for her health.
FOR TO

[3] *Why he does not prepare dinner* is good for her health.
Q

[4] *Him not preparing dinner* is good for her health.
ACC ING

[5] ? *His not preparing dinner* is good for her health.
POSS ING

[6] * *His not preparing of dinner* is good for her health.
ACTION NOMINAL

[7] ** *His not preparation of dinner* is good for her health.
NOUN

(Examples and judgements taken from Ross (1973: 163).)

Another example to illustrate gradience is plural agreement, which assigns plural marking on the main verb following a conjoined subject. Ross's judgements are shown in [8]–[13] below for a range of conjoined subjects. In these examples the rule of plural agreement is most acceptable with the most nominal subjects.

[8] *That he lost and that you won* *are/is wonderful.
THAT

[9] *For him to lose and for you to win* *are/is wonderful.
FOR TO

[10] *Him winning and you losing* ?are/is wonderful.
ACC ING

[11] *His winning and your losing* ??are/is wonderful.
POSS ING

[12] *Jack's winning of the bingo tournament and your losing of the hopscotch marathon,* were unexpected joys.
ACTION NOMINAL

[13] *Senator Phogbottom's nomination and the ensuing rebel-
lion in Belgrade* were unforeseen by our computer.
NOUN

My intuitions concerning the acceptability of the above sets of
examples agree with Ross's, both with respect to the direction of
the acceptability, and to the presence of a gradience in the degree
of acceptability.

The continuum is relevant to the present discussion, because it
will be shown that (ING) exhibits sensitivity to the nominal or
verbal status of grammatical categories, and that it manifests itself
along a continuum rather than between discretely demarcated
categories.

Occurrences of (ING) in the British data were initially
classified according to the following grammatical categories:
progressives, quasi-progressives, VP complements, periphrastic
future, appositive (non-finite) participles, pre-nominal adjunct
modifiers (subdivided according to their participial or gerundive
origin), Acc-ing, gerundive nominals, action nominals, derived
nominals, compounds, monomorphemics, proper names and
prepositions. Examples are given in [14] – [29].[2]

[14] *I'm workin'* at a caterer's on the 20th. PROGRESSIVE
(C.F. Battersea Park, London)

[15] then I *started gettin'* pains behind me ears there. QUASI-
PROGRESSIVE (K.H. Liverpool)

[16] I don't mind *watchin'* rugby. VP COMPLEMENT (R.K.
Cardiff)

[17] I've had a feeling that things *are goin'* to happen. PERI-
PHRASTIC FUTURE (J.B. Manchester)

[18] We've been to Jersey, *drivin'* all over. APPOSITIVE
(E.N. Norwich)

[19] maybe a *waitin' list,* I don't know. ADJUNCT MODI-
FIER (gerundive A.G. Edinburgh)

[20] the plain *workin' man* today in England, he either has
roast beef . . . ADJUNCT MODIFIER (participial)
(J.W. Norwich)

[21] cause it's either *you gettin' battered or 'im gettin' battered.*
ACC-ING (E.M. Liverpool)

[22] *havin' a fall,* that did it. GERUNDIVE NOMINAL
(O.M. Manchester)

[23] and I gave him *a thumpin'.* ACTION NOMINAL (M.Y.
Edinburgh)

[24] No, it's hit the outside of the *nettin',* DERIVED NOMI-
NAL (J.G. Chelsea, London)

[25] before then they were *nothing*. COMPOUND (W.T. Glasgow)

[26] it's only in the *mornins* I think MONOMORPHEMIC (B.C. Manchester)

[27] no it was *amazin'*. PREDICATE ADJECTIVE (M.Y. Edinburgh)

[28] We took a girl each and walked right on back to *Tillingham*. PROPER NAME (M.R. Essex)

[29] and then swing it over, *accordin'* to where your horses walked, you see. PREPOSITION (M.R. Essex)

Table 18.3 shows that the velar variant /ŋ/ increases in occurrence as we move towards the nominal end of Ross's continuum.

TABLE 18.3 Linear correspondence of velar occurrences /ŋ/ to Ross's continuum

THAT	FOR TO	Q	ACC ING	GER NOM	ACT NOM	DER NOM	NOUN
	11% (1260)		15% (26)	17.5% (160)	19% (158)	32% (72)	78.5% (149)

Progressives may occur in any of the three leftmost categories (THAT, FOR TO, Q), and they show the lowest percentage of the velar variant. The percentage under NOUN at the far right includes both proper names and the compounds *everything, anything, something* and *nothing*. Monomorphemic nouns such as *morning* are not shown in Table 18.3.

The monomorphemic nouns show a lower occurrence of the velar variant than do proper names and compounds, the percentage of /ŋ/ for monomorphemics being 30 per cent. They show a lower occurrence than might be predicted according to the correspondence shown in Table 18.3, even though they are well towards the nominal end of the continuum. One reason for this descrepancy is that the monomorphemics in the British data consist almost entirely of two words, *evening* and *morning*. I would predict that a broader sampling of monomorphemic words would align more closely with proper names.

The results of a variable rule analysis for (ING) and grammatical category are shown in Table 18.4. The probabilities are for rule applications of the velar variant. The grammatical categories when grouped in Table 18.4 are not significantly different from each other with respect to their probabilities. Worth noting in Table 18.4 is the separation of adjunct modifiers according to whether they are gerundive or participial in origin. The statistical analysis includes the speakers' ages as well as the geographical region. The importance of dividing the urban centres into two groups will be addressed shortly.

TABLE 18.4 Probabilities of velar variant /ŋ/ of (ING) in British synchronic data according to grammatical category, dialect region and age

	p	%	N
Proper names any/every/some/nothing	0.93	84	149
Derived nominals adjunct modifiers (+ger) compound modifiers (+ger)	0.63	33	127
Monomorphemic nouns	0.48	30	99
Gerunds gerund NP complements acc-ing verb phrase complements reduced relative clauses appositive participles absolute participles	0.36	17	735
Progressives quasi-progressives periphrastic future non-adjunct modifiers (+part) adjunct modifiers (+part) predicate adjectives	0.26	11	1229
Prepositions	0.20	13	24
Lond./Manch./Birm./Essex	0.67	31	1001
Bristol/Cardiff/Glas./Edin./ Liverpool/Gateshead/Norwich/Leeds	0.33	11	1362
Under 35	0.42	18	1446
Over 35	0.58	22	917
Input prob.	027	20	2363

Log likelihood = −912.9797; chi sq./cell = 0.90

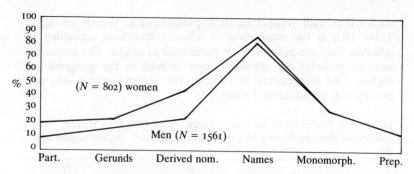

FIGURE 18.1   Percentages of velar variant /ŋ/ for men and women by grammatical category (taken from Table 18.4).

The groupings of the grammatical categories shown in Table 18.4 could not be combined further without statistical significance.[3] A grammatical effect is clearly observable in Table 18.4, and is consistent with earlier reports of such an effect for other speech communities. This grammatical effect is not reducible to other conditions. For example, Figure 18.1 shows the percentages for the velar variant by grammatical category, age and sex. The grammatical effect is evident for both men and women, although women show a higher occurrence of the velar variant overall.

I interpret the evidence shown in Tables 18.3 and 18.4 as independent corroboration of Ross's continuum. The evidence presented by Ross for the existence of a gradient ranking of acceptability judgements along a nominal-verbal scale corresponds with the observed gradient probabilities of rule applications for the velar variant of (ING) by grammatical category.

This observed continuum may be contrasted to a model which classifies (ING) into discrete lexical categories. The issue is whether the appearance of a grammatical continuum cannot be resolved according to a discrete analysis of lexical categories, eg V, N, A and P, or perhaps along some dimension of inflectional and derivational criteria.

18.3 X-bar syntax

One of the major tenets of the X-bar theory of phrase structure has been the assumption that the lexical categories of a language can be analysed into sets of discrete syntactic features (Chomsky 1970; Jackendoff 1977). The major lexical categories of English

TABLE 18.5 Discrete feature matrix (Chomsky 1970).

	+N	−N
+V	A	V
−V	N	P

assumed within X-bar theory, and their associated features, are shown in Table 18.5. The feature matrix is the analysis assumed in Chomsky (1970), and adopted in Radford (1981). The groupings of the categories in the British data corresponding to the feature matrix in Table 18.5 are as follows:

[+N −V] monomorphemics, proper names, derived nominals, compounds;

[+N +V] adjunct modifiers (gerundive/participial), pred. adj.;

[−N +V] VP complements, non-finite participles, progressives, quasi-progressives, periphrastic future;

[−N −V] prepositions.

The status of gerunds has not been clearly defined within this matrix.

Table 18.6 shows the British data arranged according to the discrete feature matrix. This regrouping of the grammatical categories results in a significant increase in the log likelihood, $p < 0.001$.

The gerunds shown in Table 18.6 were treated separately, since their status within X-bar theory in terms of feature assignment is less clear than the other categories. Yet combining the gerunds either nounwards, ie with derived nominals, or verbwards, ie with participles, was significant at 0.001. In neither instance was the fit (chi square/cell) improved over that shown in Table 18.4.

Table 18.7 shows the data modelled according to a three-way analysis. In this case the division is between the inflectional and derivational status of (ING), or roughly, between categories in which (ING) serves a grammatical function as opposed to a lexical one. Monomorphemic nouns are retained separately, forming the third group.

Action nominals were classified as derivational because of their lexical contrast to derived nominals illustrated in pairs such as *the*

TABLE 18.6 Probabilities for velar variant /ŋ/ by syntactic features (discrete feature matrix)

	p	%	N	Syntactic features
Nominals	0.82	56	320	[+N −V]
Modifiers	0.59	24	157	[+N +V]
Gerunds	0.44	17	393	
Participles	0.34	12	1469	[−N +V]
Prepositions	0.27	13	24	[−N −V]
Lond./Manch./Birm/Essex	0.67	31	100	
Edin./Glasgow/Liverpool/ Gateshead/Leeds/Norwich/ Bristol/Cardiff	0.33	11	1362	
Under 35	0.43	18	1446	
Over 35	0.57	22	917	
Input prob.	0.21	20	2363	

No. of cells = 20; chi sq./cell = 1.23; log likelihood = −961.2396

growth of tomatoes vs *the growing of tomatoes*. Gerundive nominals and acc-ing were classified as inflectional because of their aspectual function in examples such as *I don't recall anything about his having been invited*.

However the gerunds are classified, as a single group or as the subgroups just described, all such groupings were significant at

TABLE 18.7 Probabilities of velar variant /ŋ/ for inflectional/derivational model for (ING)

	p	%	N
Monomorphemic	0.79	63	248
Derivational	0.43	23	296
Inflectional	0.26	13	1819
Lond./Birm./Manch./Essex	0.61	31	1001
Edin./Glasgow/Liverpool/Gateshead/ Leeds/Norwich/Bristol/Cardiff	0.39	18	1362
Under 35	0.44	18	1446
Over 35	0.56	22	917
Input prob.	0.29	20	2363

No. of cells = 12; log likelihood = −1104.648; chi sq/cell = 2.83.

the 0.001 level. The fit is also worse, chi square = 2.83/cell, as compared with 0.90/cell shown in Table 18.4.

Based on these observations, it has been shown that the data do not conform to the categorial groups defined by currently assumed feature bundles. The elements align along a continuum, without sharp boundaries demarcating categories.

Ross (1973b) raises the issue of whether elements are equispaced along the continuum. If not, could it be the case that categories tend to bunch along it? The probabilities shown in Table 18.4 suggest a bunching tendency based on the observation that although there is an overall gradience ranging from least nominal to most nominal, some differences between categories were not significant.

For example, even though verb phrase (VP) complements are analysed as participial (ING), combining them with progressives was significant at 0.01. Yet combining them with gerunds was not significant at 0.05. Although gerunds can be distinguished from VP complements on the basis of possessive marking on the subject, *I regret him coming* vs *I regret his coming,* the contrasts in meaning between these is not sharp.

Reduced relative clauses were also combined with gerunds and VP complements without statistical significance. There are, in fact, instances of ambiguity between VP complements and reduced relative clauses. For example, the sentence *I saw the man washing his car* has two readings. The reading as a relative clause may be paraphrased as *I saw the man who was washing his car,* and the reading as a VP complement may be paraphrased as *I saw the man wash his car.* Although the ambiguity is revealed by the availability in English of two separate paraphrases, the difference in meaning is again not always significant. These types of evidence provide some basis for why the patterns of (ING) variation might exhibit bunching along the continuum.

In section 18.4 a different type of evidence will be examined in support of the continuum model for (ING), evidence which relates the past history of (ING) to its present-day status as a variable.

18.4 Diachronic evidence

The present participle of Old and Early Middle English had the suffix *ind.* (Other variants included *end* and *and.*) Moore, Meech and Whitehall (1935) in their well-known study of Middle English dialects establish that by the mid-fifteenth century, *ind* had been replaced with *ing* in the south of England. The isogloss provided by their data which indicates the area affected by this replacement *c.* 1450, is shown on Map 18.1.

The probabilities for /ŋ/ are shown on Map 18.1 by urban centre. The cities with probabilities greater than 0.5 fall within the region where *ind* was replaced by *ing*, *c.* 1450. The cities with probabilities less than 0.5 lie outside this region. Geographically, the latter represent northern and peripheral regions. A closer examination of the difference between these probabilities shows that they result from differences in frequency of /ŋ/ for the verbal categories. The northern and peripheral regions show much lower occurrence of /ŋ/ than the southern region, with respect to the categories at the verbal end of the continuum.

TABLE 18.8 Percentage of velar variant /ŋ/ for major grammatical categories inside and outside dialect regions

Categories	Inside		Outside	
	%	N	%	N
Any/every/some/nothing	90.8	79/87	77.1	27/35
Proper names	73.3	11/15	66.7	8/12
Derived nominals/modifiers (+ger.)	38.9	14/36	30.8	28/91
Monomorphemics	44.0	22/50	16.3	8/49
Gerunds/acc-ing/NP complements	26.1	46/153	11.3	27/240
Verb phrase complements	34.3	12/35	6.2	4/65
Non-finite participles	31.6	36/114	6.3	8128
Quasi-progressives	21.6	16/74	4.7	4/86
Progressives/periphrastic/ modifiers (+part.)	18.4	78/423	5.9	38/646
Prepositions	14.3	2/14	10.0	1/10
Total		1001		1362

A fanning effect can be observed in Figure 18.2. The most nominal categories for all urban centres show similar percentages of velar occurrence, with those inside the isogloss being somewhat higher. Yet there is a noticeable difference between the two geographical regions with respect to the verbal categories. This difference is interpreted as a residual effect of the earlier, historical replacement of *ind* with *ing*.

The vowel of Late Middle English in the North which preceded *nd* on the participle was represented as <a>. In contrast, the spellings <i> and <ie> frequently occurred in the South. If it can be assumed that these differences may have corresponded to some difference in pronunciation, bearing in mind these are unstressed syllables, there would be more reason to expect a confusion between *nd* and *ng* in the South, than in the North. This

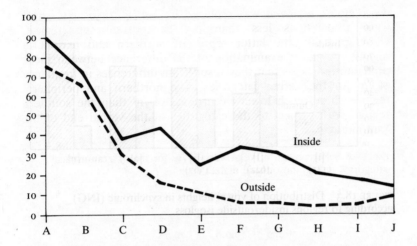

FIGURE 18.2 Graph representation of Table 18.8.
(A) Any/every/some/nothing; (B) proper names; (C) derived
nominals/modifiers (+ ger.); (D) monomorphemics; (E) gerunds/acc-
ing/NP complements; (F) verb phrase complements; (G) non-finite
participles; (H) quasi-progressives;
(I) progressives/periphrastic/modifiers (part.); (J) prepositions.

would be more likely under the condition that the southern vowel
was high and front, and that the final stops were not pronounced
(see Houston 1985 for a more detailed discussion of the historical evidence).

There is acoustic evidence that a high, front tense vowel could
contribute to the perception of a following apical stop as a velar
one. Habick (1980), using an American speech sample, measured
the following loci for F1 and F2, for high and central vowels, and
apical and velar stops:

/iy/	F1 350 Hz		/ə/	F1 550 Hz
	F2 2400 Hz			F2 1700 Hz
/g/	F1 400 Hz		/d/	F1 500 Hz
	F2 2000 Hz			F2 1800 Hz

These data show that high front tense vowels and velar stops have
similar loci. Assuming that high front tense vowels may have been
present before the apical nasals of *ind* in southern England
c. 1450, the acoustic data provide evidence for why the perception of the following nasal could have been [ŋ] instead of [n].

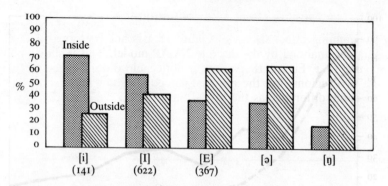

FIGURE 18.3   Distribution of vowel heights in synchronic (ING)
according to regions inside/outside isogloss

Some synchronic evidence to support such a view is provided
by the distribution of vowel quality in the British data.

Figure 18.3 shows a significantly higher proportion of centralized vowels for the regions lying outside the isogloss than for
those lying inside it. In contrast, speakers from regions lying inside the isogloss (London in particular), show a much higher
proportion of high front vowels.

In contrast to the historical change which affected the participles, the spelling of gerunds (verbal nouns) has always been
<ng> for regions lying on both sides of the isogloss. (This was
<ung> in Old English.) This provides some historical basis for
the observed similarity of velar occurrences for both regions, with
respect to the most nominal categories. There is also evidence for
a historical basis to the observed differences in the percentages
of /ŋ/ with respect to the verbal end of the continuum. Such
historical differences provide an account of why the adjunct
modifiers should separate into different groups, as shown in Table
18.4. Historically there were both participial and gerundive
prenominal adjuncts. From a purely synchronic perspective of the
models shown in Tables 18.6 and 18.7, there is no obvious way
to account for the statistically significant differences between
them in Table 18.4.

Thus the grammatical effect observed in Table 18.4 provides
support for Ross's synchronic continuum, as well as affording
some insight into processes of historical change, geographically
situated. It clearly indicates how synchronic linguistic variation
may serve to reveal a continuity with past, invariant linguistic
elements.

18.5 The Fanning effect as a continuum

The fanning effect shown in Figure 18.2 is not preserved if the data are analysed by the discrete NVAP model. This is shown in Figure 18.4. Figure 18.4 shows a noticeable difference between the two regions, but the nominal categories show approximately the same difference as the verbal ones.

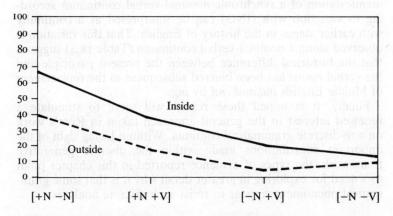

FIGURE 18.4 Percentage velar variant /ŋ/ according to discrete NVAP model

18.6 Conclusions

To summarize, I have presented evidence which provides some support for the existence of a grammatical continuum, in contrast to a model which postulates only discrete boundaries between categories.

The data presented here receive some confirmation from other reports of similar grammatical conditioning. Recall the data shown in Table 18.1. Additionally, Ross's arguments present evidence on the gradient nature of grammaticality judgements of nominal and verbal constructions based on introspective data.

The variable rule analysis has provided a means of comparing various models of the data; the discrete models shown in Tables 18.6 and 18.7 were shown to combine significantly different categories. The model which retained separately all the significant groups indicated a gradience, rather than the presence of sharp boundaries between categories. If this linear effect really is a manifestation of perceived differences in the nominal or verbal characteristics of (ING), it would be expected that the application of rules which are sensitive to the nominal or verbal attributes of a construction would result in a range of acceptability judgements. This is what Ross has tried to show.

The pattern of variation observed for the dependent variable (ING) was linked to a historically motivated difference. The manifestation of a synchronic nominal-verbal continuum according to variation with (ING) can be interpreted as a continuity with earlier stages in the history of English. That this variation is observed along a nominal-verbal continuum (Table 18.4) suggests that the historical difference between the present participle and the verbal nouns has been blurred subsequent to the replacement of Middle English *ind/and/end* by *ing*.

Finally, it is hoped these results will serve to stimulate a renewed interest in the general approach taken in Ross's work on non-discrete grammatical continua. Without losing sight of the important contributions made within the discrete generative framework, the types of evidence reported in this chapter point to a need for exploring in greater detail why it is that some grammatical phenomena appear to resist such discrete analyses.

Acknowledgement

This paper was presented at New Ways of Analyzing Variation (NWAV) XIII, October 1984.

Notes

1. Occurrences of the periphrastic future *going to* are not shown in Table 18.1 since there are only twenty-six tokens. The velar variant occurred in 4 per cent of the tokens for the periphrastic future.
2. The citations after each example indicate the initials of the speaker, the city and the tape counter number.
3. Statistical significance here is measured as significant differences between the log likelihoods of two successive variable rule analyses. For example, the difference between the log likelihood shown in Table 18.4 and the log likelihood for an analysis which combined further any of the grouping of Table 18.4, was significant at the 0.001 level.

References

ABDEL-JAWAD, HASSAN (1979) 'A report on the (ING) variable in a Philadelphia speech community (Fishtown)', unpublished 561 Report, W. Labov's research seminar on field methods.

ANSHEN, FRANK (1969) 'Speech Variation among Negroes in a small Southern community', unpublished dissertation, New York University.

CHOMSKY, NOAM (1970) 'Remarks on nominalization'. In R. Jacobs and P. Rosenbaum (eds), *Readings in English Transformational Grammar*, Waltham, Mass.: Ginn.

GREGG, ROBERT (1984) *The Survey of Vancouver English*. Excerpts from the Final Report to the Social Sciences and Humanities Research Council, Ottawa.

HABICK, TIMOTHY (1980) 'Sound changes in Farmer City: a sociolinguistic study based on acoustic data', unpublished dissertation. Urbana, Ill.: University of Illinois.

HOUSTON, ANN (1985) 'Continuity and change in English morphology: the variable (ING)', unpublished dissertation. University of Pennsylvania.

JACKENDOFF, RAY (1977) 'X̄ syntax: a study of phrase structure syntax', *Linguistic Inquiry Monograph*, No. 2. Cambridge, Mass.: MIT Press.

LABOV, WILLIAM (1966) *The Social Stratification of English in New York City*. Washington D.C.: Center for Applied Linguistics.

MOORE, SAMUEL, MEECH, SB., and WHITEHALL HAROLD (1935) *Middle English dialect Characteristics and Dialect boundaries*. University of Michigan Language and Literature Series.

RADFORD, ANDREW (1981) *Transformational Syntax; A Student's Guide to Chomsky's Extended Standard Theory*. Cambridge: Cambridge University Press.

ROSS, JOHN (1972) 'Endstation haupwort: the category squish', papers from the Eighth Regional Meeting, Chicago Linguistic Society.

ROSS, JOHN (1973) 'Nouniness'. In O. Fujimura (ed.) *Three Dimensions of Linguistic Theory*. Tokyo: Tokyo Institute for Advanced Studies of Language, TEC Company.

SHUY, ROGER WALT, WOLFRAM and RILEY WK (1967) *W.K. Linguistic Correlates of Social Stratification in Detroit Speech*. Washington: Center for Applied Linguistics.

STOLZ, WALTER and BILLS, GARLAND (n.d.) 'An investigation of the standard-nonstandard dimension of central Texas English', mimeographed. Linguistics Laboratory, University of Pennsylvania.

TRUDGILL, PETER (1974) *The Social Differentiation of English in Norwich*. Cambridge: Cambridge University Press.

WALD, BENJI and SHOPEN, TIMOTHY (1981) A researcher's guide to the sociolinguistic variable (ING). In T. Shopen and B. Wald (eds) *Style and Variables in English*. Winthrop Publishers.

WOODS, HOWARD (1979) 'A socio-dialectal survey of the English spoken in Ottawa: a study of sociolinguistic and stylitic variation', Ph.D. dissertation, University of British Columbia.

Part five

Adverbials

Chapter 19

Adverbials in English dialects

J. K. Chambers and Peter Trudgill

Most of the chapters in this book have been centrally concerned with dialectal variation in the verb system. In turning now to adverbials, we are not, in fact, leaving the verb system entirely. Although adverbials fill several semantic and syntactic roles in English, most of them involve modification of the verb, and the relation to the verb system is close. One of their best-known roles is to further specify the type of action expressed by the verb, as in

John $\left\{\begin{array}{l}\text{always}\\\text{repeatedly}\\\text{abruptly}\end{array}\right\}$ left the party.

In many languages, such specifications might be realized by affixes on the verb itself, expressing habitual, iterative and inchoative aspects.

Another role is to signal the speaker's attitude towards the propositional content of the sentence, as in

John will $\left\{\begin{array}{l}\text{surely}\\\text{necessarily}\\\text{possibly}\end{array}\right\}$ leave the party.

This function is very similar to that of the modal auxiliaries of the verbal system; the meanings indicated by the adverbs can be paraphrased with modals:

John $\left\{\begin{array}{l}\text{should}\\\text{must}\\\text{might}\end{array}\right\}$ leave the party.

The similarity between some adverbs and the modals becomes clear in Brown's discussion of double modals in Chapter 8.

Speakers whose grammar does not include double modals are usually puzzled, even mystified, when they first hear such sentences as

He might could do it.
He should can do it.

Their puzzlement usually disappears when they realize that these sentences can be paraphrased in the standard grammar by substituting an adverb for one of the modals.

He could maybe do it./He could perhaps do it.
He can likely do it./He can probably do it.

Because they have so many diverse functions in English grammar, adverbials form the most heterogeneous category among the major lexical classes. They are usually dealt with by grammarians in subclasses determined by semantic and/or syntactic criteria, as manner adverbs, temporals, locatives, intensifiers and so on. (For a useful syntactic classification, see Jackendoff 1972: Ch. 3; for a comprehensive outline, see Quirk *et al.* 1985: Ch. 7, 8.)

One of the most-discussed shibboleths of English grammar in recent years seems, from a linguistic viewpoint, to be a case of an adverb moving from one subclass into another. The use of the adverb *hopefully* with the meaning *I hope (that)* has caught on wildly in the last few decades, to the point where it is much more common to hear a sentence such as the following with *hopefully* than its more conservative paraphrase:

Hopefully, John will avoid further injury.
I hope (that) John will avoid further injury.

This use of *hopefully* horrifies purists because the adverb has traditionally been an adverb of manner, used in quite different contexts, as in

John searched the mail $\left\{ \begin{array}{l} \text{zealously} \\ \text{hopefully} \\ \text{frantically} \end{array} \right\}$ for his cheque.

$\left\{ \begin{array}{l} \text{Zealously,} \\ \text{Hopefully,} \\ \text{Frantically,} \end{array} \right\}$ John searched the mail for his cheque.

In sentence-initial position, *hopefully* has now pretty well lost its meaning as an adverb of manner. Instead, it has taken on the meaning *I hope that*, probably as a means by which speakers and writers can avoid drawing attention to themselves with the first person singular pronoun. This use was roundly condemned for several years, and sometimes still is, as a 'misuse' of an adverb of manner.

What has happened is that *hopefully* has acquired a brand-new status in a different subclass of adverbs. The modal adverbs such as *surely, necessarily, possibly* and *probably* permit the speaker or writer to express an opinion about a proposition without resorting to the first person pronoun: sentences with these adverbs mean that 'I' (the speaker or writer) consider some event to be certain, necessary, possible or probable. *Hopefully* fits into this class neatly, although it was not a member of it before. As often happens when some aspect of grammar undergoes rapid change, the new usage arouses the ire of some pundits who attempt to resist the change.

Several regional variants in English syntax involve adverbials.

The construction called '*after* + present participle' is heard in Ireland and in New World regions settled by the Irish in sentences such as

She's after coming from the mainland.
He is after telling me all about it.

The meaning is that the action of the participle is recently completed, equivalent in Standard English to the present perfect with an adverb, as in

She's just come from the mainland.
He has just told me all about it.

In parts of the United States and Canada, and perhaps ubiquitous in both, is an interesting syntactic form known as the '*ever*-exclamation' that has attracted very little attention from linguists and dialectologists. It occurs in sentences like these:

Does he ever drive fast!
Is he ever stupid!

The meaning is highly emphatic, and the sentences almost presuppose a *Wow!* at the beginning: reasonable paraphrases might be *Wow! He drives very fast!* and *Wow! He is really stupid!* The syntax of *ever*-exclamations, strangely, is the same as yes/no questions, with inversion of the auxiliary, but there is no sense of interrogation implied. The adverb *ever*, even more strangely, seems only vaguely related to its standard meaning 'at any time', as in *Does he ever drive fast?* or *Is he ever stupid?* The *ever* of exclamations means 'habitually, at all times', as it also does in the formula *Yours ever* in letter writing and perhaps in *forever*, that is, 'for all time to come'.

In Canada, the common adverbial phrase 'as well' occurs in an uncommon position, that of a sentential adverb, as in

She warned us of the dangers. As well, she told us how to avoid them.

The phrase has its expected meaning, 'also, in addition', just as in sentence-internal or sentence-final positions, where it occurs regularly in standard English. But only in Canadian English, according to H. A. Gleason, Jr (personal communication), does it occur in initial position, linking the content of two sentences. It has the same function as other sentential adverbs such as *therefore, however, moreover* and the like.

The syntactic regionalism that has perhaps drawn most attention over the years is 'positive *any more*', in sentences such as

He complains a lot any more.
Any more, they usually call it 'cottage cheese'.
War, any more, is genocide.

Sentences such as these prove to be quite baffling to listeners whose grammar does not permit *any more* in positive contexts. (Every English dialect permits *any more* in negative contexts, as in 'He doesn't complain any more'.) As Labov points out in Chapter 21, positive *any more* can usually be paraphrased by the temporal adverb 'nowadays'. But it is by no means, as he also points out, a 'simple synonym' for 'nowadays', as shown by the absurdity of sentences such as

When would you rather live, in 1920 or any more?

Semantically, positive *any more* sentences presuppose that their assertion (*eg* 'He complains a lot') was not true in the past. Pragmatically they normally imply that the speaker disapproves of the situation. (For example, if someone says, 'He smiles a lot any more', she probably means that she considers his smiling excessive, or not genuine, or the like.)

Although occurrences of positive *any more* in North American speech have been mentioned in print fairly frequently since 1929, mainly in the journal *American Speech,* very few of the articles prior to the work of Labov and his research team in the 1970s attempted any analysis. Most articles, in fact, consist of a paragraph citing a sentence or two recorded in a particular place.

Such citations are useful mainly as an indication, albeit an unsystematic one, of the geographical distribution of positive *any more.* Eitner, in Chapter 20 below, makes good use of them for that purpose. Although his article was originally published in

1949, subsequent observations have only confirmed his 'rough curve of distribution' from a core area on the Midland seaboard ('the Philadelphia-northern Delaware area') outward to the American Midwest and southern Ontario.

Eitner is aware of a geographical discontinuity in this distribution. The parts of the American Midwest where positive *any more* occurs follow, as he indicates, the inland migration of the Midland settlers. Southern Ontario was not on that route, and Eitner suggests that positive *any more* may have arrived there from a different source, 'the wave of Scotch-Irish into Ontario in the 1820s'. But before that, from 1783 to 1803, Ontario received an influx of Pennsylvanian refugees who were anti-revolutionaries in the War of Independence. Positive *any more* is one of the linguistic features that preserves the 'Loyalist' roots of inland Canadian English.

The provenance of positive *any more* remains, in our view, very much an open question. Eitner postulates a 'Scotch-Irish theory of origin', and the doughty presence of Scotch-Irish settlers in its focal region, the American Midland, lends an air of plausibility to his claim. His citations of sentences with *any more* in positive contexts from Northern Ireland and mid-Scotland should close the case, but instead they cast serious doubt upon it. It is hard to find even an oblique relation between the sentences identified as 'positive *any more*' and the Scotch-Irish non-negative *any more* sentences cited by Eitner:

There's no herring in it the day, but there'll be herring any more.

It's waarm for the time o'year an it'll be waarmer any more.

They fail all three of the criteria: 'any more' is not paraphraseable by 'nowadays' here but by 'soon'; the clauses with 'any more' do not presuppose that their assertion was not true in the past (and in the first of the two sentences the past state must be asserted *because* it is not presupposed); and the speakers imply their approval of the situations they describe, not disapproval.

In looking for the possible origins of positive *any more*, it seems quite natural to assume that it arises as an extension of standard negative *any more*. Eitner seeks philological evidence for this in collocations of *more* with *any* beginning *c.* 1330. Labov seeks empirical evidence for it by testing the extent to which the meaning of positive *any more* is inferrable by speakers of the standard dialect. The two chapters thus make an instructive contrast in the ways in which research in dialectology has been transformed since mid-century.

References

JACKENDOFF, RAY S. (1972) *Semantic Interpretation in a Generative Grammar*. Cambridge, Mass: MIT Press.

QUIRK, R., GREENBAUM, S., LEECH, G. and SVARTVIK J. (1985) *A Comprehensive Grammar of the English Language*. London: Longman.

Chapter 20

Affirmative 'any more' in present-day American English

Walter H. Eitner

The term *any more*, used adverbially in negative, interrogative and hypothetical clauses, is common in American speech. Its employment in the sense of *now, nowadays,* and *further* may be illustrated by these sentences: 'The train isn't late any more'; 'He cannot be suspected any more'; and 'If it rains any more, we'll have a flood'. Paralleling this usage regionally is the adverbial *any more* of positive, non-interrogative, and non-hypothetical constructions. Fifty-nine examples listed in the *American Dialect Dictionary (Wentworth:* 1944) show it appearing initially five times, medially ten times and finally forty-four times. The following sentences illustrate the three positions: 'Any more it's hard to get coal'; 'I forget any more how it was'; and 'He goes there a good deal any more'.

Generally, the sense of *now* or *nowadays* is still implied, sometimes seemingly in contradiction of a former condition, that is: 'Coal was easy to get, now it is hard to get'; 'I knew how it was, but now I've forgotten'; 'Before, he didn't go there very often'. This is not always true, however. In the sentence 'They still use that custom any more', there is no implied change; and John T. Krumpelmann (1939: 156) reports in *American Speech* that, in a statement made to him, 'You stay in your office too late any more', there was no necessary implication that he had formerly kept shorter office hours. The senses of the term are similar in the three positions, except in the medial one, where the term seems slightly less pointed and less emphatic, and tends more towards the connotation of *still.*

To judge from the numerous citations of the *American Dialect Dictionary,* affirmative *any more* is employed by the educated as well as by the illiterate, by the urban as well as by the country folk. It is reported in use by teachers and shopgirls; and, in one case, is defended by a native college teacher of foreign languages on the ground that *now* and other equivalents seem inadequate and flat. Krumpelmann (1939) heard it in the spontaneous and unaffected speech of an honour student and a graduate student, both of West Virginia colleges.

At this point it becomes necessary to find the geographical distribution of the term. The *American Dialect Dictionary* remains the most rewarding first source for the purpose. In its 86 definite citations, largely drawn from the pages of *Dialect Notes and American Speech* for the years 1903–44, the term is reported as used or known in Illinois, Indiana, Iowa, Kansas, Kentucky, Maryland, Michigan, Montana, New York, Ohio, Pennsylvania, South Carolina and West Virginia. It is also reported in Ontario. Of these citations, West Virginia has 47; Pennsylvania, 8; Kentucky, 6; New York, Ohio and South Carolina, 5 each; and none of the other states has more than 2. It is reported 'not observed' in central New York; it is reported unknown in western Tennessee and in Arkansas.

One's first impression from these figures is that the term is centralized in West Virginia. The entries from that state, however, include at least nineteen for the northern section, four of them specifically from Morgantown, the home of the University of West Virginia and of the dictionary's editor. It may not be unjust to conclude, therefore, that the sampling there was disproportionately large.

Of the eight citations for Pennsylvania, seven are from the southern part of the state; the other is not placed. The six Kentucky citations are from the north-eastern section; all but two of them are drawn from the pages of Jesse Stuart's books. All five New York citations are from Elmira, near the Pennsylvania border. Ohio's are from Trumbull County in the north-east, with the exception of one from Columbus towards the south. The five from South Carolina are from the central and south-western portions of the state. Illinois's informant lives in Dewitt County, in the centre of the state; Michigan's in the south-east; Montana's in the south; Ontario's in the south-west; and the remainder are not specifically located.

To augment this record there is a more recent list of citations available in *American Speech,* compiled by A. R. Dunlap, of the University of Delaware (Dunlop 1945: 12–15). He gives 250 informants, a few of whom were college graduates, but most of them were high-school graduates and members of his classes in 1944. The homes of those reporting that they had heard the affirmative *any more* in their own areas are as follows: Delaware, largely the northern part, 15; the southern part of Indiana, 3; Maryland, near the Delaware border in the north, 2; the southern part of Michigan, 2; New Jersey, close to the Pennsylvania border, 2; the southern part of New York, 3; the north-eastern and south-western sections of Ohio, 3; the Philadelphia and Pittsburgh areas of Pennsylvania, 8; the extreme south-west of Virigina, 1; the north-east and the south-west of West Virginia, 2. The others were widely distributed west of the Mississippi in Arizona, California, Iowa, Minnesota, Missouri, Nebraska, Oklahoma, Texas and Washington. Thirty-two reported that they had heard the expression in other than their home areas; a third of them cited it from Delaware and the others added Alabama, Arkansas, Florida, Mississippi, North Carolina and Tennessee to the states listed above. The number who reported the term as natives of Delaware, and the number who indicated that they heard it there, make it appear that Delaware is a point of centralization. Again this may be explained by its being the canvassing area. The chance sampling is significant in that the *American Dialect Dictionary* contains no citations for Delaware, whereas Dunlap lists only two informants from West Virginia.

The combined lists show that affirmative *any more* appears most often in these eight states, in the order of frequency: West Virginia, Pennsylvania, Delaware, New York, Ohio, Kentucky, Indiana and South Carolina. The term has a rough curve of distribution stretching from the Philadelphia-northern Delaware area westward through the southern part of Pennsylvania, southward through West Virginia, and again westward through northern Kentucky and the southern segments of Indiana and Illinois. In Ohio and New Jersey it appears in areas close to Pennsylvania. It is noticeably absent from North Carolina; but it is evident in the western half of South Carolina. Elsewhere in the southern states it appears only sporadically. It is known in the Far West, the North-west and in the Great Plains. Apparently the term is unknown in Wisconsin, but it has been noted in Iowa, Kansas, Michigan, Minnesota and Ontario Province. In New York it is found only in the south, close to Pennsylvania. It is unknown in New England.

The problem now is to ascertain as far as possible the origin of the locution in this country. H. L. Mencken (1948) seems to hold that it stems from the Germans of Pennsylvania. This view can be largely put aside because the term's distribution in Pennsylvania does not coincide with the settlement area of those people. Its obvious spread throughout the United States generally also indicates another origin. A suggestion of Welsh sources, advanced by R. Whitney Tucker (1944) is prompted in part by the prevalence of the term in mining regions. This may similarly be discounted because of its distribution elsewhere.

A more likely source is the Scotch-Irish who entered Pennsylvania through the port of Philadelphia in great numbers, beginning around 1720. Their early influx was almost as large as that of the Germans. It also almost equalled the combined numbers of Quakers and others of English origin. Leaving Pennsylvania, many of them went southward and to the interior. They then established themselves in the back country of Maryland, Virginia, and the eastern part of West Virginia. Later they moved west of the Blue Ridge, and eastward into the Piedmont. They were still moving when the Alleghenies were conquered, and were among the earliest to enter the Ohio country and to follow the Ohio River westward. Thereafter the opening frontiers as far as Oregon and Washington always had the Scotch-Irish as a part of their populations (Baugh 1935; Burr 1922: 44–7).

This general migration from the seaboard to the interior and westward coincides fairly neatly with the distribution of affirmative *any more*. Also, since the Scotch-Irish were too few and too scattered in New England to resist early absorption into the general population of those states, and thereby lost their group identities (Burr 1922: 46) it is not surprising that the locution does not appear there. This would also tend to explain its absence from the main part of New York, largely settled by migrants from New England. On the other hand, the wave of Scotch-Irish into Ontario in the 1820s (Ahrend 1934) may account for the presence of the term in that section.

The Scotch-Irish theory of origin is supported by the listings of *any more* found in the *English Dialect Dictionary* (Wright 1898) and the *Scottish National Dictionary* (Grant n.d.). The former cites the use of the term in positive as well as negative phrases to express the sense of *from now on,* and gives an undated example from North Ireland: 'A servant being instructed how to act will answer "I will do it any more".' The *Scottish National Dictionary* illustrates its use adverbially and affirmatively in the sense of *now, henceforth.* It gives two examples, dated 1928, from Argyll in mid-Scotland, which is that part of the country most convenient to North Ireland: 'There's no herring in it the day, but there'll be herring any more', and 'It's waarm for the time o'year an it'll be waarmer any more'.*

---

* *Editor's note:* These three sentences from Northern Ireland and mid-Scotland, where *any more* apparently means 'soon', sound very odd to North Americans who use positive *any more* natively. This difference casts doubt upon Eitner's 'Scotch-Irish theory of origin.'

That affirmative *any more* is a development within the English language itself may be demonstrated historically. In this regard the *Oxford English Dictionary* (*OED*) and the concordances to Shakespeare and the Bible are most helpful. According to the former, the word *any* was primarily used in interrogative, hypothetical and conditional forms of speech (*OED*, I 1, a, *s.v*, *any*). Citations date back as far as the year 1000. It was also used as an emphatic negative from a date about as early (*OED* I, 1, b, *s.v. any*). Around 1300 its use in affirmative sentences appears: 'The serpent . . . was more wise than any beast' (*Cursor Mundi*, l. 700) (*OED* I, 1, c, *s.v. any*). Shortly thereafter, around 1330, it became joined with *more*, which had also been used since 1000 in negative, interrogative and hypothetical contexts. The phrase *any more* then superseded the simple *more* in adverbial usage in a conditional sense of *further, longer, again,* (*OED* C, 4, *s.v. more*). Thus the negative, hypothetical and interrogative *any more* was established. Robert Manning of Brunne employed it in his *Chronicle* (l. 14,001) of 1338: 'And if you challenge him any more, He shall send you such as these are.'

Later (about 1400) *any* came into use adverbially with comparative adjectives (*OED* II, 7, *s.v. any*). In Caxton's *Enydos* (xix. 72) of 1490 there is the phrase 'to presse me wyth wordes ony more'. After that, affirmative *any more* appears in Shakespeare's *Richard II* (ii, ii, 208) of about 1595, 'I'll hate him everlastingly that bids me be of comfort any more', and in the Bible (1611) in the two near-negative instances, 'Saul shall *despair* to seek me any more' (1 Sam. 27:1), and '*feared* to help Ammon any more' (2 Sam. 10:9).

It appears not unreasonable to suppose, therefore, that *any more* has followed the development of *any* from the negative, interrogative and conditional into the affirmative usages. The conditional use of *more* with *any* around 1330 may easily have led to the later affirmative use. It is no broad jump from 'If we hear the voice any more' to 'We hear the voice any more'.

The tentative conclusions derived from these sources are that adverbial and affirmative *any more* developed natively in English from conditional formations; that it became localized at a later date in Scotland; than it was transplanted to North Ireland; and that it spread widely in the United States through the immigration of the Scotch-Irish and their movements further inland.

References

AHREND, EVELYN R. (1934) 'Ontario speech', *American Speech* 9: 136–9.
BAUGH, ALBERT C. (1935) *A History of the English Language.* New York: *pp* 415–21.

BURR, CLINTON STODDARD (1922) *America's Race Heritage*. New York.

DUNLAP, A. R. (1945) 'Observations on American colloquial idiom', *American Speech* **20**: 12–15.

GRANT, WILLIAM (ed.) (n.d.) *The Scottish National Dictionary*. Edinburgh: *s.v. any more.*

KRUMPELMANN, JOHN T. (1939) 'West Virginia peculiarities', *American Speech* **14**: 156.

MENCKEN, H. L. (1948) *The American Language: Supplement II*. New York: *pp* 203, 204, 234.

TUCKER, R WHITNEY (1944) 'Notes on the Philadelphia dialect', *American Speech* **19**: 29.

WENTWORTH, HAROLD (1944) *American Dialect Dictionary*. New York: *s.v. any more.*

WRIGHT, JOSEPH (ed.) (1898) *The English Dialect Dictionary*. New York: *s.v. any, p* 3.

Chapter 21

The boundaries of a grammar: inter-dialectal reactions to positive *any more*

William Labov

21.1 Introduction

As linguistics begins to turn outwards towards the speech community, it will once again be possible to offer a theory for those who are deeply committed to writing the grammar of a particular language. There are of course many open questions on the internal organization of grammar, but before anything else it must be decided what the grammars are about: I take it as agreed here that the only valid grammars will be about the language used in everyday life by ordinary citizens arguing, greeting, gossiping, calculating, persuading and running off at the mouth in countless other ways.

But we must also decide where these grammars begin and where they end – their external and internal boundaries. How broad, or how narrow is the grammar of a speech community? This is quite a different question from that of determining the boundaries of the speech community itself which is defined by a much wider range of phenomena besides its grammar: differences in vocabulary, in cultural traits, in phonetic posture and discontinuities in lines of communication. The grammars that we are discussing must be broadly conceived to include phonology, semantics and discourse rules, but they would not include the dictionary or a whole ethnography of speaking. The study of the external boundaries of a grammar is therefore a subset of the problem of drawing dialect boundaries, but the most central one for linguistic purposes. We will adhere for the present to the Chomskyan notion that the grammar might represent the knowledge that the native speaker needs to produce and understand the language in native fashion. There will be other things

that we want to say about the grammar which will not fit within
this framework: the distribution of lexical items among derivational suffixes, the differential rate of change of certain parts of
the grammar, the extent to which the morphology fits in with
general tendencies of marking and unmarking – such facts are of
no use to the native speaker, and must be put into a meta-gram-
mar. We will then have a base for the empirical investigation of
grammars that speakers actually have available, trying to discover
which speakers actually use which rules.

As we will see, 'use' is not a single dimension: there are many
ways in which a variant form may be recognized, understood,
evaluated, projected and controlled by speakers. We will examine
some of these properties first in relation to the proposition that
we only need one grammar for a language: that the knowledge
of a native speaker, potential and actual, reaches out to embrace
the patterns used by all other speakers.

21.2 The outer limits of a grammar

The notion of a pan-dialectal grammar was put forward most for-
cefully by C.-J. Bailey in 1969, at the Los Angeles Conference
on Historical Linguistics in the Light of Generative Grammar
(Bailey 1972). He pointed out that we can and should write a
single grammar to encompass all (or nearly all) of the dialects of
a language, since the competence of the (fully adult) native
speaker reaches far beyond the dialect he uses himself. Bailey
argues for such grammars on the ground that (a) as native
speakers become older, they become familiar with an increasingly
large number of other dialects; (b) they have the ability to understand and interpret the productions of those other dialect
speakers, analysing their rules as extensions or limitations of their
own rules; and (c) they can even extrapolate from their own rules
and predict the existence of dialects which they have never heard.
Bailey's argument also invoked the existence of universals of
change as proposed by Kiparsky (1968) in which the existence of
one (marked) rule ordering presupposed the possibility of another
(unmarked) order.

We can then project the possibility of a single grammar in
which various rules and environments or rules are seen ordered
along a single dimension, one implying the other, and the writing
of a single grammar justified by the uniform ordering of these
features. Such ordering may be universal, or fixed for a given
area, on the other hand, the transition to a different ordering
would be a nice argument for a separate grammar.

Simplicity considerations play an important role in such constructions. They are the basic argument for bringing together various subrules in different environments into a single rule. If native speakers do this in the rule systems they form themselves, then subdialects will be forced into alignment by the tendency to compact individual rules into a single larger rule and to simplify the environments. There is considerable disagreement on whether or not there is empirical evidence to prove the existence of such simplifying activity (Bach and Harms 1972; Schane 1972; Labov 1972; King 1969).

The argument as to whether rules are added only at the ends of grammars is also important here. If rules were added only at the end, or at the end of certain sections, then it would be possible to write general grammars down to a certain point and stop, leaving the details to be worked out in later volumes by dialectologists. This is the strategy followed by Chomsky and Halle (1968), and it is not inconceivable that native speakers follow comparable strategies. If so, any grammar of English will be pandialectal to a point, and speakers may proceed with the work of interpretation in confidence that there are no misapprehensions behind them.

Finally, we can consider the extension of this argument to bilingual communities. Gumperz (1971) argues that we can construct a single 'repertoire' for the several 'different' languages which a speaker can use. Can this repertoire be in fact a grammar? If we consider Gumperz's findings in Kupwar, it seems quite likely. Gumperz shows that the surface morphology and the lexicon are totally different for the local Marathi and Kannada spoken in Kupwar. But Gumperz has also shown that it should be possible to write a single set of grammatical categories, phrase structure rules and transformations, and a common set of output constraints on surface ordering for syntax and phonology. This would go beyond a pan-dialectal grammar, and demonstrate the ability of speakers, over a long period of time, to bring two rule systems into close approximation so that they are in effect one system.

It will first be necessary to see what kinds of evidence we might use to decide if a given rule is potentially or actively in the dialect of a given speaker. Let us consider A', a native speaker of dialect A, who has been in contact with dialect B for some time. If other speakers of A have been in intimate contact with B for long periods, we can follow Gumperz in arguing that the work of translation is apt to be quite simple: a mechanical recoding of lexical items. But if there is no history of contact, there may be deeper differences, and A' must use his own linguistic competence to ferret them out. He may not know himself how much or how little he knows about this dialect, but we should be able to put him to the test in various ways to decide how much of B he has assimilated: whether he has activated his pan-dialectal grammar or constructed one for the occasion.

There are six questions we can pose about A''s grasp of a rule of dialect B which will help us decide what kind of a rule he himself is using. A' has just heard a speaker of B use a form B_1 that is not produced by A''s grammar.

1. Does A' *recognize* B_1 as grammatical for some native speakers of English? In a word, does he know that B_1 exists? Or, faced with B_1 for the first time, can he recognize it as a possibility open to speakers of English?
2. Can he *evaluate* its social significance – that is, see it as colloquial, formal, slang, or stigmatized so that he would know in what social context to use it?
3. Can he *interpret* B_1 – not just in the normal favourable contexts, where it is supported by other forms, but in neutral and unfavourable contexts as well?
4. Can A' *label* the meaning of B_1 in zero contexts, faced with the isolated form itself? The labelling function might seem beside the point, since the normal use of language does not require it; but it will appear that in the heartland of dialect B, speakers will be able to choose the right label when outsiders fail.
5. With or without this understanding, can A' *predict* the use of B_1 in an extended range of environments – both syntactic and semantic? Finally,
6. Can he *use* B himself productively? (6) does not automatically follow from (5), since the use of language in social interaction requires a much higher degree of skill and a kind of overlearning that is not needed to predict the use of others in a reflective mode.

The six abilities we are testing seem to form three sets. The first two depend upon the broadening of wider experience beyond the vernacular as noted by Bailey; the second two depend upon the second ability to extrapolate from one's own vernacular rules and assign the new form to the proper subrule; the last two represent the deeper ability to recreate the exact form of the rule or subrule and synthesize new forms. Ability (5) is crucial for deciding if the form is represented in a pandialectal grammar in the same form as in the vernacular where it originates.

With these preliminary considerations, let us now consider some empirical investigations.

21.3 Positive *any more*

We will consider one of the most interesting and mysterious examples of divergence in English syntax. Syntactic change is an elusive process as compared to sound change; whereas we find sound changes in progress in every large city in the English-speaking world, we have comparatively little data on syntactic change. Phenomena which seem at first glance to represent change turn out to be continuations of long-standing traditions not reported by grammarians. This may be the case with the use of *any more* in positive sentences, which appears to be spreading outwards from its centre in the Midwest. In Q-SCOM-I[1] we asked our informants:

[1]   What would it mean if you asked *Who plays ringalevio?* and someone answered *A lot of cats play that any more.*

When I first encountered this use of *any more* I thought it meant 'still', and this is the impression that many outsiders have. We think of it as the opposite of *A lot of cats don't play that any more. ie* 'they still play that'. But on further exposure, it quickly becomes apparent that *any more* does not meant 'still' but rather 'nowadays'.

[2]   That's the trouble with airplanes any more.
                              (Retired railroad engineer,
                              Champaign, Illinois)

[3]   Those secretaries write most of the letters any more anyhow.
                              (Personnel manager, raised 32
                              kilometres north of Evansville,
                              Indiana)

Though we do not yet know the full geographic distribution of this form it is used automatically and frequently in Pittsburgh, western Pennsylvania, Ohio, Indiana and parts of Illinois, Kansas, Missouri, Utah and other western areas, and it is apparently spreading to other parts of the United States. In general, positive *any more* appears to be a Midland phenomenon and its incidence reported so far corresponds quite closely to the areas of Midland settlement and influence mapped by dialect geographers. It is not a social marker or stereotype, and is not evaluated by most speakers. I once asked a young woman clerk in Cleveland if it was true that people around there could say 'We go to the movies any more'. She answered no, they didn't say that; they all said *show*. I have pressed the point with speakers from this area after they used positive *any more* in actual conversations and after a while they will become confused and say that they made a mistake, and should have used *don't*. It is important to realize how far below the level of conscious awareness this syntactic feature lies. In 1969, an issue of *Life* appeared with a featured headline on one story next to a photograph of the author of a recent bestseller kneeling on her bed:

[4]   What it takes to be a lady author any more

I have been unable to trace any response or reaction to this as an odd utterance. In Q-SCOM-II we also asked for an interpretation of

[5]   We live in Columbus any more.

When we examine the pattern of reaction to [1] and [5] we find that many absorbed a negative meaning, some understood 'still', but the majority got some form of 'nowadays':

	[1]	[5]
Negative	7	4
Still	9	4
Unmarked present	–	9
Used to	–	2
Nowadays	19	15

Only thirteen informants registered 'nowadays' for both sentences, but this was a much higher number than I expected. Even linguists have been deceived about the meaning of positive *any more* when approaching it from outside. In case after case, linguists have told me that they were familiar with the *any more* dialect. When I asked them what positive *any more* means, the answer is usually 'still'. But when they are informed that the meaning is 'nowadays', they begin to recall that this was the way that they heard it used. If even a linguist can be so misguided, how can we explain this high response to *any more* in our subjects? We did not draw them from the Midwest, but from a wide range of areas in the eastern United States, reaching out for the basis of a pan-dialectal grammar from our Philadelphia location.

When we consider the geographic origins of the subjects, this puzzle is resolved. We can divide all informants into (+): those who showed some response of 'nowadays' to at least one sentence and did not contradict this meaning in the other; and (−): those who gave at least one 'negative' or 'still'. showing that they did not understand positive *any more*. The following list shows the geographic distribution of thirty-three informants from Q-SCOM-

1 according to their *any more* responses, listing them under the
area in which they lived from 4 to 13 years old.

	Midwest	Eastern Pa. and Philadelphia area	Other areas
(+)	Fla/Pittsburgh	Philadelphia	NYC
	Wisconsin	Philadelphia	
	Ohio	Philadelphia	
	Iowa	Philadelphia	
	W. Va/Pittsburgh	Philadelphia	
		Philadelphia	
		Berwyn	
		Bryn Mawr	
		Cherry Hill	
		Cherry Hill	
		Cherry Hill	
(−)		Philadelphia	New England
		Philadelphia	Massachusetts
		Philadelphia	Massachusetts
		Hazeltown	Mass/Fla
		Altoona	Upstate New York
		Cherry Hill	NYC
		Glassboro	Atlantic City, NJ
			Maryland
			Los Angeles

The pattern now becomes clear, including the one exception from
New York City. This young woman of 17 moved into Freeland,
Pa., two years ago, and apparently noticed Pennsylvania speakers
using positive *any more* as 'nowadays': she calls it 'a fad'. Otherwise, Easterners, Southerners and even Westerners fail to
recognize the meaning of positive *any more*. Philadelphia is
divided. On the other hand, all the Midwestern speakers naturally
and without comment identified the meaning and their only concern was with lexical items like *cats* in [1] which drew their
attention.

In our further investigations of *any more,* we began again with
a sentence which provides no contextual clues except the meaning
of the sentence itself.

[6] Someone said, *John smokes any more.* Do you get the idea
     that

    (a) John hasn't been able to kick the habit _____
    (b) or John has quit _____
    (c) or John wasn't smoking for a while but now he is
         _____

This sentence strikes many speakers of the *any more* dialects as odd or ungrammatical at first, because it lacks the normal contextual support as in *John is always smoking any more,* or *John smokes a lot any more* (see below). In fact, a very large number of basic *any more* speakers from heartland areas such as Kansas reacted to *John smokes any more* as 'no native speaker would say it' when they first encountered it in our grammaticality test. But when they considered it in the context [6], they unhesitatingly gave the right interpretation. Furthermore, they gave the correct response to [7] and [8] which indicate that they are quite capable of using and interpreting *any more* in [6]:

  [7] So what would you guess that *any more* means in John smokes any more?
      (a) [still]   _____
      (b) [nowadays] _____
      (c) [negative]   _____

  [8] Have you ever heard anything like that? _____ Where?
      _____ Could you say it yourself? _____

In our Kansas sample of 25 subjects, 11 answered [8] by saying that they could say *John smokes any more* themselves. But 6 of these responded to the isolated sentence in our grammaticality test by saying that 'no native speaker would say it', four checked off 'someone might but I've never heard it', and only one indicated that it was perfectly natural. This response is one of the most dramatic demonstrations of the difficulty of interpreting judgements of isolated sentences on a typical grammaticality test: if the investigator does not determine the context, various uncontrolled factors will do so for him, producing such odd and misleading responses. The basic situation here is that a sentence in which *any more* carries the main grammatical meaning without support is rare, but in a slightly larger context, quite natural for the grammar to produce.

    In further work on the matter, we introduced a second *any more* sentence directly after [6]

  [9] Someone said *Harry likes rock music any more.* Do you get the idea that
      (a) Harry's turned off rock _____

    (b) or Harry's always been a great rock fan _____
    (c) or he's finally seen the light? _____
A correct pattern of response to *any more* sentences is then [6c],
[9c], [7b]. Table 21.1 lists the overall patterns of responses from
170 subjects according to their geographic origin. A correct interpretation of *any more* is a pattern of ccb, or corresponding
answers in the earlier studies.

TABLE 21.1 Geographic distribution of subjects interpreting positive
any more as 'nowadays' in questions [6]–[9] (no. correct/total
responses)

	Geographical background of subjects (4–12 years)			
	Midwest	Phila. region	South	North East
Q-SCOM I (Phila.)	5/5	11/18		0/9
Q-SCOM II (Phila.)	2/2	6/9		0/7
Q-SCOM III (Phila.)	6/9	10/17	2/10	6/45
Q-SCOM III (Kansas)	10/11		1/4	3/4
Q-SCOM III (R.I.)			1/1	1/23
Q-SCOM III (Utah)	8/10		0/1	0/3

Again the pattern which emerges is quite clear. In Philadelphia
we get a uniformly Midwestern response except for three
speakers interviewed in Q-SCOM-III. In the Utah and Kansas
samples, there are only one or two Midwest residents who have
failed to grasp *any more*. In the South, including West Virginia
and Maryland, and in the East, we get only a small percentage
of those who understand this form: the great majority interpret
any more as negative of 'still'. The largest number of exceptions
from eastern states are those who have been in Philadelphia and
have been exposed to the pattern there. For the Philadelphia area
is plainly different from any other region: in every subsample we
find it split with about 60 per cent of the subjects understanding
any more, and the rest failing to do so. Unlike the Midwesterners,
many Philadelphians say that they have heard the form.
    But why is the Philadelphia area split? Does this represent dif-
ferential familiarity with *any more* or different abilities to
decipher an unfamiliar construction by general principles? This is
a crucial question for our study of the outer limits of a grammar.
For if two-thirds of the Philadelphians can calculate the meaning
of an unfamiliar rule by extrapolation from their own rules, positive *any more* might indeed be a candidate for a pan-dialectal
grammar.

We cannot be sure that no Philadelphian ever deciphers positive *any more* from first principles. But there is circumstantial evidence that most of these informants had heard *any more* used in positive sentences many times, undoubtedly without realizing it. For we have had many reports of such sentences in the Philadelphia area:

[10] It's the same thing to me any more. It's the same thing every year.

(Piano tuner, 70, Philadelphia)

This sentence was written down immediately[2] and preserves accurately the use of *any more* to mean 'nowadays'. The speaker was explaining why he did not watch the Mummers' Parade nowadays though he used to watch it all the time when he was young. We have other reports of *any more* being used in Philadelphia; *any more* is all about us, under the surface, but is not available for conscious judgements of grammaticality.

At first glance, the positive use of *any more* seems to be a simple extension of an isolated lexical item; in effect, a new synonym for 'nowadays', 'these days', 'lately', etc. But when we begin to analyse the different interpretations presented by our subjects, it becomes apparent that we are dealing with deeper principles of discourse and semantics. Let us first consider the meaning of *any more* in negative sentences as in *John doesn't smoke any more*.

[11]   *Past*   *Present*

x is the case   doesn't any more
x is not the case

I will introduce the term 'head' to indicate the assertion made by *NEG + any more* about the present: 'that he does not smoke now'. In addition there is a 'tail' indicating what was the case in the past: 'that he did'. If the head is an assertion, is the tail also? Or is it a presupposition, an implication or consequence? Does *John doesn't smoke any more* presuppose that he used to smoke, imply it, or assert it? One test for presuppositions is to see what happens on negation, since by definition presuppositions are not affected by negation. But we cannot simply reverse *doesn't* to *does;* it is generally considered that we must also change *any more* to *still* when we do so. In this case, we find that the tail is unaffected, and we must conclude that it is a presupposition of *NEG + any more*.

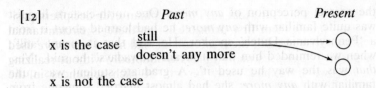

That is, *still* and *any more* are opposed only in their heads, not in their tails. But when we turn to the sentence *John smokes any more* as understood in the Midwest, we find that both head and tail are reversed:

[13]

	Past	Present
x is the case	NEG + any more	
x is not the case	POS + any more	

Thus we see that *any more* is more than a new lexical item. It represents the filling of a new grammatical category which did not exist before except in lexical form: but it involves the implicit restructuring of *NEG + any more* so that the tail is no longer a presupposition but an implication or a simultaneous assertion with the head. This now means that *still* and *any more* are not polar opposites as in other dialects.

Given the abstract character of this semantic shift, it is no wonder that speakers outside the *any more* dialect area ('outsiders') are not able to decipher *any more* correctly. Although our first results made it seem possible that *any more* was a good candidate for a pan-dialectal grammar, it now seems as if there are indeed two separate dialects with different understandings of the meanings of *any more*. The development of positive *any more* is not the filling of an empty hole, which might be done by the extrapolating and generalizing ability of the native speaker; instead, an understanding of *any more* requires actual contact with the new use and new attitude towards the discourse structure of *any more*.

Outsiders persistently interpret the tail of positive *any more* as a presupposition. The fact that this presuppositional analysis is well below the surface may be responsible for the strong recoding effect. In each area that we have investigated, we find linguists who have regularly encountered *any more* in natural speech and interpreted it wrongly through their own framework. While they may have interpreted it correctly at first, the recoding mechanism seems to produce the wrong result again and again. There seems to be no connection between linguistic insight and the correct perception of *any more*. One north-eastern linguist was quite familiar with *any more*: he had learned about it from a 'Pennsylvania Dutch' speaker. He said that it meant 'still'; when we reminded him that it meant 'nowadays', he said, 'Yes, *that* was the way he used it'. A graduate student was quite familiar with *any more*: she had almost married someone from Oberlin who had used it, and it had irritated her very much. It meant 'still', she said. When we reminded her that it meant 'nowadays' she said, 'Yes, *that* was the way he used it'. A linguist from one of the Midwestern areas was present in a group where we were using Q-SCOM-III: he was the only person present not raised in the Midwest, though he had lived there himself for several decades. In the discussion that followed, he disagreed with our analysis by pointing out that *any more* meant 'still'. The native Midwesterners contradicted him, identifying it as 'nowadays'.

This recurrent pattern of sophisticated but erroneous responses demonstrates more clearly than anything else that positive *any more* is not part of a pan-dialectal grammar. It is true that linguistic tradition has turned attention away from meaning towards distributional questions. But if linguists do not have built into their grammars a mechanism for properly interpreting positive *any more*, we can conclude that it does not belong in any general grammar for English speakers. We are dealing with an irreducible difference between two grammars.

But we do not mean to imply that there is no transition between the two. Many people first react to a discussion of positive *any more* as if it were an interesting example of lexical change, but no more than a synonym for 'nowadays'. This view dissolves as we begin to probe more deeply into other changes in the quantifier system which accompany this shift. I cannot do more than sketch lightly here some of the issues involved and the areas of investigation, but I will try to indicate the general directions of our current research in Philadelphia and its environs.

First we note that there is a cline of *any more* possibilities for all dialects. In Q-SCOM-III we follow [8] with a question which asks the subject to predict parallel uses of *any more*:

[14] *Any more* actually means 'nowadays' in these sentences, the way it's used in the Midwest. Would you guess that if someone says *John smokes any more,* meaning 'John smokes nowadays', that he would also say

(a) That's the trouble with airplanes   _____
    any more.

(b) Any more I don't go there.   _____
(c) Any more football is more popular   _____
    than baseball.
(d) Any more you're talking!   _____
(e) It's so hard for him to walk across   _____
    the room any more.
(f) Where is he any more?   _____
(g) That's impossible any more.   _____
(h) It's hard to do that any more.   _____
(i) It's easy to do that any more.   _____
(j) When would you rather live, in   _____
    1920 or any more?
(k) When was the best beer brewed?   _____
    Any more.
(l) Secretaries write most of the letters _____
    any more anyhow.

It is clear that *any more* is not just a simple synonym for *nowadays*, since speakers everywhere laugh at *j* and reject both *j* and *k*. There is an implicational scale of *any more* used which may be shown as

[15] (a) It's impossible to do that any more.
      (b) It's so hard to do that any more.
      (c) It's hard to do that any more.
      (d) It's easy to do that any more.

As the strength of the negative presupposition falls off, the use of *any more* becomes less likely. For outsiders, [15a] is perfectly acceptable, [15b] can be questionable (though we have observed it in actual speech from a New Haven resident), and [15c, d] are out of the question. It is interesting to note that Midwestern speakers who use all four naturally seem to find it very difficult to know which of these forms would be used by Easterners, but we are only beginning to explore this converse view of the matter.

The factivity dimension is a very sensitive one here, for [14g] is generally much less acceptable to outsiders than [15a]. The presence of the non-factive *for-to* complementizer seems to strengthen negative presupposition. If the negative presupposition is strong enough lexically, we can begin to observe the use of positive *any* even beyond the *any more* construction. Question [16] is based on a sentence spoken to me by a Philadelphia druggist:

[16] Someone said, 'These razor blades are going like hot cakes. I hope there's any left.' What would he mean?

One of the most striking things about [16] is that in the course of our investigations, not one speaker failed to interpret it correctly. There is no tendency whatsoever to supply a negative meaning to *any* after *hope*. We therefore observe that the movement of *any* into positive contexts is not limited to *any more*.

Finally, we may point out the dramatic implications of [14b] for another rule of English grammar. To the extent that one recognizes a connection between *any* and *any more*, it appears that this sentence violates the categorical rule of negative attraction. It is therefore not surprising to find that this is the most limited context for the application of positive *any more*. Table 21.2 shows the implicational scale which proceeds from our Kansas exploration of *any more*. Each *any more* subject is identified by a triplet such as ccb indicating his pattern of response to the basic questions ([6]–[9]). The + or − following the triplet indicates whether or not the informant stated that he would say *John smokes any more* himself. Thus in the basic pattern we see three ccb+ speakers and one ccb− subject: differing from them on only one point, there are five other ccb+ subjects. Next is a group of five informants who differ on two points, including two cbc− types, and three whose responses showed no resemblance to the native *any more* pattern on ([6]–[9]), listed as xxx−. Only one of these appears among the first ten in this matrix, but several are listed at this lower level. Conversely, as we look further down the matrix, we find only one ccb+ subject at a lower level (see below).

At the bottom of the implication scale we find subjects who predict only [14e, h] and reject all other forms. In the intervening area, there is a set of five subjects who generally do not accept the fore grounding of *any more* in [14c, b] or the use of *any more* in WH-questions [14]. This includes one ccb+ type and two ccb−, so this pattern seems to have some claim to native status.

We have only begun to explore the linguistic implications of a matrix such as Table 21.2, and to study the intermediate stages in the marginal Philadelphia area. But the data presented here should be sufficient to indicate that we are dealing with deep-seated differences in the section of the grammar that deals with quantifier systems. The difference between the *any more* grammar and the outsiders appears in Table 21.2 as a gradual expansion of the conditions under which *any more* is predicted in positive sentences. Yet the strong recoding process in sophisticated speakers, and the sharp cleavage in reactions to ([6]–[9]) makes it doubtful if we can justify the inclusion of the positive *any more* dialect in a pan-dialectal grammar. Table 21.2 is an

TABLE 21.2 Predictions of positive *any more* in environments of question [14]

Subject	e	h	a	g	i	c	l	b	f	k	j	d
	Sub-cases of [14] *Predicted that* any more *speakers would say*											
I, I, I, 2	I	I	I	I	I	I	I	I	I	0	0	0
I, I	I	I	I	I	I	I	I	I	I	0	0	0
4	I	I	I	0	I	I	I	I	I	0	0	0
I	I	I	I	I	I	I	I	I	I	0	0	I
I	I	I	I	I	I	I	I	I	0	I	0	0
,4	I	I	I	I	I	I	I	I	I	I	0	0
3	I	I	I	I	I	I	I	I	0	0	I	0
4	I	I	I	I	I	I	I	0	I	0	0	I
3	I	I	I	I	I	0	0	I	I	0	0	0
4	I	I	I	I	I	I	0	I	I	0	0	0
2, I	I	I	I	I	I	0	I	0	0	I	0	0
4	I	I	I	I	I	0	0	0	I	0	0	0
2	I	I	I	I	I	0	I	0	0	I	0	0
4	I	0	I	I	I	0	0	0	0	0	0	0
4	I	I	0	0	I	0	I	I	0	0	0	0
4	I	I	0	I	0	I	0	0	I	0	0	0
4	I	I	0	I	0	0	0	0	0	0	0	0
2	I	I	0	0	0	0	0	0	I	0	0	0
4	I	I	0	0	0	0	0	0	0	0	0	0

Subject code:	answers to	[6]	[9]	[7]	[8]
	I	c	c	b	+
	2	c	c	b	—
	3	c	b	c	—
	4	x	x	x	—

overview of a number of sub-grammars. Further investigations may modify our view, but the weight of current evidence says that in the grammar of Easterners and other outsiders only the strong presupposition of a negative outcome will allow *any more* in a positive sentence. At this point their grammar comes to a stop, because further extensions seem to demand a new analysis of *any more* which challenges and defeats their linguistic imagination.

Notes

1. Q-SCOM-I, II and III refer to interview protocols developed at the University of Pennsylvania in order to find out how well subjects could understand dialects of English other than their own.

2. This example illustrates the strong tendency of outsiders to recode positive *any more,* and the unreliability of their information unless it is written down immediately. Teresa Labov has been able to elicit several spontaneous examples of positive *any more* from several Philadelphians, and was alert to the use of this form. She heard [10] and wrote it down immediately. At the end of the day she told me that she had observed someone say, 'We watch the Mummers' Day parade any more'. She had recoded *any more* to the meaning of 'negative', even though the example clearly shows that it means as always 'nowadays'.

References

BACH, EMMON, and HARMS, ROBERT T. (1972) 'How do languages get crazy rules?' In Stockwell and Macaulay (1972: 1–21).

BAILEY, CHARLES-JAMES N. (1972) 'The integration of linguistic theory: Internal reconstruction and the comparative method in descriptive analysis.' In Stockwell and Macaulay (1972: 22–31).

CHOMSKY, NOAM, and HALLE, MORRIS (1968) *The Sound Pattern of English.* New York, Harper & Row.

GUMPERZ, JOHN, and WILSON, ROBERT (1971) 'Convergence and creolization: A case from the Indo-Aryan/Dravidian border'. In Hymes, Dell (ed.) (1971) *Pidginization and Creolization of Languages.* Cambridge: Cambridge University Press: 151–68.

KING, ROBERT (1969) 'Historical linguistics and generative grammar'. New York, Holt, Rinehart & Winston.

KIPARSKY, PAUL (1968) 'Language universals and linguistic change'. In E. Bach and R. Harms (eds) *Universals in Linguistic Theory.* New York, Holt, Rinehart & Winston, *pp* 171–204.

LABOV, WILLIAM (1972) 'The internal evolution of linguistic rules'. In Stockwell and Macaulay (1972: 101–71).

SCHANE, SANFORD (1972) 'Natural rules in phonology'. In Stockwell and Macaulay (1972 199–229).

STOCKWELL, ROBERT P., and MACAULAY, RONALD K. S. (eds) (1972) *Linguistic Change and Generative Theory.* Bloomington, Ind.: Indiana University Press.

Part Six

Conclusion

Chapter 22

Dialect grammar: data and theory

J. K. Chambers and Peter Trudgill

Dialect grammar, as we have already observed, has been much less studied than phonology and vocabulary. The most common reason proffered by dialectologists to explain the discrepancy is the relative infrequency of syntactic or morphological variants as compared to phonological or vocabulary variants. In other words, it is harder to gather examples of the former for study.

The claims about differences in frequency are obviously true. If one is gathering data on, say, *h*-dropping, an hour-long conversation with a speaker who occasionally says *'appy, 'ome* and *'ealth* rather than *happy, home* and *health* will almost inevitably include dozens of words that count as data. By contrast, a one-hour conversation may not include more than one or two instances – perhaps none at all – of, say, positive *any more* sentences or double modals. It is our view, however, that the infrequency of data should be considered as an obstacle to the analysis of grammatical variants rather than a cause for ignoring them.

At least as significant a factor in the relative paucity of dialect grammar studies – perhaps more significant, because it is more insidious – is the very elusiveness of the data. Grammatical variants evade the conscious awareness of listeners and speakers – even professional listeners and speakers, as it were, such as linguists or dialectologists – in a way that phonological or lexical variants do not. As Labov, in Chapter 21 above, notes: 'Syntactic change is an elusive process as compared to sound change. . . . Phenomena which seem at first glance to represent change turn out to be continuations of long-standing traditions not reported by grammarians'. The relative infrequency and the elusiveness of syntactic variants are not, of course, unconnected. Certainly the accumulation of numerous instances of a variant will heighten awareness of its existence, and vice versa.

At least as important in making grammatical features hard to discern, we suggest, is their functional role in speech acts. Grammatical elements are linked to the propositional content of language more integrally than phonological elements. They are the conveyors of the message in a discourse or conversation. As such, they are less easily dissociated from the discourse itself and made into the subject of paralinguistic comments or observations. Contextual cues, felicity conditions and implicatures disguise (or perhaps compensate for) unusual syntactic structures in a conversation, whether those structures are the result of performance factors (false starts, ellipses, blends) or dialect differences.

The lack of awareness of syntactic variants is well known anecdotally. Labov cites an example above, when he asks a Cleveland store clerk if it is true that people there could say 'We go to the movies any more'. The clerk replies that they all say 'show', not 'movies', thus fastening on a lexical item in the test sentence and ignoring its positive *any more* construction altogether.

Similarly, a linguistics class reacted with puzzled silence when they were read a set of sentences as examples of a new construction being used by teenagers in and around Toronto. The sentences included these:

> I can usually put them to bed at twenty to seven, 'cep'fer she's learning to tell time now.
> We have to mail this letter, 'cep'fer Charley might want to write something in it.

Having been told at the outset that the sentences illustrated a change in usage, the best guess as to what this change was that the students could make was a stab in the dark about sequence of tenses. Yet the novelty of the sentences was readily recognized when the spoken version replaced *'cep'fer* with the full phonetic form *except for,* or when the sentences were presented in written versions. Only then did the students recognize that *'cep'fer/except for* is here functioning as a complementizer, introducing a clause (Chambers 1987), whereas, traditionally, it has functioned only as a preposition (as in *Men aren't usually sensitive to colours, except for interior decorators*). Thus sentences like the ones above are simply overlooked when they occur with normal phonology and intonation, and the construction goes virtually unnoticed in ordinary conversation. Other things being equal, we might expect that it will continue to spread colloquially in the region for a couple of generations until it becomes common enough that it

occurs in writing. At that point, it will probably be noticed as a
'new' form and perhaps be subject to comment in classrooms,
letters to the editor and elsewhere.

Further evidence of the invisibility of syntactic variants comes
from tests of comprehension. In one test, groups of native and
non-native speakers were asked to choose among possible meanings for sentences such as this one (Trudgill 1983):

Don't jump off while the bus stops.
(a) Nonsense
(b) . . . when the bus stops
(c) . . . while the bus is stopping
(d) . . . until the bus stops
(e) _____

Sentences like this one are widely used in parts of northern
England with the meaning (d). Most of the subjects guessed
either that it would mean (c) or that it was nonsensical. The native speakers were hardly better at the task than the non-natives,
in spite of the fact that these sentences are in widespread use, in
some cases as little as 40 kilometres from their homes.

Once grammatical forms are identified as dialectal variants, it
is true that their infrequency does then pose problems for
analysis. However, this problem can often be solved, at least partially, methodologically. Linguistic interviews can be designed in
such a way as to maximize opportunities for the occurrence of
particular forms. For example, investigations of passive sentences
should steer the conversation towards patients rather than agents,
and investigations of the progressive aspect should discuss dura-
tive events rather than punctual ones.

Some constructions, however, remain intractable even with the
most ingenious field methods. Most dialectologists are well aware
that there is no entirely satisfactory substitute for data gathered
in spontaneous conversation, but necessity requires that there be
supplementary methods. A common one enlists teams of ob-
servers to record chance occurrences of the form for a common
data-file. The accumulation of published notes over a long period,
such as the citations of positive *any more* from *American Speech*
and elsewhere used by Eitner in Chapter 20, has the same effect.
If a cautionary note is needed about the analytic difficulties with
a corpus gathered randomly, though, one might look at
Wolfram's analysis of *a*-prefixing (Ch. 17), in which his systematic
corpus from Appalachia allows him to make numerous refine-
ments on previous proposals based on less complete data.

Supplementary information on rare forms can also be gathered by tapping speakers' intuitions directly. Labov uses several gambits for this purpose with positive *any more* in Chapter 21. Butters (1973), in an attempt to discover the combinatorial possibilities for double modals in the American South, presented speakers with sentences with paired modals such as *might could, might ought to, might should, might shouldn't,* and others, which obviously could only have been elicited in spontaneous speech in numerous hours of interviewing (if at all). He asked the speakers to rate each sentence on the following scale:

1. I have never heard this construction used.
2. I have heard this construction used by others, but it isn't a part of my normal speech patterns.
3. I've used this construction in informal conversation as a part of my own normal speech patterns.
4. I've used (or might use) this construction generally, including in writing, as part of my own normal speech patterns.

In this way, he was able to draw conclusions about permissible combinations and other aspects of double modal usage that might otherwise have remained inaccessible.

As studies of dialect grammar increase and their methods become more refined, their potential significance for theoretical syntax will naturally grow. So far, as we noted in Chapter 1 the points of contact between the two fields have been minimal. To some extent, the fault may lie with dialectologists for paying less attention to grammar, especially syntax, than other aspects of language structure. They have not, however, ignored it completely or treated it summarily. The chapters of this book indicate something of the high quality of existing research and the extent of its coverage.

The fault must then be shared by the theoreticians. Their domain of investigation has been narrowly, though seldom explicitly, confined to standard language. (Non-theoreticians sometimes claim that theoreticians take a much narrower view even than this, looking only at Standard English, but if that had some polemical value twenty or twenty-five years ago, it is certainly has none today.) Familiarity with non-standard syntax could potentially sharpen theoretical arguments as much as do imported 'exotica' from Kenyarwanda or Ponapean.

A straightforward case in point occurs in Chomsky (1989), where he constructs an argument based on the assumption that declaratives with unstressed *do* are 'illegitimate'. Summarizing his chain of inferences as briefly as possible, his argument goes as follows. He notes that the D-structure for English interrogatives such as

Q John I AGR write books

will not yield a well-formed S-structure because certain universal principles cannot apply to it. He postulates that the English-specific rule of *do*-support 'saves' the D-structure from yielding no output by inserting *do* in the modal position. AGR and I can now adjoin to *do,* and will then be raised to Q, forming

Did John write books?

Chomsky notes that this same derivational history, 'however, permits the illegitimate form "John did write books" (*do* unstressed) alongside of "John wrote books", both deriving from the declarative form corresponding to' the D-structure above. In attempting to explain why *do*-support occurs in interrogatives but not (he assumes) in declaratives, he proposes that language-specific rules, such as *do*-support, can apply only when universal principles are blocked.

This part of his argument obviously depends upon the non-existence of declaratives with unstressed *do* as grammatical structures in English. But declaratives with unstressed *do,* of course, exist hardily in Wessex English, as shown in detail by Ihalainen in Chapter 12 and Gachelin in Chapter 16.

For Chomsky's argument to be maintained in the face of the Wessex counter-evidence, two possible avenues might be attempted. First, one might try to demonstrate that Wessex periphrastic *do* has a source other than *do*-support – that it is, say, a true modal or, at any rate, something other than a mere tense-carrier. Ihalainen, however, provides ample evidence that it is a tense-carrier and nothing more. Second, one might decide to mark Wessex grammar as an exception to Chomsky's generalization, where language-specific rules are allowed to compete, as it were, with universal principles in a derivation. But if so, the generality of Chomsky's claim simply dissolves, rendering it vacuous. Neither avenue holds much promise for maintaining the theoretical claim.

We hope, then, that this book will help to bridge this gap between theoreticians and dialectologists, to the mutual benefit of both parties. More grammatically sophisticated treatments of non-standard dialects are needed, and so is a more empirically based approach to grammatical theory. We would like to think that this collection will stimulate further research into the grammar of non-

standard dialects, further methodological developments and
further insights into the nature of grammatical variability in
language.

References

BUTTERS, RONALD R. (1973) 'Acceptability judgements for double modals
in Southern dialects'. In C-J. N. Bailey and R. W. Shuy (eds) *New
Ways of Analyzing Variation in English*, Washington, DC: Georgetown University Press, *pp* 276–86.

CHAMBERS, J. K. (1987) 'The complementizer *'cep'fer'*, *American Speech*
62: 378–9.

CHOMSKY, NOAM (1989) 'Some notes on economy of derivation and
representation'. In I. Laka and A. Mahajan (eds) *MIT Working Papers in Linguistics 10: Functional Heads and Clause Structure*,
pp 43–74.

TRUDGILL, PETER (1983) *On Dialect: Social and Geographical Perspectives*.
Oxford: Basil Blackwell.

Notes on contributors

Keith Brown is currently Research Professor in Linguistics in the University of Essex. Between 1965 and 1984 he lectured at the University of Edinburgh. He was published a number of books and articles on the descriptive syntax of English and Edinburgh Scots; he is the author of *Linguistics Today* (1984) and co-author, with Jim Miller, of *Syntax: an Introduction to Linguistic Structure* (1980).

Jenny Cheshire lectures in Linguistics at Birkbeck College, University of London. She is the author of *Variation in an English dialect: a sociolinguistic study* (1982) and *Describing Language* (co-author, 1987), as well as papers on different aspects of sociolinguistics and dialectology. She has edited collections of papers on dialect and education and on English as a world language.

Donna Christian is Co-Director of the Research Division of the Center for Applied Linguistics, Washington, DC. Her publications include *Dialects and Education: Issues and Answers* (1989), *Variation and Change in Geographically Isolated Communities: Appalachian English and Ozark English* (1988), and *Appalachian Speech* (1976), as well as articles on dialects and on issues related to language and education. She is Editor of *AAALetter*, the newsletter of the American Association of Applied Linguistics.

Edina Eisikovits is a Lecturer in Linguistics at Monash University. Her main interests are in sociolinguistics and child language development and she has written particularly about Australian English.

Crawford Feagin is a visiting scholar at the University of Pennsylvania where she is completing research for a book on change in progress in the phonology of Alabama English. She was recently Visiting Lecturer in sociolinguistics at the University of Texas at Austin.

J-M Gachelin is Professor of English at the University of Rouen. He has written a thesis on *W. Barnes, Linguiste et poète* (1981) and a monograph on *W. Barnes and the Dorset Dialect* (1988), besides articles on English dialectology and Scots as a literary language, particularly in W. L. Lorimer's *New Testament in Scots*. He has also contributed to the *Oxford Companion to the English Language* (1990).

John Harris lectures in Linguistics at University College London. He is the author of *Phonological variation and change* (1985) and articles on non-standard English, phonological theory and language change.

Martin Harris is presently Vice Chancellor of the University of Essex, having been Professor of Romance Linguistics at the University of Salford from 1976 to 1987. He has published a number of books and many articles on the Romance languages, of which the best known is the *Evolution of French Syntax* (1978). He has recently edited *The Romance Languages* (1988) with Nigel Vincent. He is co-editor of the Longman Linguistics Library.

Ann Houston received her Ph.D. in linguistics from the University of Pennsylvania in 1985. She was a lecturer at the University of Pennsylvania between 1985 and 1987 and taught both graduate and undergraduate courses in sociolinguistics and syntax. She also held a post-doctoral Fellowship at Pennsylvania, and served as Research Faculty for the Language Analysis Project. She has published papers on the quantitative analysis of English syntax and on English morphology within a socio-historical context. More recently she has worked in industry as a computational linguist in the area of natural language processing. She currently holds the position of Development Scientist at Ascent Technology in Cambridge, Massachusetts, and is working in several areas related to artificial intelligence.

Ossi Ihalainen is Professor of English Philology at the University of Helsinki. He has written extensively on dialectal syntax and is currently working on a book on Somerset English. He is also compiling a large machine-readable, grammatically tagged corpus of dialectal British English.

William Labov is Professor of Linguistics and Psychology at the University of Pennsylvania, and a co-editor of *Language Variation and Change*. He is the author of *Sociolinguistic Patterns, Lan-*

guage in the Inner City, and many articles on linguistic change in progress. His current research concerns the effect of language change on comprehension across dialects.

Harold Paddock is a Professor of Linguistics at Memorial University of Newfoundland. His publications include *A Dialect Survey of Carbonear, Newfoundland* (1981), several articles in the areas of language variation and experimental phonetics, as well as two volumes of poetry.

Walt Wolfram is Professor of Communication Arts and Sciences at the University of the District of Columbia and Co-Director of the Research Division at the Center for Applied Linguistics. His publications include *The Study of Social Dialects* (1974) *Appalachian Speech* (1976), *Dialects and Education: Issues and Answers* (1988), *Dialects and American English* (1990), and numerous articles on a wide variety of vernacular dialects in the United States.

Index

Index entries are arranged in word-by-word alphabetical order, in which a group of letters followed by a space is filed before the same group followed directly by another letter. *'As well'* therefore precedes *'aspect'*.